GERMANY

REMAGEN: First permanent floating bridge across the Rhine River, opened for traffic 11MR45.

05-11AP: Close engineer combat spt of 9th Div

20JA-04AP: Corps combat engineer support

NETHERLANDS

24DE-04JA: Battle of the Bulge: close engineer combat support of 84th Div

RHINE RIVER

BRUSSELS
- 32-07FE45
- 33-15FE45
- 34-01MR45

Liège
- 35-03MR45
- 36-05MR45
- 37-08MR45
- 38-09MR45

- 44-07AP45
- 43-04AP45
- 45-19AP45
- 42-31MR45

- 23-22DE44
- 24-25DE44
- 25-30DE44

- 19-01OC44
- 26-02JA45
- 27-03JA45
- 28-08JA45
- 29-20JA45
- 30-28JA45
- 31-02FE45

- 39-22MR45
- 40-27MR45
- 41-28MR45

- 22-18DE44
- 20-23OC44
- 21-06NO44

- 18-17SE44

LUX

255-mile motor movement for assignment to Third Army

05-19JA: Close engineer combat support of 82nd Abn & 75th Divs

GERMANY

GERMANY

21AP-04MY: Close engineer combat support of 86th Div & III Corps

23OC-17DE: Lumber production for 1st Army winterization. 29 sawmills, 2.6 million bd feet.

29 Million

23OC-17DE

FRANCE

INGOLSTADT: 324-ft Cl 40 Treadway Bridge. First bridge across the Danube River in III Corps.

- 46-21AP45
- 47-25AP45
- 48-26AP45
- 49-27AP45
- 50-29AP45
- 51-30AP45
- 52-03MY45

DANUBE RIVER

MUNICH

1 Debarkation Liverpool	18 Martelange	35 Frotzheim
2 Llanelly, Wales	19 Mont Rigi	36 Monehhof
3 Highnam Court, Glos.	20 Champion Femenn	37 Esch
4 Bournemouth	21 Marche	38 Bad Neuenahr
5 Southampton	22 Ciergnon	39 Kalenborn
6 At Anchor	23 Maffe	40 Gullesheim
7 Utah Beach	24 Clavier	41 Rothen-bacher Lay
8 Hebert	25 Maffe	42 Rodenhausen
9 Haut Verney	26 Modave	43 Dainrode
10 La Chappell-en-Juger	27 Xhoris	44 Kustelberg
11 Le Bourg	28 Scoumont	45 Neustadt
12 St. Symphorien-les-Monts	29 Vielsalm	46 Petersaurach
13 Desertines	30 Recht	47 Gunzenhausen
14 Neufchatel-en-Saosnois	31 Herresbach	48 Lohrmannshof
15 Gas	32 Ober Forstbach	49 Gaimersheim
16 Perles	33 Langschoss	50 Geisenfeld
17 Rozoy-sur-Serre	34 Rotgen	51 Attenkirchen
		52 Kirchasch

BRIGADIER GENERAL HARVEY R. FRASER.
COMMANDING OFFICER, 51ST ENGINEER COMBAT BATTALION
FROM DECEMBER 14, 1944 TO JULY 7, 1945

From the collection of Harvey Fraser

THE 51ST AGAIN!

An Engineer Combat Battalion in World War II

By Barry W. Fowle and Floyd D. Wright

 WHITE MANE PUBLISHING COMPANY, INC.

Copyright © 1992 by Harvey R. Fraser

The authors and copyright holder have donated their royalties from the sale of this book to The Corps of Engineers Historical Foundation, a non-profit organization dedicated to preserving and making better known the history of the United States Army Corps of Engineers.

ALL RIGHTS RESERVED—no part of this book may be reproduced in any form without permission in writing from the publisher, except by a reviewer who wishes to quote brief passages in connection with a review.

This White Mane Publishing Company, Inc. publication
was printed by
Beidel Printing House, Inc.
63 West Burd Street
Shippensburg, PA 17257 USA

In respect for the scholarship contained herein, the acid-free paper used in this book meets the guidelines for permanence and durability of the Committee on Production Guidelines for Book Longevity of the Council on Library Resources.

For a complete list of available publications
please write
White Mane Publishing Company, Inc.
P.O. Box 152
Shippensburg, PA 17257 USA

Library of Congress Cataloging-in-Publication Data

Fowle, Barry W., 1930-
   The 51st again! : an engineer combat battalion in World War II / by Barry W. Fowle and Floyd D. Wright.
     p.   cm.
   Includes index.
   ISBN 0-942597-35-4
    1. United States. Army. Engineer Combat Battalion, 51st--History. 2. World War, 1939-1945--Regimental histories--United States. I. Wright, Floyd D., 1923- . II. Title. III. Title: Fifty-first again!
D769.335 51st .F68   1992
940.54'1273--dc20   92-8981
                                                                            CIP

PRINTED IN THE UNITED STATES OF AMERICA

DEDICATION

*This book is dedicated to the
Men of the
51st Engineer Combat Battalion
who gave their lives
during
World War II*

PFC Cecil C. Blackburn
PVT Gerald C. Brown
SGT L.D. Conley
1LT Paul W. Curtis, Jr.
T/5 Paul Dufallo
S/SGT Alex George
PFC Ray Haywood
PFC Edgar L. Mathis

S/SGT William W. Rankin
S/SGT Floyd P. Rich
PFC James M. Shanes
PFC James M. Snow, Jr.
CPL Jerry R. Stephens
PVT Carl Strawser
PFC Raligh Tillman
PFC David L. Wotton

Introduction

The 51st Again is the story of an Engineer combat battalion at war in Europe during World War II. At the end of the war there were 42 divisional and 147 non-divisional Engineer combat battalions located in Europe. The 51st Engineer Combat Battalion (ECB) was just one of many Engineer combat battalions.

But the 51st ECB was special. It stood out because it held a 40-mile front against the Germans in the Battle of the Bulge in December 1944. For this they were awarded the Presidential Distinguished Unit Citation, the highest honor that can be given to any unit in the Armed Forces of the United States for heroic achievement in combat. It stood out because it constructed so many bridges in the Allied drive across Europe, bridges across major rivers such as the Roer River for the 9th Infantry Division, the Rhine River at Remagen where it built the second bridge across the Rhine, and the Danube which it bridged for the 86th Division while under enemy fire two weeks before the war ended. The 51st stood out because it had an outstanding battalion commander, then Lieutenant Colonel Harvey R. Fraser, and because it had outstanding officers, non-commissioned officers, and enlisted men, who were willing and hard-working Engineers.

Fraser and the 51st joined forces just before the Battle of the Bulge. They stayed together until the war ended. In December 1984, Fraser told the students of the United States Army Engineer School at Fort Belvoir, Virginia, how he became commander of the battalion and his first two weeks on the job.

> In early December I was languishing in Brittany with the Communication Zone and managed to get ordered to Paris. I took the occasion to visit BG John Hardin, Deputy Engineer, ETO. I told him I was ashamed to draw my pay for sitting out the war and wasting my talent in Brittany. I had been pressuring him for six

months to get me into a combat outfit. So he said, "Dammit, Harvey, I'm going to fix it so you won't be ashamed to earn your pay anymore. You get your gear and report to Colonel Bill Carter, Engineer First Army at Spa, Belgium." Carter assigned me to command the 51st Engineer Combat Battalion, the rearmost engineer battalion in First Army area. I said, "Holy Smokes, Colonel, I wanted to get out of the Service of Supply." He replied, "You go down there and do a good job and we may move you forward."

As you have already surmised the Germans saved him from moving me by moving the action to the front door of the 51st CP. On 12 December I reported to Colonel H. W. Anderson, Commander of the 1111th Engineer Group at Trois Ponts for briefing. On the 14th I reported to the battalion in Marche with the mission of operating 32 sawmills cutting timber for winterization and bridging for the expected Rhine River crossing. Prior to noon on the 16th, I managed a session with the staff and Headquarters Company and a visit to all line companies and their sawmills. At about 1600 the S-4 of the 1111th Group interrupted the company commanders meeting to report that the Germans had broken through the U.S. lines in Schnee Eifel and were racing for the Meuse River and the port of Antwerp. He said, "Colonel Anderson orders you to send one company to Trois Ponts to defend and prepare the bridges there for destruction and to set up a barrier line along the Ourthe River from Hotton to Bastogne — only about 20 miles."

I directed my battalion executive officer, Major Yates, just returning from the hospital, to move with Company C to Trois Ponts. Remember that the battalion was scattered all over "Hell's half acre" in more than 32 places. Gathering the troops and combat loads for movement took some time. Yates and Captain Scheuber, commanding Company C, took off and arrived at Trois Ponts at midnight on the 17th.

By now I was, as you can realize, an expert terrain analyst of the area because I had visited 32 sawmills in the previous three days. The company commanders and the staff already knew the area well. We looked for road nets, bridges, defiles and towns that were bottlenecks and could be made even more impassable. I can't remember how many barriers were planned but at least 20-30, sometimes 2-3 deep, that is, blow one and fall back to the next. I will not try to describe them all, but will discuss only three important and effective ones that changed the course of the battle.

INTRODUCTION

You have already heard about the exploits of the 51st at Trois Ponts on 18 December. They faced the spearhead of the Fifth Armored Panzer Army and stopped them in their tracks. Major Yates and Captain Scheuber had 8 bazookas, 10 machine guns, 140 men, one 57-mm. antitank gun and lots of guts.

Colonel Joachim Peiper, the Commander of the First Panzer Regiment of the First SS Panzer Division, hit Trois Ponts early on 18 December with 20 tanks and armored infantry. By dint of good planning and a little luck all three bridges in Trois Ponts were blown just in time. Later Peiper said, "We proceeded at top speed toward Trois Ponts in an effort to seize the bridges there. If we had captured them intact it would have been a simple matter to drive through to the Meuse early that day." Score one for 51st ECB. The Trois Ponts detachment held out until 21 December when they were relieved by the 82d Airborne Division.

Next I will discuss the bridge and battle at Hotton on the Ourthe River. Our map reconnaissance told us this was a very important defile, first because U.S. troops, shell-shocked and scared, were retreating across this bridge, and secondly, it was a natural place to effectively delay the Germans, and thirdly, the bridge and road were absolutely necessary for the U.S. counterattack which we hoped would soon begin.

Hence, we assigned one whole platoon of company B at this bridge with two tanks, one 90-mm. antitank gun, and one 37-mm. antitank gun, plus one platoon of a 40-mm. antiaircraft battalion who stopped retreating and volunteered to fight with us. There were no other Americans in Hotton when we set up our defense there on the 17th, but late on the 20th the 3d Armored Trains moved into this location.

On the 21st we received mortar and small arms fire at Hotton when five or six German Tiger tanks appeared followed by motorized armored infantry troops which occupied a hill overlooking the town. It was hot and heavy for several hours. We stood ready with our detonators to blow the bridge, but those 40-mm. guns shooting horizontally, our small arms fire, our 90-mm. antitank gun, and our mines kept the Germans off of the bridge and held them all day until Combat Command Reserve of the 3d Armored moved in the late afternoon and the Germans turned tail and started south.

The Fifth Panzer Army had been frustrated at Trois Ponts so the lead passed to the Sixth Panzer Army in the south. General Kreuger ordered his troops to strike while the iron was hot to gain the bridgehead at Hotton before the United States could establish a blocking line. General Manteuffel, CO, 116th Panzer Division paid tribute to the bravery of the American Engineers at Hotton because failure to secure the bridge was decisive for the future of the LVIII Panzer Corps and the Sixth Panzer Army. Both the German corps and army commanders praised the feat of arms by a group of embattled Engineers.

The corps headed south and the thrust of the Sixth Panzer Army shifted to Ortheuville where the German troops had wrested a bridge from the 158th Engineer Combat Battalion. The Germans were across in force but Company A of the 51st had set up a platoon-sized barrier at a place called Champlon Crossroads just three miles north of Ortheuville. The barrier was probed late on the 21st but small arms fire and mines turned back the probe and things were relatively quiet all night.

The Germans missed big chances on the 21st, but on the 22d they moved with determination and power. We held the Champlon Crossroads until the 7th Armored Trains could escape from La Roche and head for Marche. We also delayed the Sixth German Army for most of the day until we were driven out. This allowed the 84th Division to prepare to defend the line from Marche to Hotton for a big fight which started on the 23d. The Champlon gang blew other demolitions as it withdrew towards Marche further delaying the Germans for the 84th. The 84th had moved from the Ninth Army area south to Marche on 21 December and by noon on that day had been ordered to defend the line Hotton-Marche. The battle for the 84th started at dawn on the 22d.

The bulk of our roadblocks had been executed by 22 December, but we still had blocking positions in the Celles-Ciney area. But on the 23d we received the following information from one of our roadblocks, "Tell your old man not to worry anymore because the 'Big Deuce' is here." That is, the 2d Armored Division.

On the 24th, with our battle area now reinforced by bigger and stronger units, we started to assemble and regroup north of Marche. The 51st had been relieved by the 82d Division at Trois Ponts, the 3d Armored at Hotton, the 84th Division and a British divi-

INTRODUCTION

sion in the Marche area, and by the 2d Armored at Ciney and Celles. This was probably the first and only time in military history that an engineer battalion had been relieved by five divisions.

Finally I'd like to make a few general comments: First, the only order I ever received from anybody during the entire period was via the S-4 of the 1111th Group on 16 December. We had no intelligence from anybody but ourselves. In fact, we knew more about what was going on in the area during 16-22 December than anybody else. All decisions to blow demolitions, to hold or to withdraw, were made by the 51st. There was no interference from higher headquarters.

Second, I want to tell you that the U.S. Army does not retreat in good order. You cannot believe the confusion created by stunned and scared units racing hell-bent-for-election for the Meuse River. The 51st CP was the only stable headquarters in the area. We had hordes of visitors night and day demanding information, chow, gasoline, and even counseling. We made every visitor sign in by unit and destination in our log so we could report on those who had passed through. We invited all to join us in our efforts — some did!! I remember well Henry V's eve of battle speech, "He who has no stomach for this fight, let him depart now, but he who sheds his blood with me shall be my brother, and gentlemen now abed in England shall think themselves accursed they were not here." In addition to the retreating U.S. troops, the roads were clogged with all sorts of frightened civilians in various conveyances and on foot.

Third, I wish to emphasize Stonewall Jackson's remarks: "Don't take counsel of your fears." This does not mean that you disregard the dangers of the battlefield. It does mean you do not worry about all the things that might happen because if fear dominates your thinking the resulting paralysis increases the hazards. Worry takes blood from the feet to the brain and if you worry long enough, you get cold feet. The feet of the 51st Engineer Combat Battalion never got cold from fear.

Finally, I would like to congratulate General Carter on his enlightened decision to send Harvey Fraser to the rearmost battalion. The 51st was a superbly trained, experienced, combat outfit and it was my great privilege to cast my lot with them. We did not save the First Army front, but we sure as hell helped save its rear.

THE 51ST AGAIN!

After the Battle of the Bulge, Fraser instituted a change he felt would increase the pride the men had in the battalion. Most Engineer units posted signs on their construction projects which listed the unit designation. Fraser changed that by posting signs saying, "51st Again." It was not much of a change but it meant much. The 51st soon became known as the "51st Again" all over Europe.

An indication of the high state of morale in the 51st was the two nicknames given Fraser by the personnel of the battalion. Neither was used to his face, but both were fondly and freely applied out of his hearing. One, "Scrappy," pointed up his scrappy nature, his reluctance to turn down an assignment, and his persistence in doing a job and doing it well and on time. The other, "Hurry-up Harvey," came from his constant, but gentle, admonition to the men to "hurry-up, hurry-up, hurry-up," while at the same time patting them on the rump.

When the war ended the 51st ECB was involved extensively in reconstruction programs in Germany before returning to the states where it was deactivated on October 27, 1945.

Readers of this history will find this a story of men who won a war with hard work and perseverance. Men, sent to do a job, who wanted to finish that job in the shortest possible time and make the world a better place to live in.

This story of Engineers is an example of what all Engineers everywhere were doing in World War II. Their story is an example and an inspiration to today's Engineer on how to get the job done.

Acknowledgements

This book is the idea of Brigadier General Harvey R. Fraser, commander of the 51st Engineer Combat Battalion from December 1944 to June 1945. Without his desire and push it might never have reached fruition.

The 51st Again is the product of many people. Contributions have been made by a number of personnel who served in the battalion during WW II. Colonel Floyd D. Wright wrote chapters 1, 2, 3, 4, and 9, and contributed greatly to most of the rest of the chapters with anecdotes concerning Company A, and some about the battalion. He also carefully read and commented on each of the ten chapters. He was ably assisted by his wife "Ed" who provided Floyd with much-needed typing skills and who contributed the 51st Proverb. Sam Scheuber, and Joseph B. Milgram Jr. provided information concerning Company C, with Milgram providing much of the information on Chapter 5. Preston C. Hodges provided material concerning Company B and other information on the battalion. Colonel Charles J. Attardo, Assistant S-3, provided a number of insights into the composition and early organization and training of the battalion. Major General Jack Barnes contributed extensively from his personal files, drawings of bridges, and a personal diary, as well as other information collected while he was the battalion S-3. Lieutenant Colonel Maurice E. Coats, the S-4, wrote the draft of chapter 10 and contributed a number of other anecdotes concerning the battalion. Dr. T. Reed Maxson contributed several humorous anecdotes. Wright, Hodges, and Scheuber did an outstanding job of digging into their attics and coming up with a number of pictures which were used in this book.

General Fraser contributed a number of anecdotes to the various chapters as well. He also carefully reviewed chapters 5-10, making suggestions and recommendations.

THE 51ST AGAIN!

Finally, Dr. Frank N. Schubert, Army Center of Military History, read a draft of the book and made numerous recommendations, and to him I owe a debt of thanks.

Although many contributed mightily to this work, as the compiler and editor of the book I accept sole responsibility for any errors or omissions.

Barry W. Fowle
Editor

Contents

Chapter		Page
I.	ACTIVATION AND BASIC TRAINING	1
	Cadre Training	3
	The Move to Plattsburg, New York	5
	Individual and Basic Training	9
II.	ADVANCED TRAINING	14
	Reorganizing the Regiment	14
	Unit Training	15
	Advanced Training	21
	Combined Training	25
	XIII Corps Maneuver Area	27
	Fort Belvoir, Virginia	29
III.	ENGLAND BY WAY OF NORTH AFRICA	31
	Preparation for Movement	31
	Fort Dix to North Africa	32
	North Africa	35
	England	38
	Preparations for the Continent	40
IV.	UTAH BEACH TO THE ARDENNES	46
	The Landing	47
	Normandy	48
	Operation Cobra	53
	The Drive into Belgium	57
	Belgium	59
	Sawmill Operations	67

Chapter		Page
V.	THE ARDENNES CAMPAIGN: TROIS PONTS	71
	The Enemy Objective	72
	Trois Ponts	76
	Stavelot Road	79
	The 505th Parachute Infantry Regiment	82
VI.	THE ARDENNES CAMPAIGN: HOLDING THE LINE	87
	Preparing the Defense	89
	The Battle of Hotton	92
	Delaying Action on N4: Ortheuville to Marche	96
	Champlon Crossroads	99
	The Battle of Rochefort	101
	Standing Firm	108
VII.	THE AMERICAN COUNTER-OFFENSIVE: FROM THE ARDENNES TO THE RHINE	113
	Support to the Divisions	114
	Bridging at Grand Halleux	120
	Germany and the Roer Crossing	127
VIII.	THE RHINE CROSSING AND THE REDUCTION OF THE RUHR POCKET	139
	Planning for Bridging the Rhine	141
	Building the Bridge	143
	Germany and the Ruhr Pocket	154
IX.	THIRD ARMY AND THE DRIVE TO BAVARIA	158
	The Long March	159
	Assault Crossing of the Danube River at Ingolstadt	161
	On to the Isar Canal	169
X.	POSTWAR OCCUPATION	172
	VE Day Reactions	172
	Occupation Duties	179
	The Road Home	183

		Page
EPILOGUE		187

Appendices

Appendix A.	Awards	190
Appendix B.	Lineage and Honors	192
Appendix C.	The Engineer Officer Candidate Course	194
Appendix D.	Panel Bridge, Bailey Type, M2	196
Appendix E.	Letter of Appreciation	201
Appendix F.	Memorandum Commemorating Activation Day	203
Appendix G.	Courses of Instruction and Instructors for Two-Week Specialist School	204
Appendix H.	Officer and First Sergeant Assignments, 51st ECB, on Departure from England	205
Appendix I.	Letter of Commendation from 505th Parachute Infantry	206
Appendix J.	Presidential Unit Citation	207
Appendix K.	French Croix de Guerre avec Etoile d'Argent	208
	Translation of Appendix K	209
Appendix L.	The 51st Proverb	210
Appendix M.	Salute to the Engineers	211
Appendix N.	Acronyms, Abbreviations, and Initials	212

Maps

1.	World War II European Theater	Inside front cover
2.	Enroute via North Africa	35
3.	Between the Salm and the Meuse	70
		Inside back cover
4.	Trois Ponts	75
5.	Hotton Area	88
6.	The Rhine Crossing	138
7.	First Army Crossings on the Rhine	140
8.	Road March	160
9.	Final Operations	162

CHAPTER I

ACTIVATION AND BASIC TRAINING

Camp Bowie, near the small town of Brownwood, is close to the geographical center of Texas. A Texan once described Camp Bowie as located in a beautiful valley with mountains on each side. However, recruits approaching Camp Bowie on a Greyhound bus in 1942 could see it from 20 miles away. The camp was in a valley about 15 miles wide, but the mountains on each side were about three feet higher in elevation than the floor of the valley. Once in the camp, the new men faced the faded wooden mess halls and headquarters buildings, the pyramidal tents with wooden floors and frames, sandy roads and trails, mesquite bushes, and the blowing dust. The extreme summer heat created a Texas size desire for something very tall and cool to drink. But because Camp Bowie was in the middle of a "dry" county, the thirsty soldier had to drive for miles to satisfy his craving. The nearest large city was Abilene, about 75 miles to the northwest.

The regiment was brand new. The War Department had constituted it as the 51st Engineers (Combat) on May 5, 1942. When activated at Camp Bowie on June 13, it consisted of a Headquarters and Service (H&S) Company, two battalions (the 1st and 2d), and 3 lettered companies in

THE 51ST AGAIN!

each battalion, A, B, and C in the 1st Battalion, and D, E, and F in the 2d Battalion. The regiment also included a medical detachment. First Lieutenant Martin F. Massoglia assumed command as the senior officer present on the day the unit was activated.[1]

Initially, Massoglia was busy with administrative details in preparation for receiving officers and enlisted men scheduled to join the regiment. During the last half of June 1942, 76 soldiers came to the regiment from the 37th and 39th Engineer Combat Regiments with a wide variety of experience. When the need arose, almost any skill could be found within their ranks. Among them was Corporal Loyd E. Sweatt, one of the few men from this group who remained with the unit for most of the war.[2]

On June 21, 1942, Colonel Edwin P. Ketchum was assigned and assumed command of the regiment. The unit continued to grow. June

LIEUTENANT PRESTON C. HODGES LEAVING THE POST EXCHANGE.
CAMP BOWIE, TEXAS. SUMMER, 1942.
From the collection of Preston C. Hodges

ACTIVATION AND BASIC TRAINING

was a banner month for this fledgling regiment as the 6th Officer Candidate Class (OCS) at the Engineer School, Fort Belvoir, Virginia held its graduation exercise on the 24th and assigned 15 new second lieutenants to the 51st. Among them were Preston C. Hodges, Karl G. Pedersen, James A. Ross, Jr., Clifford P. Schroff, and Floyd D. Wright. Five days later Massoglia assigned those officers the following duties: Ross — adjutant and S-1; Hodges — personnel, adjutant, and assistant S-1; Pedersen — commanding officer, H&S Company: Schroff — commanding Officer, Company C; and Wright — motor officer. From the 7th OCS at Fort Belvoir, graduating on July 8, 1942, came 17 more second lieutenants, including Arnold H. Carver, assigned to H&S Company, David H. Henry, assigned to Company F, and Albert E. Radford, assigned to Company E. The 8th OCS class at Fort Belvoir graduated on July 22, 1942 and sent the regiment nine more officers. All the officers from OCS had a wealth of background experience. Some of them had been squad leaders, company clerks, carpenters, truck drivers, supply sergeants, and platoon sergeants, to name only a few former duties. First Lieutenant John C. Paronsky, Dental Corps, joined the regiment in late July as the dental surgeon.[3]

Cadre Training

During July and August the 76 enlisted men and some 50 officers of the regiment stayed extremely busy. During the morning hours, schools were conducted and administrative duties performed. An administrative school under Lieutenants Ross and Hodges instructed first sergeants and company clerks. Lieutenant Fleetwood conducted a school for company motor sergeants and mechanics, and Lieutenant Massoglia directed a school for supply officers and supply sergeants. The unit also constructed and rehabilitated buildings for company supply rooms, mess halls, storerooms, and recreation buildings. Individual and organizational equipment was received and made ready for issue to filler personnel when they arrived. In the afternoons, the schedule included close order drill, marches, physical conditioning, unarmed defense, and organized athletics.

The arrival of 250 enlisted men on July 25 interrupted those daily activities. On paper those men were assigned to the 37th Engineer Combat Regiment, but because that unit had relocated to prepare for movement overseas, the men were assigned to the 51st for three weeks of intensive training before being sent to the 37th. Reviewing the condition of the 51st Engineer Combat Regiment at this milestone in its development, any rational person would have concluded that it was

THE 51ST AGAIN!

absurd to give it the mission to qualify 250 enlisted men for overseas movement within three weeks. The men of the 51st did not know the assignment was absurd, so it sent each of its six lettered companies about 42 men each and the training began. After three weeks of fast-moving training the 51st sent 250 completely trained soldiers to Camp Claiborne for their assignment to the 37th Engineer Regiment.

After that interlude of full-time training, the regiment went back to its schedule of working in the morning and training in the afternoon. The men noticably improved the area. Roads and walks were installed and most of the buildings neared completion. Much work still needed to be done before filler personnel arrived. The inside of mess halls had to be painted, and shelves and storage bins constructed in unit supply buildings. With the small number of people in the regiment to do the work, each man had to give his best effort.

On August 17, Colonel H. Wallis Anderson assumed command. He set the example by putting on his fatigues, grabbing a paint brush or hammer, and jumping in to work with the lieutenants and enlisted men. He laid the foundation for the development of teamwork and esprit de corps that bound the 51st together for any task. Each day he marched the men barefoot on the hot sand, a standard cure for the athlete's foot that was prevalent in those days. Each man marched whether he had athlete's foot or not.[4]

During the first week of August 1942, Second Lieutenant John W. Barnes joined the regiment from Fort Belvoir. He was assigned to command H&S Company. After a month of duty with the regiment, Second Lieutenant Pedersen was reassigned to Company C and Wright to Company A, both as platoon leaders.

During September 1942 an Engineer Officers Candidate School (OCS) Board was appointed in the regiment. The stated policy of the board was to send as many qualified enlisted men as possible from the regiment to the OCS at Fort Belvoir. That action reflected the Army's effort to expand rapidly so that it could fight on two sides of the globe at the same time. Members of the board included Captain McCollam, First Lieutenant Massoglia, and Second Lieutenants Hodges, Oberdorf, and Schroff.

By the end of September, Second Lieutenants Glade S. Wittwer, James D. Spurrier, and Clifford P. Schroff commanded Companies A, B, and C respectively. To assure himself that everyone was fully trained and qualified, Colonel Anderson arranged for all officers to attend classes every Tuesday and Thursday evening between 1900 and 2100 hours. The subjects ranged from first aid to map reading, and included the functions of S-1 (personnel), S-2 (intelligence), S-3 (operations), and S-4 (supply).

ACTIVATION AND BASIC TRAINING

The Move to Plattsburg, New York

By October the unbelievable had become routine. The regiment was now given orders to load its men, tools and trucks onto railroad cars and move to Plattsburg Barracks, New York, located on Lake Champlain, about 20 miles south of the Canadian border.

Because of a shortage of men, the task of packing and loading the large quantity of organizational equipment acquired during the regiment's three months of existence was almost overwhelming. Officers and soldiers working together loaded the 46 flatcars and boxcars. The few individuals who knew how to drive the unit's vehicles were in great demand. Convoys drove to the railroad yard, loaded vehicles onto flatcars, then returned to the regimental area in one vehicle. The drivers set up another convoy and returned to the railroad yard. This was repeated, using officers and enlisted men to drive, until the task was completed. Lieutenants Oberdorf, Pedersen, and Schroff were given considerable credit for planning and supervising the loading details.

About 25 officers and 75 enlisted men travelled by train to New York. The rest went by car. The train left Camp Bowie on its 2,016-mile trip on October 15, 1942. It took 45 hours. Any sleeping that took place was done in a sitting position or on the floor of the train coach.

Second Lieutenant Nevio (Pete) Petrini was appointed mess officer and issued a sum of cash to purchase food for the trip. Pete believed that any money he could save on food could be used by the companies in Plattsburg to purchase athletic equipment and other recreational items. With his determination to save money, and his ethnic background, nothing but salami sandwiches appeared on the menu for what seemed to be three times a day. In any event, when the train pulled into Plattsburg, New York at 1400, October 17, 1942, all aboard sincerely hoped they would never again see a salami sandwich. Needless to say, the money saved by Pete had to be turned over to the finance officer and was never seen again.

On arrival at Plattsburg the 51st was assigned to VI Corps. Equipment and men were unloaded and moved to Plattsburg Barracks, a mile or so south of town. Plattsburg Barracks was an old regular army post dating back to the War of 1812. In the late 1880's there had been rumors that the post would be abandoned. Strong public pressure to continue a military presence in the area influenced the construction of a permanent installation in 1891. The post was constructed to house an infantry regiment, the largest concentration of troops in peacetime that Congress would permit until preparation began for World War II in the late 1930s. The first reserve officer training corps (ROTC) camp was held

BACHELOR OFFICERS QUARTERS #25. PLATTSBURG BARRACKS, NY.
From the collection of Preston C. Hodges

THE BARRACKS HOUSING FOUR COMPANIES OF THE 51ST ECB. THEATER, GYM AND PX ARE ON THE RIGHT. PLATTSBURG, NY, 1943.
From the collection of Preston C. Hodges

ACTIVATION AND BASIC TRAINING

there in 1914, and such training was known as the Plattsburg Idea for many years.⁵

The post centered on a large, oval-shaped parade ground. On the south end the post headquarters complex consisted of the quartermaster, hospital, commissary, and post exchange. Behind this grouping were the stables for the horses assigned to the post. On the east side of post, located on the edge of Lake Champlain, were barracks for the enlisted men and office space for company orderly rooms. All buildings on the post were brick structures two to three stories high and heated with steam. The kitchens for each company were located on the ground floor facing Lake Champlain. For 1942, they were quite up-to-date and modern. On the northwest corner of the oval were bachelor officer quarters (BOQs), while on the west side of the oval were eight-room brick duplexes for the married officers. This was a long way from Camp Bowie, both in distance and facilities.

Within three days of arriving in Plattsburg a training program was started. Among other things the program included specialized training for officers and enlisted men in supply, motor maintenance and administration. After a thorough reconnaissance of the immediate area, Macomb Reservation was selected as the field training area for the regiment, and a mobilization training program prepared by the S-3. Other than rifle ranges, one indoors for .22-caliber firing, and the other outside for .30-caliber firing, all other training sites had to be constructed. Training continued through the month of November. At the same time preparations continued for the arrival of more people.

One of the first banner days in the history of the 51st Engineers occurred on November 17, 1942 when Captain Robert Yates took command of the 1st Battalion. His leadership would have a positive impact on the battalion. That same date Lieutenant Pedersen, formerly commanding officer, 1st Battalion, was reassigned to command Company A. The previous commander, Lieutenant Wittwer, was reassigned to the 2d battalion as adjutant.

Other assignments continued as the regiment expanded. Major James A. Kirkland became the executive officer on November 21 and Captain McCollum was reassigned to regimental S-3. Lieutenant Carville became the assistant S-3. Lieutenant Massoglia, having completed the Field Officers' Course at Fort Belvoir, was appointed Commanding Officer, 2d Battalion, vice Second Lieutenant Earle O. Baird.

Colonel Anderson, who had served in Europe during World War I, believed that his troops must be strong enough to survive the hardships of war. It was not surprising to anyone when, on November 24, he ordered a regimental march to Macomb Reservation for an overnight bivouac, followed by a return march the next day. The total distance covered was 24 miles. None of the younger men in the regiment could complain about the march for it was led by Colonel Anderson on foot, both to and from Macomb Reservation, named after Alexander Macomb, Chief Engineer, US Army, from June 1, 1821 to May 24, 1828. That was the beginning of many marches to and from Macomb.

Additional officers arrived. Ten more second lieutenants came on November 28 from the 16th OCS class at Fort Belvoir. Among these were Lieutenants Raymond L. Bailey, Elmer G. Baldwin, Richard I. Green, and Fred L. Nabors. More enlisted men arrived at the Plattsburg railroad depot on Christmas Day, 1942, and at odd intervals thereafter until January 10, 1943. The men, from all corners of the United States, had been inducted into the Army, issued uniforms, and sent by rail to Plattsburg without any training. The majority were from the south, southwest, and mid-Atlantic regions of the country. During these 16 days the strength of the regiment increased from about 150 officers and men to over 1,600. The regiment was now ready for training.

The shock of the weather in Plattsburg was rather severe for the men from warmer climates. When they stepped off the train there was some eight inches of snow on the ground and a temperature below zero Fahrenheit. They were quickly moved from the depot to the post gymnasium for processing. The regiment was well prepared for their arrival. The gymnasium had been divided into areas, one for each company, a classification section, and a medical section. The men had a wide variety of education and experience. The challenge for the classification section was to insure that each company received an equal share of men with education and experience, as well as those with nothing to offer but a strong heart and a willingness to do their very best. As the men entered the gymnasium, they were interviewed to determine the type of work they could most easily take up within the regiment. Based on that finding, the men were assigned to the companies. Within each company this procedure was repeated when assigning a man to a platoon, squad, or section. Following their assignments the men were given complete physical and dental examinations in the gymnasium. They then received orientation talks by the commanding officer, executive officer, surgeon, and chaplain of the regiment, before marching to their company areas.

Because of the limited cadre of NCOs within each company many of the new arrivals had to be placed in positions of responsibility as acting corporals, sergeants, and staff sergeants. There was no lack of

ACTIVATION AND BASIC TRAINING

second lieutenants in the regiment, but there were shortages of first lieutenants, captains, majors, and lieutenant colonels. With all positions filled by cadre or acting personnel, basic training began.

Individual and Basic Training

The regiment issued a master training schedule which specified the what, when, and where of the training. Each company then submitted to its battalion a detailed schedule which specified who would do the training and how. The basic organizational element in training was the platoon. The second lieutenants, cadre NCOs, and acting NCOs administered the training. The training started with the basics of close-order drill and right- and left-face movements.

The training was consonant with the dual mission of combat engineers. Their primary mission was engineering but their important secondary duty required they fight in combat as infantry. To be an infantryman the engineer soldier had to learn infantry subjects beyond those normally encountered in basic training. These included training on crew-served weapons such as the .30-caliber machine gun and the .50-caliber machine gun that were assigned to all combat engineer companies. They also learned how to use the 2.36-inch rocket launcher (bazooka), the 37-mm. anti-tank gun, the grenade launcher, which was attached to the muzzle of a .30-caliber rifle, and the flame thrower. The Engineer learned small unit tactics up to battalion sized operations.

For defensive operations the Engineer had to know explosives and demolitions in order to destroy bridges, knock down trees to form abatis, destroy tunnels, and blast craters in roads. He also had to be able to lay minefields, build field fortifications, obstacles and barbed wire entanglements for delaying the enemy. For the army on the offensive, the Engineer had to build bridges, both fixed and floating, build and maintain roads and airfields, and clear mines and obstacles.

The combat engineer squad of about 14 men was the smallest unit, and as such, the core of the battalion. Three of these squads made a platoon led by a staff sergeant and a lieutenant for a total of 44 men. Three of these platoons and a headquarters platoon made a company of 175 officers and men, including a captain as company commander, and a first sergeant. Three of these line companies (A, B, & C) plus a Headquarters Company and staff, formed an engineer combat battalion, commanded by a lieutenant colonel with a major as the executive officer. There were 649 total officer and enlisted personnel in the battalion.

The squad was led by a three-stripe "buck" sergeant with a corporal as an assistant squad leader. The capabilities of this squad were immense. Within it there was a carpenter, technician 4th grade (T4), carpenter helpers, riggers, demolition men, electricians, and one or two basic engineer soldiers. The squad traveled in a 2½-ton dump truck with tool chests along each side of the truck bed that served as seats for the squad. These chests included a carpenter's tool chest with the tools for that trade, a demolition chest, and two pioneer chests with shovels, axes, adzes, wood mallets, machetes, rope, double blocks and snatch blocks, to name only a few of the items.[6]

At each organizational level above the squad were additional tool chests with equipment for the squad to use when needed. These included mine detectors, additional shovels, picks, axes, explosives, anti-tank mines, and other tools and engineering equipment. All members of the squad were cross-trained to assist each other. Carpenters had to be able to help the riggers when a boom made of logs and rope was to be constructed, and the demolition man had to assist the carpenter when a timber trestle bridge was constructed. So, in addition to routine training, some of the men had to learn how to use hand saws, how to drive nails with a hammer, how to use an axe to fell a tree, and how to use an adze to level two sides of a log for use in the construction of a bridge. Many soldiers were taught to drive trucks and operate construction equipment.

About January 15, 1943, approximately 100 new men joined the regiment. A provisional training company was established to give these late arrivals ten weeks of basic training in six weeks. Afterward, the men were sent to their assigned companies on an equal training status with the rest of the regiment.

During January, the War Department assigned VI Corps Headquarters overseas, and replaced it with XIII Corps. In addition to military training the regiment started elementary education classes in several areas. A number of Spanish-speaking men from the southwest attended classes in speaking, reading, and writing English. There were also men in the battalion who could not sign their names, and some platoon leaders insisted that these men learn to do so. Once they learned to sign their names the line on payday moved faster since an officer did not have to witness the man's "X" mark.

Extremely cold weather prevailed all through the basic training period. Temperatures reached 35 degrees below zero on several occasions. In most places the ground was covered with snow to a depth of

ACTIVATION AND BASIC TRAINING

two feet. Lake Champlain was frozen over with ice three feet thick. In spite of these conditions, training was conducted outside. All floating bridge training had to be accomplished on the ice. The pneumatic floats, the 25-ton ponton bridge, and the floating footbridge were constructed on the shore, then pushed out over the lake as if they were floating. Then they were dragged back to shore and disassembled. In the short space between the barracks and the lake ice an obstacle course was constructed to strengthen the stamina and self-confidence of each soldier. Many of the men came down with colds, but after extensive physical conditioning, the health of the unit returned rapidly. The sick rate was considerably below average, clear evidence that morale was high.

Competitive tests during the last half of January measured progress in training. These tests consisted of squad, platoon, and company close order drill, military courtesy, extended order drill, infantry tactics, rigging, and bridging. Only explosives and demolition training, and firing on the rifle range were postponed until warmer weather. To fire on the rifle range for qualification in sub-zero weather would have been extremely difficult. Shooting—taking in a deep breath then expelling half of it and remaining perfectly still while adjusting the sights to the bullseye and squeezing the trigger until the rifle fired itself—could not be done with any degree of proficiency with the soldier shivering from the cold, his hands numb.

Explosives and demolitions training was postponed because dynamite, when frozen, became sensitive. For safety reasons it had to be destroyed by burning. Frozen dynamite could be thawed out slowly by the judicious use of steam heat, but this was a slow and risky process. Dynamite, because of its sensitivity, was never intended as a military explosive; however, due to the shortage of trinitrotoluene (TNT), dynamite was extensively used for training. TNT, one of the least sensitive military high explosives, was stable in any climate, unaffected by moisture, and quite durable for underwater use.

To complete basic training, the men had to qualify in fixed bridging. Each company was given two tactical bridges to be constructed under blackout conditions during the hours of darkness. The temperature during this exercise ranged down to 40 degrees below zero. The first bridge was a standard double bent timber trestle bridge. These bridges were usually constructed with 8 × 8 or 10 × 10-inch timbers, depending on the design.

Prior to building the bridges, the battalion constructed a road to the site, in one instance, a deep ravine. It removed all the trees and brush at the site, then stacked all bridge building material at the site such as the correct sized timber, bolts, drift pins and nails for use by the company building the bridge. After the company completed the bridge, it disassembled it the following morning, and restacked the timbers in the appropriate location for the next company assigned to build the bridge.

The second bridge constructed under blackout conditions was a combination timber trestle and H-10 bridge designed to carry loads for an Army corps. It could span a 130-foot gap, some 30 feet deep. That cumbersome combination was the only portable fixed bridging material available for long and high level spans until the English engineer, Sir Donald Bailey, invented the bridge that carried his name and was widely used throughout World War II.

The H-10 steel bridge was in the form of a deck truss which consisted of two such trusses fastened together by stiffeners and cross bracing. A cross section looked like a box beam constructed of angle iron. A launching nose with a large steel wheel on the end was attached to the front of this structure. The construction procedure called for assembly of the H-10 on the bank, then attaching a winch to the nose of the bridge and pulling it down into the ravine and up the opposite bank. The theory was that the front of the bridge would roll on the steel wheel while the rest of the bridge would be dragged like a sled. Many problems developed trying to follow this procedure, making the H-10 one of the most difficult bridges to build. The most serious problem was its tendency to tip over on its side when dragged over uneven terrain. It was hard to move over stumps and rocks and often lodged behind or between them. Once in place down in the ravine a standard timber trestle bridge was constructed on top of the H-10 to complete the bridge.

The night that Company A built this type of bridge, the temperature hovered between 30 to 40 degrees Fahrenheit below zero. The weather was so cold that the canteen cups stuck to the lips unless the coffee was hot enough to heat the cup. Under blackout conditions, "in the very dead of winter," Company A dragged its H-10 into the ravine. Because winching the bridge was a stop-and-go situation, the truck driver had to sit for long periods of time while waiting for instructions to be hollered to him. At one point in the early hours of the morning there was no response from the driver when told to take up on the winch. Lieutenant Pedersen assumed that the driver had fallen asleep and opened the truck door and hollered at him. Still no response. The driver was so cold he could not move. He was taken from the truck in a sitting position, wrapped in blankets, placed in the rear of a truck, and driven to the post hospital where he finally thawed out. After a few days rest in the hospital he returned to duty. In the meantime the bridge was

ACTIVATION AND BASIC TRAINING

completed by daybreak, then dismantled in preparation for the next company.

At another fixed bridge site, the company stockpiled material in preparation for the construction of a bridge made of logs and small saplings. This was a daylight problem and each platoon was rotated to the site under tactical conditions prior to constructing the bridge. On arrival the unit established local security by preparing defensive positions for riflemen and machinegunners in the event of attack. When the positions were completed outposts were established to watch for the enemy while the rest of the platoon began construction of the bridge. If an enemy approached, the outposts sounded the alarm and the men grabbed their weapons to defend the site. Upon completion of this training, each platoon was deemed capable of moving into any wooded area with only their own hand tools and cutting down trees for a vehicular bridge.

During January 1943 some of the second lieutenants in the regiment were promoted to first lieutenant. John W. Barnes was promoted on January 11 and on January 23, nine others pinned on the silver bars. Among them were Karl G. Pedersen and Clifford Schroff. Promoted to major on the same day was the regimental S-3, Albert E. McCollum. During February, Captain Robert Yates attended the Field Officers Course at Fort Belvoir, Virginia, and on February 25, Second Lieutenant Preston C. Hodges took command of Company B.

Basic training continued into February, and separate schools for officers and NCOs continued in the evenings twice a week. Those schools, and preparation for the next day's training, left little spare time for the officers and NCOs. In the 8th week of basic training, a number of specialist schools were started. Schools for intelligence, camouflage, gunnery of all types, rigging, driving, mechanics, engineer equipment operators, chemical warfare, and carpentry were included. Schools were also started for future first sergeants and supply sergeants. These were held during half of the day. The rest of the day was devoted to basic training.

By the end of February, reconnaissance and planning was started by the S-3 section for advanced training sites at Macomb Reservation. Shortly thereafter the companies began construction of a 37-mm. fixed and moving target range, a .30-caliber and .50-caliber fixed and moving target range, a .45-caliber submachine gun fixed and moving range, and a range for anti-aircraft fire.

CHAPTER II

ADVANCED TRAINING

By early 1943 major changes in organizational structure were taking place throughout the Army. The old square infantry division of World War I fame with two brigades of two infantry regiments each was being changed to a triangular configuration. The new triangular division, tested by the 2d Infantry Division during the late thirties had three regiments and was typically deployed with two regiments forward and one in reserve. The square division had a total strength of just over 28,000 men whereas the small triangular division had around 15,500 men. The new division was much easier to control and maneuver.[1]

Reorganizing the Regiment

These changes had a direct impact on the Corps of Engineers. The old division had a regiment of combat engineers with two battalions to support four infantry regiments. The new division had one engineer combat battalion with three line companies to support the three regiments.

For separate engineer combat regiments like the 51st there were also changes. The regimental headquarters became a group headquarters. As a result the group became primarily a tactical or operational head-

ADVANCED TRAINING

quarters with limited administrative and supply responsibilities. The group headquarters could have attached any number or type of engineer battalions depending on the group's assigned mission. Separate companies such as floating bridge companies, treadway bridge companies, and light equipment companies could also be attached to the group as needed.

These changes took effect for the 51st Engineer Combat Regiment at Plattsburg near the end of its individual and basic training period. Effective March 18, 1943 the regiment was reorganized and redesignated the 1111th Engineer Combat Group. Provisional staffs and H&S Companies were formed prior to the redesignation so that they could become functional on the effective date of reorganization. The former 1st Battalion of the regiment was redesignated the 51st Engineer Combat Battalion, and the 2d Battalion became the 238th Engineer Combat Battalion.[2]

Colonel Anderson became the commander of the newly formed 1111th Engineer Combat Group (ECG). Major James A. Kirkland was his executive officer and Major Albert E. McCollam became the group S-3. The group sergeant major was Gilberto G. Solis. Captain Martin F. Massoglia became the commander of the newly formed 238th.

The group commander appointed Captain Robert B. Yates as the first commander of the new 51st Engineer Combat Battalion. The strength of the battalion was 815, with 130 in H&S Company, 230 in Company A, 220 in Company B, and 235 in Company C. The redesignation had no effect on the companies and basic training continued as before. The overstrength of enlisted men was reduced by reassignment of those not physically qualified or over age.[3]

Promotions continued. On March 2, 1943, Second Lieutenants Hodges, Radford, Carver, and Henry were promoted to first lieutenant as was Wright two days later. Many of the enlisted men who joined the battalion in December and January were rapidly promoted to fill vacancies. With the approach of spring, training became a little more pleasant and basic training was soon completed.

Unit Training

On April 7, 1943 the 1111th Engineer Combat Group, along with the 51st and 238th Engineer Combat Battalions, moved to Macomb Reservation to begin unit and combined training. A base camp was established where the officers and men were to sleep on the ground in pup tents. Colonel Anderson again set the example for the officers and men by enduring all of the hardships of outdoor life. Although large squad tents were available for administrative work, they were not used for sleeping. When it came time to sleep everyone crawled into his pup tent. Even with the cold, the snow, the rain, and the mud, no soldier could complain because the commander and his staff lived under the same conditions. At the end of the first night at Macomb the men woke up to a new layer of snow about four inches deep.

Macomb Reservation was an excellent training site. Its approximately 5,000 acres varied from wet and spongy marshland in the eastern part to rolling hills and rugged mountains in the west. Thick forest covered most of the reservation. Within the training area a small stream emptied into Salmon Lake. The lake was well suited for training in river crossing operations and in the construction of floating bridges. The most difficult task facing the soldiers in river crossing operations was in learning how to paddle the plywood and pneumatic assault boats in a straight line. To the landlubber both of these boats appeared to be designed to travel in circles, or at best, in a zigzag line. With perseverance and practice most of the squads finally mastered the skill.

The issue of new immersion heaters used by the company kitchens greatly alleviated hardships in the field. They proved to be worth their weight in gold. One of those gas-fired heaters immersed in a 30-gallon garbage can full of water produced boiling water in about 20 minutes. The hot water filled numerous needs for the men. It was used for washing messkits, shaving, and taking spit baths from steel helmets when the courage could be mustered to do so in the chilly weather.

Training was conducted on the reservation five days each week, then on Friday afternoons the battalion returned to Plattsburg Barracks. Most of the time the 12-mile trip back was made on foot. Saturdays were reserved for cleaning the barracks, cleaning and repair of equipment, inspections, and parades. If necessary, training for the correction of deficiencies was also conducted on weekends.

Passes were issued on Saturday nights so that the men could visit the city of Plattsburg. In remembering those early days, warm and friendly smiles spread across the faces of the veterans who frequented the Fife and Drum, the favorite "watering hole" in the city for the 51st ECB. During the stay of the battalion, the owner surely realized a handsome profit. All areas have their favorite drink, and in Plattsburg it was Canadian Club and gingerale. Some of the soldiers met their future wives in that beautiful northern city.

Sundays were set aside to pamper aching muscles, tend blistered

ADVANCED TRAINING

feet and fingers, and go to church. Monday morning found the troops hiking back to Macomb. Several times during unit training, extended tactical exercises required the troops to spend the weekends on the reservation.

The battalion conducted frequent air alerts all during the winter and spring. It alloted each company an area to defend against paratroop or airborne attack. The air alerts were practiced under complete blackout conditions. Some considered this training to be a joke at the time but it would be put to good use during the Battle of the Bulge in the Ardennes during December 1944.

On April 10, Captain Yates returned from training at Fort Belvoir and reassumed command of the 51st Engineer Combat Battalion. By that time the rigorous training during the winter in upstate New York was already molding the battalion into a well-trained, well-disciplined, and coordinated unit, with a high esprit de corps.

Near the end of April 1943, XIII Corps conducted mobilization training program tests for the battalion. These tests were given to determine the effectiveness of basic training just completed by the 51st ECB. The battalion's average score was 83 percent, the highest rating of any similar organization in XIII Corps. Company A scored 75 percent, Company B, 89 percent, and Company C, 84 percent.[4]

As part of the infantry training program, the 1111th ECG devised a tactical problem employing both of its battalions. The 238th ECB was assigned to occupy and defend a mountain top position. It immediately set about preparing defensive positions in anticipation of an attack. The 51st ECB was assigned the mission of the aggressor, attacking from a distance of about 10 miles. It had to move on foot during the night, perform a tactical river crossing, and take the high ground controlled by the 238th ECB by dawn the next day.

Although it was April the temperature often dropped to freezing and below. The night of the exercise was extremely cold and, with no moon, pitch dark. The 51st successfully completed the exercise, but not without incident. While driving under blackout conditions a Company A truck driver ran off the road and down an embankment, injuring 16 men. The injured were taken to the post hospital. Fortunately, none of the men were seriously hurt.[5]

Without any let-up in training, changes in battalion personnel continued throughout the spring. On May 7, Lieutenant Richard I. Green, Company C, was promoted to first lieutenant. Losses included a cadre of 4 officers and 60 men, sent to Camp Van Dorn, Mississippi, to form the 163d Engineer Combat Battalion. The officers sent to be potential company

CO. A, 51ST ECB, ON PARADE IN THE CITY OF PLATTSBURG, NY. SPRING OF 1943.
From the collection of Floyd D. Wright

LIEUTENANT FLOYD D. WRIGHT PLACING EXPLOSIVES FOR CREATING A CRATER AS AN ANTI-TANK OBSTACLE. CO. A., 51ST ECB. PLATTSBURG, NY.
Photo by Cpl. Al Bolha

CASTLE CONSTRUCTED OUT OF CONCRETE BY THE 51ST ECB AT MACOMB RESERVATION DURING MARCH 1943 TO BEAUTIFY THE AREA AND SHOW THE ENGINEERS WERE THERE.
From the collection of Floyd O. Wright

MAJOR ROBERT B. YATES AND FIRST LIEUTENANT PRESTON C. HODGES AT COMPANY B, MACOMB RESERVATION, NY 1943, 51ST ECB.
From the collection of Preston C. Hodges

MOCK-UP OF TACTICAL EXERCISES. LIEUTENANT RICHARD I. GREEN KNEELING. 51ST ECB TRAINING AT MACOMB RESERVATION. APRIL-MAY, 1943.
From the collection of John W. Barnes

THIS IS A GIN POLE WITH A MOVEABLE BOOM. THE MEN ARE MOVING A 55 GALLON DRUM TO PROVE THAT IT WORKS. TRAINING SITE AT PLATTSBURG BARRACKS.
From the collection of Floyd D. Wright

ADJUSTABLE (THE CROSS BEAMS COULD BE MOVED UP OR DOWN ON THE ALUMINUM POLES) ALUMINUM TRESTLES FROM THE 25-TON PONTON BRIDGE. JULY 21, 1943. ABERDEEN PROVING GROUNDS, MARYLAND.
Photo by Cpl. Al Bolha

H-15 TIMBER-TRESTLE BRIDGE, CONSTRUCTED BY COMPANY C, ACROSS THE SALMON RIVER. MACOMB RESERVATION, PLATTSBURG, NEW YORK. APRIL-MAY, 1943.
From the collection on John W. Barnes

DOUBLE-DOUBLE BAILEY BRIDGE (40 TONS) WITH A FOOT WALK. JULY 21, 1943, CO. A, 51ST ECB, ABERDEEN PROVING GROUNDS, MARYLAND.
Photo by Cpl. Al Bolha

commanders were Second Lieutenants Petrini, Garrity, Levitus, and Hulce. The enlisted men, most of whom had five or six months of service, were to train filler personnel assigned to the newly formed 163d ECB.

Additional personnel losses for the 51st occurred on 30 May when Second Lieutenants Brucker, Kelso, Johnson, Fossett, Conklin, and Baugh transferred out to fill individual vacancies for overseas assignment. The one addition to the battalion occurred on 18 May, when Captain Alfred H. Rawlins arrived as the executive officer of the 51st ECB.

Advanced Training

At Macomb Reservation a number of the newly designed Bailey bridges arrived at the battalion motor pool in 2½-ton trucks and were unloaded by men who wondered how all the steel panels, beams, and braces would be put to use. The Bailey Bridge, a through-truss highway bridge, was to be used primarily to span gaps from 30 to 210 feet in length. However, the bridge could be assembled to meet varying conditions.

Each lettered company was issued one training manual that named and described the various parts. The book also described the many ways the bridge could be constructed. The panels, which were the major components of the bridge, weighed about 577 pounds. These were called truss sections and were 10 feet long and 61 inches high. Each section was connected end to end by panel pins to form a truss. With a steel panel on each side and connected by an I-beam, called a transom, plus decking, the bridge was called a single-single Bailey Bridge. If two panels were placed on each side with an additional panel on top of each of these panels it was called a double-double Bailey. The bridge could be constructed anywhere between a single-single to a triple-triple, depending on the length of the span and the load to be carried by the bridge.

The Bailey was the best military bridge invented up to that time. It could be loaded and unloaded from trucks, constructed, and disassembled using only manpower. The transom was the heaviest component of the bridge. It was a reinforced, 10-inch, steel I beam about 20 feet long, and weighed 618 pounds. A crew of 8 men was used to place the transom. After a full day of such work a soldier was ready for a full meal and a good night's sleep.

The bridge was built on rollers with a skeleton launching nose that allowed it to be pushed across the gap until it came to rest on rollers on the far bank. The only critical element was the counterweight. A sufficient counterweight to the bridge proper was needed on the near bank until the launching nose rocked down to rest on the rollers on the far bank. When feasible, a 20-ton mobile crane was used to assist in the construction of the bridge, greatly reducing the manpower required.[6]

The lieutenants and sergeants spent many hours poring over the technical manuals, learning the nomenclature of the parts. After gaining some book-knowledge the companies moved to the training sites where they began constructing their first Bailey bridges. It was truly a school of hard knocks, and everyone learned by trial and error. Within a short period of time the men of the battalion mastered the bridge, and everyone knew that he could construct the bridge at any time, either in daylight or in total darkness. Before the war ended, the 51st built many of those bridges throughout Europe.

To hone the skills of the two battalions and to make life a little easier, the 1111th built several buildings on the reservation. Using salvaged lumber, three buildings were constructed for group and battalion headquarters. Shower facilities accommodated 2,000 men with hot and cold water. An outdoor theater was built with a 24 × 36 foot stage, and a seating capacity of 2,000 persons. On occasion the local population came out to enjoy a movie under the stars with the men. A 24 by 36 foot building was constructed for the Post Exchange.

Portable generators powered an electric lighting system for each of the buildings. Lights were connected for the headquarters, theater, each company kitchen, and the Post Exchange building. That work provided valuable training not only in the building trades, but also in construction, supervision, and organization of such projects.

During May the 51st constructed a number of pillboxes. These were organized into a fortified area so that each company could be trained in the techniques for assaulting a fortified position. Normally a combined team of infantry and engineers worked with support by indirect artillery and by aircraft. Advancing with the infantry, the engineers used flame throwers to force the enemy to close the openings in the pillbox with either sandbags or steel doors. They then placed satchel charges (prepared bundles of TNT in a canvas satchel, with a blasting cap, a time fuse, and a fuse lighter), on the pillboxes to blast a hole through the concrete. The engineers also learned to clear lanes through concrete obstacles called "dragon's teeth" to provide lanes for tanks to move through.

Each company rotated through the fortified position site. To conserve TNT, and for safety reasons, live explosives were not used. Hundreds of blocks of wood measuring two inches by two inches by four inches, with .25-inch holes drilled in one end simulated ½-pound blocks

ADVANCED TRAINING

of TNT. These were used to make satchel charges, and to learn how to attach explosives to destroy bridges, fell trees, make booby traps, and destroy railroad rails. Before the training in explosives and demolition was completed, the troops were permitted to use real dynamite and TNT to drop two or three trees and to split a steel railroad rail.

During demolition training, a squad was formed into a circle with each man holding the two wires to a live electric blasting cap. The caps, enclosed in a copper shell .25-inches in diameter, were about 2.5-inches long, and filled with tetryl or PETN, a sensitive high-explosive used to detonate TNT or dynamite and other explosives. The electric caps could be ignited with a flashlight battery or a blasting machine activated by twisting the handle. With the blasting caps swinging between their legs, the men were taught the difference between arranging the caps in a parallel circuit and a series circuit. On one occasion a soldier, using a flashlight battery, did not believe that putting one wire on the positive terminal of the battery and the other on the flat end of the battery would cause an explosion. He learned the hard way. The blast injured all members of the squad who were immediately sent back to the post hospital. The doctor applied an antiseptic solution to each puncture in the skin and sent them back to the reservation for full duty. Those men with copper shrapnel imbedded in the skin were told that the fragments would either work their way to the surface where the men could remove them with their fingers, or they would remain embedded under their skin and never cause any problems.

The 1st Platoon, Company A had to construct an infiltration course before May was over. The course was about as long and as wide as a football field. At one end a seven-foot trench ran the width of the field. At the other end two .30-caliber machine guns were emplaced so that they could command the entire length of the field. When live ammunition was fired it passed about 20 inches above the ground. Between the trench and the machine guns were barbed wire entanglements, craters, and trip wires that would set off explosives when moved. While the machine guns swept the entire field with live ammunition, a platoon crawled out of the trench, rifles cradled in their arms, and moved forward on their bellies, avoiding the craters and trip wires and keeping their butts low to the ground. At the barbed wire they turned on their backs so that they could hold the wire up with their hands as they wiggled under it.

As the platoon finished construction of the course, Captain "Bull" Yates, the battalion commander, arrived on the scene. He asked Lieutenant Wright if his platoon had constructed the course. Wright replied proudly, "Yes, Sir, 1st Platoon, Company A." With that, Yates directed

Wright to get into the trench at the far end and crawl toward him while he fired one of the .30-caliber machine guns. Yates was going to find out if the infiltration course was safe for the rest of the battalion by using Wright as a guinea pig. No matter which direction Wright crawled, Yates kept the machine gun fire directly overhead. The rest of the platoon thought this little exercise to test their work was extremely funny. When the results of the test proved the course had been properly constructed, the platoon became the first group of men in the battalion to crawl through the course, as Yates and Wright manned the machine guns. Afterward, every member of the battalion completed the course as part of their qualification for shipment overseas.

On June 4, 1943, Major Victor J. Reafsnyder took command of the 51st Engineer Combat Battalion. Captain Yates then became battalion executive officer, and Captain Alfred H. Rawlins the assistant division engineer (ADE). The ADE's primary job was to maintain liaison with the next higher headquarters above battalion, normally a group, but sometimes a division or corps headquarters.

Captain Yates was promoted to major on June 11, 1943. By then the battalion had fired for qualification on the rifle range with the .30-caliber M1 rifle, and the order of classification in arms was published. H&S Company had 3 experts, 24 sharpshooters, and 64 marksmen. A total of 83 percent of the men qualified. Company A had 1 expert, 47 sharpshooters, and 95 marksmen, with 79 percent of the men qualifying. Company B with 15 experts, 48 sharpshooters, and 106 marksmen, had 88 percent qualify. Company C qualified 90 percent of the men with 10 experts, 64 sharpshooters, and 83 marksmen. The medical detachment had 1 expert, 1 sharpshooter, and 11 marksmen, qualifying 72 percent of its men. Eighty-five percent of the men of the battalion qualified. Sergeant Hervie L. Middleton, Company B, who had come to the 51st at Camp Bowie in the summer of 1942, had the highest score in the battalion with 206 points out of a possible 210.

The school at Fort Belvoir continued to turn out second lieutenants for the 51st. On July 4, 1943, Lieutenants Charles Attardo, Bruce W. Jamison, Leo Nolan, and Richard Pulawski joined the battalion. Jamison had attended a refresher course at Belvoir after earning his commission through ROTC. The others were graduates of the 33d class at Officers Candidate School.

On July 7, 1943, Company A was ordered to move by motor convoy to Aberdeen Proving Grounds, Maryland. After a full day's journey, the men of Company A pitched their pup tents on the parade ground of the Military Academy at West Point, New York, and spent the night. The next night was spent on the floor of a gymnasium in Pennsylvania.

ADVANCED TRAINING

The following day the company arrived at Aberdeen, Maryland, about 22 miles northeast of Baltimore, the Ordnance Corps' testing and proving grounds for Army vehicles and tanks.

Company A's mission was to construct short spans of all the fixed vehicular bridges presently in the Army's inventory. The Ordnance Corps wanted to know how their tanks and trucks would perform on those bridges. The bridges were built on flat terrain, so considerable time and effort was spent beforehand in establishing manmade abutments. These were made of wood-timber cribbage with earth piled behind them to make an approach ramp and a foundation for the abutment so that the finished bridge would be a few feet above the ground. Among the bridges constructed were the Bailey bridge, a bridge which utilized the adjustable aluminum trestles from the 25-ton ponton bridge, a bridge using the treadways from the steel treadway floating bridge and the standard timber trestle bridge. Several roads and wood-timber box culverts were also constructed. Within 12 days the job was completed.

Although the company received valuable training in building the bridges, culverts, and roads, the most memorable part of the trip to Aberdeen had to do with the fact that it was home base for several battalions of the Women's Army Corps (WACs). The Army trained those female soldiers to drive, test, repair, and maintain every vehicle and tank that the Army owned. Those soldiers of Company A lucky enough to get a pass to Baltimore will never forget the late night train ride back to Aberdeen. The coaches were 95 percent filled with WAC passengers, and 5 percent Company A, all singing in perfect harmony as the train chugged back to Aberdeen.

With a job well done and a letter of commendation from the commanding general to prove it, Company A returned to Plattsburg, New York, on July 24.

On July 12, while Company A was in Aberdeen, First Lieutenant Schroff replaced Lieutenant Ross as the battalion S-3.

Combined Training

When Company A returned, the 51st began combined training. This training included platoon, company, and battalion field exercises; squad and platoon combat firing; attacking fortified areas; combat in cities; laying and removal of mines; and intensive bridge and road construction. In addition the battalion conducted a review of basic and unit training.

THE 51ST AGAIN!

The battalion continued to conduct full field pack hikes to Macomb Reservation each Monday morning. The men were challenged to beat the walking time of the previous Monday. Coming back each Friday afternoon was easier. All the men looked forward to warm quarters, a soft bed with sheets, and passes to town.[7]

At that point in the Army's mobilization program the only antitank weapon available to small units was a towed 37-mm. antitank gun. In addition to the three squad trucks assigned to a combat engineer platoon, an armored half-track vehicle, which towed the 37-mm. gun, was included. The half-track was armed with a .50-caliber and .30-caliber machine gun mounted on a sliding rail. Altogether this half track packed a lot of firepower. Commanded by a weapons sergeant, with a crew from the three squads, the half-track was used extensively in all tactical training exercises. However, the 37-mm. gun could not penetrate the thick armored plate of the German tanks. Eventually it was replaced by the hand-held, 2.36 inch rocket launcher (bazooka).

To round out combined training, various competitive exercises were held between the companies. These included bridge building and squad and platoon combat firing. Company C had the best record in squad and platoon combat firing. It also had the best time in ponton bridge and H-10 bridge construction. Company B set the pace in the construction of the floating footbridge.

By this time most soldiers felt that they had done all of the training that could be done. They could not have been more wrong. More individual training was needed for the battalion. Selected soldiers went to special schools to become medical aidmen for each platoon. Others went to group headquarters to learn how to use and maintain tactical radios. When the course was completed, these men were assigned to operate the radios at company headquarters, and the portable back-pack radios authorized each platoon. Other soldiers went to Cooks and Bakers School, probably the most important school attended by the men in the battalion, because the quality of the meals affected the morale of everyone in a company. Soldiers can put up with most any unbearable condition as long as the unit has a good mess sergeant and good cooks.

Second Lieutenants Mueller and Coats became first lieutenants on July 28, as did Baldwin and O'Neil seven days later. On August 4 the battalion S-3, Captain Schroff, became the first officer promoted to that rank from the original cadre of second lieutenants sent to Camp Bowie. Captain Richard F. Huxman joined the battalion on August 31 and was assigned to headquarters.

In retrospect, when considering the outstanding training received by the 51st Engineer Combat Battalion at Plattsburg Barracks and the unit's high state of readiness, credit goes to many. Colonel Anderson, the group commander, and Major McCollam, his S-3 during most of the period, planned and organized the entire program. Major Yates, commander of the 51st ECB during most of the training period, executed the training under realistic conditions. The young lieutenants and NCOs, who led the companies and platoons and performed the actual training, did outstanding jobs under extremely adverse conditions. As old soldiers know, the backbone of any Army unit is its noncommissioned officer corps. The 51st was extremely fortunate to have an outstanding group of NCOs from first sergeant down to corporal. The training could not have been effective without them.

The buck privates in the rear ranks, the private first class, and the technicians—T/5s and T/4s—of the 51st were among the best soldiers in the United States Army. They had the mental alertness and physical stamina to master the many and varied skills they learned at Plattsburg under severe weather conditions. Throughout the history of the 51st, much credit has accrued to the officers and NCOs for their heroic achievements, and justly so. But the mud-sloggers who actually did the work with their bare hands must also get full credit and should never be forgotten for their contributions.

XIII Corps Maneuver Area

During the first three days of September 1943, the 51st prepared for movement from Plattsburg Barracks to the XIII Corps Maneuver Area in the mountains of West Virginia. All of the authorized unit equipment went on two trains. After the experience of moving to Plattsburg, New York, from Camp Bowie, Texas, this loading operation moved along like a well-oiled machine. The train pulled out of Plattsburg at 1800 hours on September 3, and 46 hours later, arrived at Elkins, West Virginia. After unloading the train, troops and equipment moved to a bivouac area about eight miles east of the city.

Located in the northeastern part of the state, Elkins is about 40 miles southwest of the Maryland state line. It has an elevation of 1,930 feet above sea level, and is on the edge of the Monongahela National Forest. Peaks within the park range well over 4,000 feet. The bivouac area for the battalion was on the side of a steep mountain. If a soldier twisted and turned in his sleep, the next morning he would find his body halfway out of his pup tent. The 1111th ECG frequently ordered changes of unit bivouac areas to provide the units training in putting up and taking down tents, and in the establishment of new command posts (CPs).

LIEUTENANT PRESTON C. HODGES ON A 40-TON BAILEY BRIDGE BUILT IN ONE DAY NEAR DAVIS, WV.

From the collection of Preston C. Hodges

The 51st's mission at Elkins involved construction of facilities within the maneuver area to make it usable by other units. Within nine days all of the tasks were completed. Company A had built roads and culverts and a timber unloading platform at the railroad siding. Company B built an airplane landing strip and a Bailey bridge near the small town of Davis, and Company C constructed a fixed target, known distance range, about two miles from Davis. Some of the lucky soldiers working near Davis managed to go into town for a hot bath in one of the local barber shops for twenty-five cents. The work done by Companies B and C was for the XIII Corps field artillery brigade. The commanding general commended both companies for their outstanding effort.[8]

ADVANCED TRAINING

Fort Belvoir, Virginia

Early on September 16, the battalion departed West Virginia by motor convoy for Fort Belvoir, Virginia. The route took the battalion across the Appalachian mountain range on steep grades and hairpin turns. Those roads provided valuable training in convoy discipline and driving skills. The most important lesson learned by the drivers was how to gear down on the steep grades to slow the fast-moving vehicles rather than riding the brakes which quickly burned out the vehicle brake linings.

By early afternoon the convoy arrived in Winchester, Virginia, near the upper end of the Shenandoah Valley. There the 51st bivouacked overnight in the same town that Union and Confederate soldiers had occupied several times during the American Civil War. As T/5 Thomas G. Banks, H&S Company recalled, all the mothers called their daughters home the night the 51st arrived. Perhaps their grandparents did not have fond memories of the days long ago when other soldiers spent the night in their town.[9]

At 0500 hours the next morning, with each vehicle's gas tank topped off, the convoy left for Fort Belvoir. Once the vehicles were unloaded, the troops moved into wooden barracks in the First Battalion area of the Engineer Replacement Training Center. The anticipation of sleeping in a real bed once again loomed large in the minds of everyone. Watching the cheerful soldiers, a casual observer would think that they were checking into the Ritz. That luxurious living lasted only 12 days.

During their short stay, the battalion was attached to the Engineer School as demonstration troops. To keep busy when not putting on demonstrations for students, the battalion held a close order drill competition between the nine line platoons of the battalion. Scheuber's platoon from Company B won first place, closely followed by Wright's platoon from Company A. At the end of 12 days the commandants of the Replacement Training Center and the Engineer School, expressed their appreciation in writing for the excellent work. Several of the officers and men of the 51st ECB received personal commendations.

The return to Fort Belvoir had been like a homecoming for the officers of the 51st ECB. Within the short span of 16 months, at least 90 percent of the officers of the battalion had completed the 90-day course of the Officers Candidate School and earned the well-known title of "Ninety Day Wonders," along with their second lieutenant's gold bars. The remaining 10 percent in the battalion had recently completed refresher training courses at Fort Belvoir.

THE 51ST AGAIN!

On September 22, while at Fort Belvoir, Virginia, Karl G. Pedersen, Company A, was promoted to captain. Karl had the honor of being the first company commander in the 51st to be promoted to captain.

Eight days later Warrant Officer Junior Grade Wilfred G. Morin joined the battalion as the personnel officer and assistant adjutant. On the next day the 51st Engineer Combat Battalion left Fort Belvoir by motor march, bound for Fort Dix, New Jersey, where it would prepare for shipment overseas.

CHAPTER III

ENGLAND BY WAY OF NORTH AFRICA

Preparation for Movement

The 51st Engineer Combat Battalion arrived at Fort Dix at 0800 hours, October 1, 1943. The unit put all of its organizational equipment into the best possible condition, then crated, waterproofed, and marked it for shipment overseas. Showdown inspections of individual clothing and equipment were also conducted. Shortages were filled and overages turned in. Because each squad, platoon, and company had organizational tool and equipment chests to pack for shipment, everyone in the battalion had an opportunity to sneak personal items into them, and many did so. The items squirreled away varied from civilian shoes and clothing to favorite canned foods and bottled beverages. All of the units' equipment that did not accompany the troops was sent by rail to the Los Angeles Port of Embarkation (POE) at Wilmington, California. Chief Warrant Officer Keesing was in charge of the supply detail that accompanied this shipment.[1]

Fort Dix was the last meeting place for the married men of the battalion and their wives. When the battalion left Plattsburg for West

Virginia most of the wives returned to their home towns for the duration of the war. Some ventured to Elkins, West Virginia, for the possibility of one or two more visits, and most of those wives journeyed to Fort Dix for one last rendezvous.

While at Fort Dix, New Jersey, First Lieutenant Radford was promoted to captain on October 18, as was First Lieutenant Barnes on October 27. On October 28, the addition of 25 men from the 22d Armored Division, and 25 men from Elkins, West Virginia, brought the battalion up to authorized strength. Warrant Officers Junior Grade Morin and Keesing were promoted to chief warrant officer on October 29. Warrant Officer Junior Grade Julius J. Horecka joined the battalion on November 1 and was assigned as assistant motor officer.

Fort Dix to North Africa

On November 5, Second Lieutenant Raymond C. Trafford joined the battalion just in time to leave by rail that same day for Camp Patrick Henry, Virginia. It was an overnight trip and by 0900 hours the next morning the battalion had moved into temporary buildings in Block 7 of the staging area. Camp Patrick Henry was about 13 miles southeast of Williamsburg and about five miles from Yorktown. There General Charles Cornwallis surrendered to General George Washington in 1781 while the British band played an old British tune, "The World Turned Upside Down." For the men of the 51st in 1943, the world was also topsy turvy. They did not know where they were going, when they would get there, or if they would ever return.[2]

At Camp Patrick Henry final preparations were completed for overseas movement. All of the men were inoculated against yellow fever, and typhus and cholera shots were started. Final shakedown inspections of individual clothing and equipment were also conducted. Once again men were transferred into and out of the battalion to bring it to within the allowed two percent of authorized strength, a requirement for overseas shipment.

Training films emphasized the importance of protecting secret information. "Loose lips sink ships" was everyone's slogan. Each individual was required to sign a statement to the effect that he had received orders for overseas movement, and that he understood that if he went absent without leave (AWOL), he would be guilty of desertion. Desertion in time of war was punishable by death by firing squad.

In spite of this threat, one soldier in Company A went AWOL. Upon investigation, it was learned from his squad leader that the soldier had

ENGLAND BY WAY OF NORTH AFRICA

recently met a beautiful blonde woman in New York City. His squad leader was sure the soldier did not intend to desert, just visit his lady friend. The sergeant felt he could convince the man to come back if he could get a two day pass to go to New York to talk to the soldier. This was a serious situation because passes were not authorized for anyone. On the other hand going AWOL at this time was even more serious. Captain Pedersen, the company commander, agreed to let the sergeant have two days to go to New York and return with the soldier. The morning report would be padded to show both men present for duty for the two days. If, on the third day, both men were not present for duty, they would be reported AWOL. On the third day, when the morning report was submitted, the two men were reported as AWOL. Within two hours of submission of the morning report they returned to duty. They were immediately given company punishment, an appropriate punishment under the circumstances. Each soldier had to perform extra duty within the company. Since no soldier can be punished twice for the same offense, company punishment was given by Pedersen to prevent higher headquarters from giving a more severe punishment as prescribed for desertion.

The battalion commander was furious. He immediately reduced the sergeant to private, fined him two thirds of his base pay for six months, and transferred him to another company. Obviously the ploy by Pedersen did not work. However, before the war ended the sergeant won back his stripes.

The battalion divided itself into two parts for the 13-mile rail trip to the Hampton Roads Port of Embarkation. The first element, commanded by Major Reafsnyder, departed on November 12, 1943. It consisted of the battalion staff, H&S Company, Companies A and B, and the First Platoon of Company C under Lieutenant Nolan. This element boarded the Liberty Ship H.R. 650, S.S. *Calvin Coolidge*. Major Reafsnyder was troop commander of all troops on board ship. The second element, commanded by Major Yates and consisting of the remainder of Company C, departed the next day aboard the Liberty Ship H.R. 656, S.S. *Richard Rush*. Also on board were Company A, 49th Engineer Combat Battalion, minus one platoon, and Company C, 237th Engineer Combat Battalion, minus one platoon. Major Yates was assigned as the commander of all troops on board that ship.

While standing on the dock waiting to board ship, each soldier received a small cloth bag with a drawstring from Red Cross volunteers. This bag contained, among other things, a small pencil, a writing pad, chewing gum, hard lemondrop candy, and a deck of cards. This gift proved useful while on the high seas.

THE 51ST AGAIN!

The convoy of 74 Liberty Ships and 17 escort vessels left Chesapeake Bay on November 14, 1943. An entry was made on each soldier's service record stating that he had left the United States for service overseas. The exact destination of the convoy was not known, but a southerly course was followed almost to Bermuda. From there the convoy turned toward the Straits of Gibraltar. After a few days at sea, most of the men got their sea legs and made good sailors. They encountered heavy seas for about three days and many men lost more than their sea legs as their stomachs rebelled. The convoy often changed course while zigzaging across the ocean, and the radar screen sometimes detected unknown objects while on the 19-day trip. Perhaps some were submarines.

Life on a Liberty Ship was a new experience. Sleeping and living in the ship's hold was almost impossible. The soldiers occupied bunks six or seven tiers high. Only the most seasoned sailors could watch the swinging back and forth of the packs and rifles hanging from these bunks without getting seasick. Each day the troops were brought to the top deck of the ship for organized calisthenics. As the men became accustomed to the rolling and heaving of the ship, they ventured out on deck on their own initiative to view the windswept ocean and the beautiful skies. The decks of the ship were always covered with oily soot from the ship's smokestack. No matter where one sat there was always a mixture of salt spray and oily soot. As a result, the soldiers' uniforms were soon covered with brine, sweat, and a greasy residue. The men tried to launder their clothes in the salt water provided for washing but never had good results.[3]

The food was probably the worst aspect of the journey. Galley personnel had installed a large steam pot in the hold of the ship. There C-rations were opened, tossed into the pot, and then heated. Twice a day the troops would pass by this pot and receive two scoops in their mess kits along with a couple of hard C-ration crackers.

With only two meals a day, food was always on the mind of the soldiers on board ship. The ship's crew had their own galley and food and ate a normal three meals a day, without the soldier's dull C-rations or K-rations. This arrangement had the potential to become explosive. The potential grew when some of the ship's crew, in order to fatten their wallets, sold steak sandwiches to the soldiers for twenty dollars. Eventually some of the men broke into the ship's cargo of C-rations and K-rations in an effort to get more food. Cooler heads soon prevailed. The men were admonished for breaking and entering, but no one was punished and no serious problems developed.

On one occasion a man from the 51st, Technician Fifth Grade Thomas Banks, volunteered for a detail to clean out the ship's refrigerator and freezer. In the process he managed to hide a large bologna sausage under his coat. Once back in the hold of the ship with the sausage, Banks could not feed the multitudes, but about 50 soldiers did get a taste of something different.[4]

On November 20, while still at sea, Captain Schroff was relieved as battalion S-3 and assigned as the assistant division engineer (ADE). Captain Huxman replaced him as the S-3.

The 51st was still on the high seas when a conference took place in Teheran, Iran, that influenced the conduct of the entire war and even changed the direction in which the 51st was going. President Franklin D. Roosevelt, Prime Minister Winston Churchill, and Premier Joseph Stalin, decided that the war in Europe would have first priority over the one in the Pacific. As a result, the 51st was diverted from India and given orders to prepare for movement to England. The equipment that went from California to India would now be issued to other units once it was learned that the 51st was going to Europe. All the scheming that went into shipping unauthorized items went for naught when the booty went to the units who received their equipment in the China-Burma-India (CBI) Theater of operations.[5]

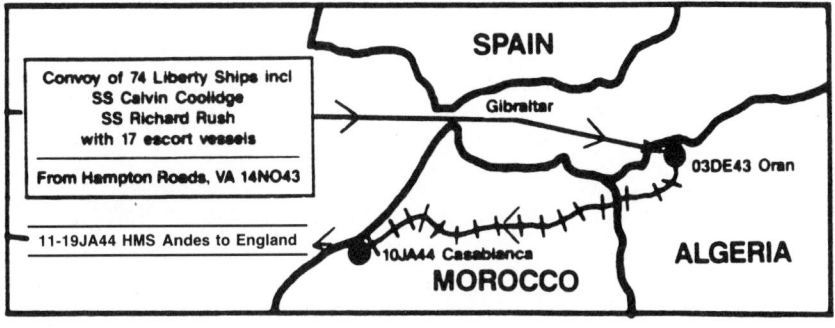

Courtesy of Major General John W. Barnes, USA (Ret.)

––––––––––––––––––– North Africa –––––––––––––––––––

The convoy entered the European-African-Middle Eastern Theater of Operations on November 23, 1943. On December 1 the men sighted the Rock of Gibraltar. As the convoy reached the coast of Oran, Algeria, the ships carrying the 51st, along with several others, steamed out of the convoy and headed for the foggy Port of Oran. With fog horns blaring it looked as if ships were going in all directions. Adding to the confusion was an unidentified aircraft passing over the convoy earlier in the day. The battalion had received orders around November 28 directing it to disembark in the Mediterranean Base Section for trans-shipment to England.

The ships dropped anchor in the harbor of Oran. The next day, December 5, the battalion disembarked and moved about 12 miles by truck to Staging Area Number 2 near Fleurus, Algeria. They were billeted in pyramidal tents in Area 18 for a stay that lasted about 30 days. Physical conditions made it appear much longer. Near the campsite steep Lion Mountain overlooked the Mediterranean Sea. The men had to climb that mountain many times during their 30-day stay in North Africa as part of their physical conditioning.

Without organizational equipment, training was limited. However, the lack of equipment did not prevent the establishment of a full schedule of activities. A provisional company was formed for the purpose of conducting military ceremonies. The company, composed of a platoon from each line company, was commanded by Captain Barnes. It participated in retreat parade ceremonies held in Oran with Major Reafsnyder as the reviewing officer. The G-3 Section, Mediterranean Base Section, highly complimented the company on its performance.

With only a few days since the last changes in personnel, the battalion continued to play musical chairs with assignments. On December 7, Lieutenant Boies moved from Company A to the battalion staff to become reconnaissance officer, exchanging places with Lieutenant Trafford. Captain Schroff, who had been ADE for just 17 days, was reassigned as commanding officer, Company C, changing positions with Captain Barnes.

While the battalion waited for a ship to England, someone decided that the troops could be used as stevedores in the Port of Oran. It was a two-shift operation with about 150-200 men on each shift. The dock assignment was a chore performed with mixed emotions. The men had to unload all types of munitions from merchant ships in torrential rains. At other times they loaded crates of food and Post Exchange supplies. Once in a while one of these crates accidentally dropped and split open. When that happened the men would help themselves as long as the port supervisors were not present.[6]

Some of the men of the 51st thought that North Africa had a warm or hot climate. They were surprised to find that in December and January the weather was cold and wet. Early mornings found the campsites muddy after the evening rains and often frozen. The sun shone for brief periods during the day but when it went down the weather turned cold.

ENGLAND BY WAY OF NORTH AFRICA

The Arabs knew how to dress for this kind of weather, using several layers of loose fitting clothing. Banks of H&S Company, who drove a truck moving them to and from the docks, remembers Arab dock workers carrying a loaf of bread and a bottle of wine in the crotch of their baggy trousers.[7]

On December 23, all men and officers became eligible for the European-African-Middle Eastern Theater Campaign Ribbon and medal because they had been in the theater for 30 days. Christmas Day, two days later, was not a joyous occasion. There were no letters or packages from home. The folks in the USA knew only that the 51st was still enroute to some unknown destination overseas. They ate their turkey and that was it.

The battalion departed Oran by rail on January 6, 1944 on the "Arab Cannonball" in 4-wheel "40 and 8" cars. During WW I that type car was used to transport 40 men or 8 horses. In Oran, 30 men and all their equipment were jammed into each car along with C-rations and five-gallon cans of water to last for 48 hours. The 420-mile, two-day trip to Casablanca was miserable for everyone. The train made frequent stops for fuel and water and for the troops to answer the call of nature.

Everyone was happy to arrive in Casablanca. The battalion was met by trucks and moved two miles to Camp Don B. Passage. This camp, with its high security fence around the pyramidal tents inside, looked like a prisoner-of-war facility. At least there were cots to sleep on and three good meals every day. While there Lieutenant Mueller, the S-1, experienced heart trouble and was transferred to the Detachment of Patients, 6th General Hospital, Casablanca, as a patient. Captain Barnes assumed Mueller's duties. From January 8 to 11 the battalion prepared for another ocean voyage, this time to England.

On January 12, 1944, the 51st and men from four other engineer combat battalions boarded a British vessel, the HMS *Andes*, and sailed for Liverpool, England, normally a three-day trip. They were unescorted on their journey because the *Andes* was said to be fast enough to elude submarine attacks. That is precisely what the *Andes* did for nine days, dodging submarines picked up on the ship's radar by zig-zagging all the way to England. After sailing west for two days, the *Andes* turned north, almost reaching Iceland before heading into the North Channel, then into the Irish Sea, reaching port at Liverpool on January 20, 1944. According to the ship's crew, at one point in the journey, HMS *Andes* was just 24 hours east of New York. The three-day cruise had lasted nine days during which time the ship pitched and rolled in the wild seas of the North Atlantic, an area notorious for its terrible winter storms. The men had quite an interesting time in their "slippery cafeteria."

England

On the same day that the *Andes* arrived in Liverpool the battalion left by train for Llanelly on the south coast of Wales, arriving on January 21, 1944. Since there were no military billets, the men of the 51st were assigned to commercial buildings in the city. H&S Company was assigned to the Exchange Drapery Building, Company A to the Furniss Camp building, Company B to Richard Thomas Institute, and Company C to the Corona Works. The battalion was assigned to the First United States Army commanded by Lieutenant General Omar N. Bradley.

Training was conducted in the outlying areas of Llanelly without organizational equipment. The battalion went back to basics immediately. Drill, tactical exercises, and physical conditioning became the order of the day. Because all five of the engineer combat battalions diverted to England from Africa were without equipment and supplies, training schedules had to be coordinated with the delivery schedules of the new organizational equipment. During the battalion's stay in England the movement of officers within the 51st, and out of it, continued unabated.

Beginning on February 10, 1944, the 51st moved by companies from Llanelly to Highnam Court, two miles northwest of Gloucester, England, where on February 11 the battalion was attached to the 1128th Engineer Combat Group. The movement was completed on the 13th with the arrival of H&S Company, battalion headquarters, and the medical detachment.

At Highnam Court, the battalion faced a supply problem. Requisitions for all organizational equipment had to be prepared and carried to the nearest supply depot. Supply Sergeant Paris Pugh prepared the requisitions and took them to the depot for quick action. He returned soon afterwards with the news that the depot supply personnel would not honor their requisitions because the 51st was not on any United Kingdom authorized supply list. Lieutenant Coats, the battalion S-4, reported the information to the executive officer, Major Yates. He responded, "Coats, take my jeep (one borrowed from another unit) and go to Base Section Headquarters, and don't come back until you have approval to draw our equipment." Needless to say, Coats left for Base Section Headquarters before daylight the next morning to carry out Yates' orders. Once there he was confronted at every level with the comment, "We don't have the 51st ECB on our list of units scheduled to be in England."[8]

By mid-afternoon, Coats finally got to see the Deputy Commander, Base Section, who listened to his supply problems and gave him the same responses as the others. However, he did promise to send a cablegram to Washington to "get this cleared up." He told Coats to stay overnight for he expected a reply the next morning. Coats, acting on orders from Major Yates, was not about to go back to Highnam Court without supply approval. Sure enough, the next morning the answer to the deputy's cablegram came back. It said, "We are not sure why the 51st ECB is in England, but take immediate action to issue the full allowance of organizational equipment."

As the battalion continued training in the vicinity of Gloucester, a steady stream of equipment arrived. Training now included day and night construction of Bailey bridges, mines and booby traps training, camouflage training, and tactics. Not many stones were left unturned. Some men of the 51st went to special schools in England for advanced training in aircraft recognition, minefields and booby traps, Bailey bridging, unit gas officer, bomb reconnaissance, intelligence, and whatever else was available to assist in battalion training. This schooling was used to excellent advantage when the men reported back to their units and passed their new-found knowledge to others in the battalion.

The 51st ECB also conducted training for other units. A secret letter and movement order from Headquarters, First United States Army, dated February 16, 1944, called for Company B, 51st Engineer Combat Battalion, to go to the Western Base Section, Oulton, Cheshire, England, on February 22, to give basic and engineer training to fillers at the 19th Replacement Depot. The training lasted for about six weeks. All members of Company B rejoined the battalion by April 3, once their mission had been accomplished.

The work of Captain Preston C. Hodges and his Company B had been outstanding. Lieutenant Colonel Craighill, commanding officer of the 86th Replacement Battalion, characterized in a letter the work of the officers and men of Company B as an "exceptionally meritorious performance...they have shown a constant devotion to duty, and by their example, in discipline and soldierly bearing, have assisted me greatly in my program of discipline for the Replacements." A second letter of commendation came from Colonel Louis P. Leone, commanding officer, Field Force Replacement Depot #4, with endorsements by the Commanding General, First United States Army, the Commanding Officer, 1111th Engineer Combat Group, and Major Reafsnyder, battalion commander. The battalion was justifiably proud of the men of Company B.[9]

On March 1, 1944 the 51st Engineer Combat Battalion was detached from the 1128th Engineer Combat Group and attached to the 1111th

THE 51ST AGAIN!

Engineer Combat Group which Colonel Anderson still commanded. The 51st was back home again with the 1111th Group, the original parent headquarters.

To commemorate the battalion's first anniversary, Major Reafsnyder issued a memorandum praising the men for their excellent work of the past year. He then set the day aside for commemorative activities including softball, volleyball, and football, pitting company against company within the battalion. Company C grabbed the brass ring on this day with victories in three sports. An awards and decoration ceremony followed during which 238 enlisted men of the battalion were presented good conduct ribbons for exemplary behavior, efficiency, and fidelity.[10]

The anniversary program ended with the entire battalion, less Company B, passing in review. Company B was on detached duty at Oulton on this date. The question of whether Company B could have earned sports laurels that day against Company C still remains a subject of good-natured debate.

Throughout March the battalion continued to draw bulldozers, bridging, and other equipment needed to bring the 51st to full Table of Organization and Equipment (TO&E) authorization. Training continued without let-up. An evening two-week specialist school started on March 27, 1944 with classes conducted by the officers and NCO's of the 51st. Men trained to be first sergeants, platoon sergeants, motor sergeants, supply sergeants, company clerks, mechanics, electricians, and radio repairmen, as well as specialists in other fields authorized under the TO&E. Tractor and truck driver schools consisted of actual on-the-job experience on projects under way by the battalion. Water supply and radio operator schools were held later.[11]

The "head shed" was not sitting idly by. The commanding officer, executive officer, and staff, plus key headquarters and section personnel, and company commanders, participated in a command post exercise which started at 1320 hours and concluded around 2100 hours on March 31, 1944. Exercises included selection of bivouac areas, establishment of CPs and outposts, reconnaissance, movement of a CP to a new location, and simulated erection of a floating bridge. Camouflage, camouflage discipline, vehicle dispersal, command post procedure, column control, and battalion standard operating procedures (SOP) were also stressed.

Preparations for the Continent

On April 13, 1944 alert orders for movement under the provisions of "European Theatre of Operations for Overseas Movement, Short Sea

ENGLAND BY WAY OF NORTH AFRICA

Voyage" were received. Movement orders were scheduled to be posted on or after April 30. Detailed instructions on administrative and supply procedures were immediately implemented. Loading plans for movement were completed in which all impedimenta and personnel were assigned to specific vehicles to avoid confusion at loading time. The commander divided the battalion into forward and rear elements and they prepared to move separately as scheduled.

Intense training continued during April on such subjects as construction of the Bailey bridge, fixed timber bridges, and the M-3 pneumatic floating bridge. Other subjects included mines and minefields, explosives and demolitions, road construction, chemical warfare, physical conditioning, and night operations. In addition, the group held a group command post exercise on April 25 and 26 with the battalion command post established at Newent Woods, Gloucestershire. Emphasis was on reconnaissance and communications, radio transmission, the laying and retrieving of landlines, and cryptography.

1 LT. MAURICE COATS, BN S-4, AND SGT. EDWARD F. FARRELL, BN SUPPLY SERGEANT.
From the collection of Maurice E. Coats

LEFT TO RIGHT. CPT. SAM SCHEUBER, LT. FRED NABORS, LT. _____ MILLNE (first name unknown), AND LT. JOHN NORTON, COMPANY C OFFICERS. LT. GREEN AT SCHOOL IN ENGLAND.

From the collection of Sam Scheuber

COLONEL H. WALLIS ANDERSON, COMMANDING OFFICER, 1111TH ENGINEER COMBAT GROUP, PINS SOLDIER'S MEDAL ON T/5 THOMAS G. BANKS, H&S COMPANY, 51ST ENGINEER COMBAT BATTALION.

Photo from After Action Report, 51st Engineer Combat Battalion

ENGLAND BY WAY OF NORTH AFRICA

In the midst of all this training, Staff Sergeant Russell E. Watson, Company B, was developing a breakdown modification of the standard mine marker. The modification made the marker collapsible, making it easier to transport and store. His proposal was submitted through channels to Headquarters, First United States Army on April 25, 1944. Shortly thereafter, word came back down through channels to Sergeant Watson that his modification was "considered to be of merit." It was published and sent to all Engineer elements of First Army as Engineer Intelligence Memorandum No. 13. Watson received the congratulations of the entire battalion.

On May 1, Reafsnyder was promoted to lieutenant colonel and Trafford to first lieutenant.

In spite of the intensive training, the men of the battalion found time to pursue other endeavors. Often the men hiked into the city of Gloucester to the local pub to dine, dance, or enjoy an evening with the residents. Tempers flared one night between men of the 51st and black soldiers of a nearby outfit, resulting in a mild melee. All that was hurt was the pride of all the combatants on both sides, who lost their passes pending resolution of the underlying causes of the fight. The solution to the problem was to issue passes on alternate days.

On the lighter side, selected personnel of the 51st participated in a "Salute to the Soldier Week" program organized by the British at Newent, Gloucestershire, on May 13, 1944. Money raised by admission fees went to the British War Loan. Members of the battalion, under the supervision of Captain John W. Barnes, played exhibition baseball games (with running commentary by Barnes and First Lieutenant Richard I. Green), and football (with commentary by Green and Lieutenant Vincent J. Harwood). Local citizens displayed considerable interest in those two typical American sports. In addition, the men of the battalion won second place in an 880-yard relay. They also won a tug of war for which each participant received 15 shillings as a prize. The battalion had, in a small way, "done their bit" to help the war effort. At the same time the participants and local onlookers enjoyed a brief respite from the war.

Finally, on the evening of June 5, 1944, the battalion received the code word "Adoration" which imposed radio silence on all units in England except those actually involved in the invasion. Shortly after midnight on June 6, 1944, much unusual aerial activity aroused suspicions among the men that the long awaited invasion was about to begin. For an hour or two, the sky was filled with low-flying planes, all traveling in a southerly direction, showing green, red, and amber lights. D-day had arrived, confirmed by radio reports the next morning that the landings had already begun on the coast of Normandy.[12]

THE 51ST AGAIN!

Two days after Normandy the battalion received General Order Number 21, First United States Army, awarding the soldier's medal to Technician Fifth Grade Thomas G. Banks, H&S Company. While working in the motor pool, Thomas saw a man nearby whose greasy and oil-soaked clothes had caught fire. He told the man to lay down and roll over, but the man was too excited to obey. So Thomas knocked the man down and threw himself on top of him to smother the flames, saving his life in the process. A review to honor Banks and present his soldier's medal was held at Highnam Court, Gloucester on June 10. The 51st, 291st, and 296th Engineer Combat Battalions participated in the ceremony during which Colonel Anderson of the 1111th Engineer Combat Group presented the award to Banks before reviewing the troops.

More than ever, readiness was now the name of the game. Late arriving ringmounts were installed on 2½-ton trucks on June 14. The rings, mounted above the passenger seat of the truck, were designed to accommodate a .50-caliber machine gun which could provide some antiaircraft protection for convoys. Waterproofing of vehicles, radios, and other equipment was also completed at this time. Normal administration, supply, and training functions became a problem since organizational transport and equipment, now prepared and packed for shipment, could no longer be used.

In accordance with a letter from Headquarters, European Theater of Operations, United States Army, on June 17, the authorized strength of enlisted personnel in the 51st was reduced from 632 to 602. At 2230 hours on the same day an order came down to the radio message center in Gloucester to hold the battalion in readiness for movement orders. Those orders, received by the battalion at 0600 hours on June 18, gave instructions for the 51st to move via motor convoy to the marshalling area at Bournemouth, England. The forward element, consisting of 24 officers, a warrant officer, and 524 enlisted men, was to move at 1025 hours that same day.

Some pre-loading had been accomplished already. The balance of packing and loading was started immediately. The forward element assembled at 1015 hours, then moved to the marshalling area, arriving at 1830 hours. On July 2, the small rear element of 5 officers, 2 warrant officers, and 98 enlisted men, followed the same procedure.

Vehicles were lined up outside the battalion area and personnel marched to their assigned locations. All drivers remained with their vehicles once they refueled and drew de-waterproofing kits for them for use once the channel was crossed.

Each man was issued blankets, two days' rations (one day's K and one day's C), a carton of cigarettes, halazone tablets for water purification, a can of canned heat, vomit bags, and a partial pay of four dollars. British money was exchanged for French "Invasion" money. When the battalion departed England it had 29 officers, 3 warrant officers, and 622 enlisted men.[13]

In retrospect, one might wonder why the 51st received alert orders on April 13, 1944 with movement orders to be issued on or after April 30. Yet the battalion remained in a training status at Highnam Court until a further alert order was issued on June 17 with embarkation at Southampton Port two days later. Perhaps the answer lies in the fact that planning had been based on a May landing, weather permitting.

CHAPTER IV

UTAH BEACH TO THE ARDENNES

The hour had arrived at Southhampton. By 0800, June 19, 1944, battalion headquarters and H&S Company began boarding the Liberty Ship SS *Charles D. Poston*, while Company B filed on to the SS *Joseph H. Johnson*, and Company A and Company C boarded the SS *Abiel Foster*. By early the following morning, all personnel and equipment were securely on the three ships, which then moved to a location between the Isle of Wight and the mainland, where they dropped anchor. There they, and 120 other Liberty Ships, waited out a severe storm then pounding the beaches of France.[1]

The ships had loaded with the intention of making a one-day crossing of the English Channel so neither sleeping facilities nor kitchens were provided for the soldiers. As time aboard ship dragged from one to eight days, tempers became short and food supplies ran out. When the two days of rations carried by each person were consumed, small boats came alongside and delivered ten-in-one rations to each ship. These rations, designed to feed ten men for one day, contained cans of food such as sliced bacon and green beans that had to be cooked. To solve the cooking problem the troops were issued small one-burner gasoline stoves. Unfortunately few men knew how to cook properly and chaos followed. Food was either half-done or burned. Bacon grease saved from breakfast to season supper's green beans turned bad during the heat of the day. The result was long lines of men at the limited toilet facilities aboard ship with the "G.I.s" or "trots." Those squads with a soldier whose mother had required him to help with the cooking at home were indeed blessed.

Because sleep did not come easy to those stretched out on the steel deck of a liberty ship, most men of the 51st spent the nights watching fireworks in two directions. To the south, from across the channel, flashes of cannon fire from the Normandy beaches lit the night sky. To the north and northeast German bombers dropped their loads on England. The response of the anti-aircraft fire, with occasional bursts of tracer ammunition, added to the display.

While the battalion waited for orders to cross the channel, General Omar Bradley went to Omaha Beach on June 22 to inspect the damage caused by the storm. The desolation greatly exceeded that of D-day. Operations on Omaha Beach had been brought to a standstill. In four days the storm over the channel had threatened OVERLORD more gravely than had all the enemy's guns in the 14 days ashore.[2]

The Landing

Finally, on June 26, orders arrived to cross the channel. Originally destined for Omaha Beach, the 51st's assignment changed just before landing, and the three ships headed toward Utah Beach and dropped anchor late in the evening. The next day, June 27, the 51st landed in France. On this day, counting the days crossing the Atlantic Ocean to Oran, North Africa, and the days from Casablanca, Algiers, to Liverpool, England, the men of the 51st logged their 37th day of sea duty. Captain Preston Hodges, of Company B probably reflected the feelings of many of the men in the 51st when he said, "I never was a good sailor. After eight days on the stormy English Channel, I would have gone ashore on Utah Beach if a German machine gun was aimed directly at me."

The unloading was two days of utter chaos. Hundreds of ships of all sizes ran around in all directions—Rhino barges pushed by small boats, LCTs (landing craft tank, carrying 36 men or one 3½-ton vehicle), LCMs (landing craft medium carrying 120 men or one 32-ton vehicle), and all types of amphibious vehicles which could operate on either land or water. The most famous of the latter was the 2½-ton, 6×6 truck

- 47 -

known as the DUKW. When any of the smaller landing craft came alongside the ship, the troops would board them by means of a rope net or gangplank.

Aboard the SS *Abiel Foster*, the men of Companies A and C were preparing to disembark when one soldier's rifle disappeared. Apparently a member of the ship's crew looking for a war trophy picked it up, not fully realizing the seriousness of his action. The ship's captain was quick to assemble his entire crew on deck and lay down the law. If the rifle was not returned to a designated location within ten minutes the wrath of all his authority would descend on the whole crew. Fortunately for all concerned the rifle was returned and the soldier disembarked with weapon in hand.

To prepare for that important day, the battalion had trained extensively in England. It had test-driven the waterproofed vehicles through man-made mud holes containing several feet of water. Waterproofing of vehicles meant sealing their electrical system from water, to include plugs, distributor, and dashboard, with a putty-like substance. The exhaust pipe and air intake on the engine were extended into the air to keep water out. It was not enough. By the time the 51st arrived on the beach, the Army had learned that waterproofed vehicles driven through salt water quickly developed serious problems with their wheel bearings and braking systems. For this reason, some of the companies had to wait several hours for the tide to go out so they could drive ashore on dry land.

About half of the vehicles and men were unloaded and moved to Transit Area B during daylight on June 27, 1944. On the next day Captain Stearns of Headquarters, First United States Army, guided the battalion to its bivouac areas at Hebert, near Ste. Mere Eglise. The battalion command post (CP) opened at 1500 on June 28, 1944. By 2200 the last troops of the forward element had arrived in the bivouac area. In spite of much confusion on the beach the 51st Engineer Combat Battalion landed with no mishaps.[3]

Normandy

The companies spent the next day de-waterproofing vehicles, digging in, establishing CPs, drawing rations and preparing to perform their primary missions. Engineer reconnaissance teams went out to determine the condition of roads. This survey included checking road surfaces, base materials of the roads, width and drainage facilities, condition and capacity of bridges, and the location of road and bridge material. Roads were assigned to the companies from Carentan to Montebourg; Ste. Mere Eglise to Ravenoville; and Ste. Marie Dumont to Carentan. On orders from the 1111th Engineer Combat Group, the battalion began its mission of road maintenance and repair on June 30, 1944.

The 51st found its first CP area strewn with all types of enemy ammunition, clothing, and equipment. American troops had also littered the area with shelter halves, gas masks, socks, sweaters, and other personal items. Mae West jackets and water buoyant belts, no longer needed, were also scattered about.[4]

By July 1, the S-4 section, under Captain Maurice E. Coats, had established two water points for supplying the troops in the area with potable water. With these facilities in operation, the 51st ECB was fully deployed and ready to perform its primary mission which was to assist, by engineering works, the advance of the army. At that time, the front line was approximately ten miles from Utah Beach. Carentan, the most forward position in the battalion area of operation, was some two miles north of the established front.[5]

Roads had deteriorated rapidly in the congested area of the beachhead. The battalion filled the potholes in the asphalt roads with cold mix (emulsified asphalt mixed with crushed gravel). Gravel roads were graded, and drainage ditches and culverts cleaned and repaired. The unit constructed by-passes between major routes to ease the flow of traffic. Entrances to ammunition and supply dumps, hospitals and bivouac areas commanded constant attention from the road crews. Many areas were swept with mine detectors to clear German mines. Each company established guards on the bridges it maintained within its assigned area.

Because the battalion was in a static position many of the men not assigned duties moved about in the surrounding combat areas. They saw the results of war first-hand. Moving through St. Marie DuMont, Ste. Mere Eglise, and the Carentan marshes near the exposed beach areas, the truth of battle emerged. Many fresh American graves had appeared. The quartermaster grave registration units had trouble keeping up with the numbers of American dead. Remains were picked up, placed on 2½-ton trucks, and moved to cemeteries. There the personal effects were removed from the dead and identification established. Enemy dead remained where they fell. War booty, in the form of enemy weapons, bayonets, daggers, rifles, machine guns, insignia, medals, clothing, and personal items, was abundant, but the smell of death became a part of the booty and was hard to remove.[6]

Some of the officers ventured to the Utah Beach area where they observed the results of the destruction of German concrete bunkers by

51ST ECB VEHICLES ON LST 498 AT UTAH BEACH ON NORMANDY.
Courtesy of Joseph B. Milgram, Jr.

CONVOY WITH 51ST ECB HEADING FOR UTAH BEACH, NORMANDY. BARRAGE BALLOONS OVERHEAD.
Courtesy of Joseph B. Milgram, Jr.

naval gunfire. Unexploded American 500 pound bombs littered the area. There were few German dead. They had either lightly manned the bunkers or withdrawn during the bombardments. The abundant personal clothing and equipment left behind, as well as large quantities of liquor bottles, small arms ammunition, mines, and potato masher grenades, indicated a hasty retreat.[7]

They wandered into a minefield area where the shelling had effectively destroyed the barbed wire entanglements and "Achtung Minen" signs. The officers knew they were in the middle of a minefield because the "S" mine prongs and trip wires were now evident. Teller mines, box mines, and booby traps were visible along the seashore bank. The trespassers combined their technical knowledge to get out safely. They spaced themselves so that one explosion would not kill them all, then gently probed their way out of the mine field.[8]

Many 82d and 101st Airborne Division troops wandered around the area. Most of these paratroopers had been in the initial fighting. Their unpleasant experiences, such as the loss of buddies during the air drop and the hard hand-to-hand fighting, showed in their faces. They knew they were lucky to be alive. These stragglers roamed around as if they had completed their job and their war was over. They were generous with their limited booty. But most of all they were happy to be back in the rear. The 51st never refused them the hospitality of the mess kitchens. The hot C-rations and other warm foods were luxuries for the veterans.[9]

During this initial flurry of activity the battalion had its first combat casualty. On July 12 Private Colon A. Barco, Company C, was struck in the abdomen by a stray piece of anti-aircraft flak and evacuated. Late in the afternoon of the same day, about two miles from the battalion CP, an ammunition dump near Audoville caught fire. All available men and equipment were sent to assist in extinguishing it. The ammunition was packed in wooden boxes or crates, and stacked in long rows several feet high with lanes in between to provide access for loading and unloading. When elements of the battalion arrived at the dump they saw flames licking up the sides of the wooden crates and black smoke billowing from the top of the stacks. Shells of all descriptions exploded throughout the area. It took nerves of steel to move into and around this inferno while trying to control and put out the fire.

Backfiring isolated the fire. Bulldozers and tankdozers plowed lanes and covered burning material with dirt. Master Sergeant Lee N. Raper of H&S Company operated a D-7 dozer belonging to a man who had been injured on another job. Without regard to his own safety he drove the dozer into the blazing dump amid flying shell fragments, smoke and flame. Other men in the battalion also risked their lives. Major Yates, Captain Barnes, Lieutenants Murphy and Henry, and Private Cash were in the forefront of those who hastened to put out the flames. The battalion suffered no casualties in this action.[10]

Some of the common tasks performed by the Engineers included bomb disposal, mine clearing, and deactivation of booby traps. Lieutenant Colonel Reafsnyder did not appreciate the actions of PFC Robert Myer, H&S Company, when he dug a German 88-mm. shell from the stone wall of one of the buildings in the bivouac area and brought it to Lieutenant Attardo, the battalion bomb disposal officer. The two were admonished by the battalion commander to dispose of the dud properly. Attardo attached a one-half pound block of TNT to the shell and put it in a six-foot deep hole. All traffic in a one-half mile radius was stopped by a well-placed squad of men hollering "fire in the hole." The explosive was then set off.[11]

Early in the evening of July 18 a German plane strafed a Company C truck containing seven men near Jean de Daye. The vehicle was badly damaged and five men were wounded. Late in the next afternoon four German 88-mm. rounds landed in and around the bivouac area of Company A. The shelling partially destroyed the clothing and bed roll of the company commander, Captain Pedersen. If he had been in the bed roll he would have been killed. No casualties occurred from the shelling, but the men of company headquarters learned to identify the sound of incoming artillery shells for the first time.

By July 23, the battalion had its first combat fatigue casualty. The unit diary noted, "A member of Company A was evacuated as a nervous exhaustion case." The soldier liked taking care of .50-caliber machine guns, and had volunteered to man those on the perimeter of the Company A bivouac area that were used for aircraft defense. These were manned during daylight hours, and when needed at night. He had manned the guns steadily for almost a month before his breakdown. The battalion learned an important lesson from that unfortunate event. From then on it used the buddy system on guard duty, especially at night, and frequently rotated the duty of manning the machine guns.[12]

Shortly before the nervous exhaustion incident occurred a gas attack alarm in the company area sent the men scurrying for their gas masks. They had rehearsed gas alarms many times during training in the States, but no amount of training can create the anxiety, fear, and apprehension that occurs when threatened with the real thing. The masks were worn for what seemed hours but probably amounted to a much shorter period of time before the all clear sounded.

Rumor circulated in the company area that a soldier on the front line had detected the smell of new-mown hay or fresh corn. All soldiers had been taught to associate this odor with phosgene gas, one of the deadly chemical gases available during World War II. The soldier immediately gave the alarm for gas. The alert spread rapidly along the line and back to the rear.

Happily for everyone in the 51st ECB, what the soldier had smelled was actually fresh cut vegetation and not phosgene gas. For a long period after this false alarm most soldiers kept their gas masks close at hand. Some members of Company A felt that the false gas alarm was a contributing factor to the combat fatigue the soldier experienced. As the medics removed the man from the company area he clutched his gas mask in his arms and would not let go of it.

On July 24 the battalion suffered its first fatality. A cave-in at a gravel pit crushed Private First Class James M. Shanes, Company C. The pit was operated as a source of gravel for the repair and maintenance of battalion roads.

Operation Cobra

Operation Cobra, the breakout from the Normandy beachhead in preparation for the drive across France, had been planned for about 2 weeks. It was delayed several times but finally began on July 24. Preparation for the attack called for American bomber support prior to United States troops jumping off. The weather turned bad, but before the order to abort the bombing mission was received, about 300 American bombers dropped their bombs 2,000 yards short of the reference line, a road running from St. Lo to Periers, killing 25 men and wounding 131 men of the 30th Infantry Division.

At 1100 hours the next day Operation Cobra went for broke with 1,500 B-17 and B-24 heavy bombers, 380 medium bombers, and over 550 fighter bombers in support. The target, about 2 miles west of St. Lo, on the south side of the road, was a rectangular area 7,000 yards wide and 2,500 yards deep. This small objective was saturated with bombs in one of the largest bombing efforts that the world had ever known. Most bombs landed on target or south of the target, but 35 heavy bombers and 42 medium bombers dropped their ordnance within American lines.[13]

COMPLETION OF A CULVERT, SEEN THROUGH THE ARCH, AT TESSY SUR VIRE ON AUGUST 6, 1944.

Courtesy of National Archives

DESERTINES, FRANCE, ROAD JOB AFTER COMPLETION. AUGUST 19-26, 1944.

Courtesy of National Archives

The 51st ECB was maintaining roads within two miles of the St. Lo—Periers road when the bombers dropped their loads. The ground shook, and shock waves fluttered the legs and sleeves of the men's fatigue clothing as though they stood in a gale-force wind. As the bombs began to fall short, the 51st received orders to unload tool chests and send the squad trucks forward to move infantry units out of the threatened area. As a result of the nearly 300 United States casualties sustained in the two-day bombing by American planes, General Eisenhower resolved that he would never again use heavy bombers in a tactical role.[14]

In spite of these early setbacks, the 9th, 4th, and 30th Infantry Divisions raced through the area. The 2d and 3d Armored Divisions followed quickly, exploiting the breakthrough. The race was now on to Paris and Belgium.

During the drive toward Paris, the battalion made four moves to keep up with forward elements. It performed a wide variety of engineering tasks throughout this period in addition to the routine but important jobs of providing potable water and sweeping areas for mines before units could move in to establish bivouacs, or supply and maintenance points. The 51st removed hedgerows to make an entrance and exit to an army supply point, constructed and backfilled a culvert at a quarry, placed five truckloads of rubble at the entrance to the First United States Army headquarters, buried dead cattle at the site of the 128th Evacuation Hospital (a continuing task because of aerial and artillery bombardment), constructed a low-water bridge over the Vire River, and widened intersections on major roads.

During August, the 51st lost a well-liked member. The 51st's medical officer, Captain Seymour Weinstein, left for a new assignment to a hospital. "Doc" was well liked by everyone so all the officers of the battalion gathered at the headquarters to bid him a fond farewell.

At this time Warrant Officer Junior Grade Julius J. Horecka, assistant motor officer, distinguished himself by designing and installing a valve lubricator for gasoline engines used with water purification units. The lubricator prevented carbon from forming on the upper parts of the valve stem when using high octane gasoline in an air-cooled engine. This modification increased by four or five times the life of the valves. Horecka's invention went through engineering channels to the Office of the Engineer, First Army, where it was accepted as an important improvement. The design was published as Engineer Intelligence Memorandum Number 23 on August 14, 1944, requiring all engineer units to incorporate the design into their equipment.[15]

THE 51ST AGAIN!

With the rapid movement across France, the major effort of the battalion shifted to bridge building. The 51st began to replace portable Bailey bridges with semi-permanent wooden bridges on major roads. The Bailey bridges were then moved forward to be used again in tactical situations.

With the frequent movement of the battalion, a standard procedure was developed. On a routine road movement to a new location an advance party went first to guide the units to their new locations. The order of march began with Company A, followed in order by B, C, and H&S Company. In the lead company, the order of march normally began with the 1st Platoon, followed by the 2d and 3d Platoon, then Company Headquarters Platoon. Quite often the battalion moved at night under blackout conditions. Around 2300 hours on August 29, 1944, the battalion went about 100 miles from Neufchatel-en-Saosnois to Gas, France, some 20 or 30 miles west of Paris. Each line company was equipped with a Harley-Davidson motorcycle which was used by messengers or scouts, and for convoy control when on a motor march.

In Company A, the motorcycle driver was Pfc Carlton (Carl) E. Moore. On the night of the move to Gas, Major Yates, the battalion executive officer, was back in the convoy enjoying a nighttime ride in a command car (a four-door sedan with canvas doors and top, and four-wheel drive). As was his custom, when his extraordinary leadership ability was not needed, Yates had a bottle of whiskey at his side to make the evening a little more pleasant. It was pitch-black but no lights could be used except blackout lights. The driving conditions were hard on all drivers, but especially so on motorcycle drivers. Apparently the good major felt sorry for Carl and decided to relieve him. While Yates mounted the motorcycle, Carl relaxed in the comfort of the command car.

A lieutenant in the convoy's lead jeep had stopped at a crossroad where no guide was posted, to determine directions. With his raincoat over his head to hide his flashlight, he scanned his map and decided that he should turn right. At that moment Major Yates roared up on the motorcycle. In his booming voice he yelled, "Don't you know where in the hell you are going? Follow me." With that he turned left and roared off into the darkness. The lieutenant was in a stew. He knew that if he followed the major, somewhere down the road in the darkness of the night, the entire battalion convoy of close to 100 vehicles and heavy equipment would have to turn around. It was a nightmare situation for anyone leading a convoy. With the courage that only comes from being too young to know better, the lieutenant turned right and led the battalion to the correct location.

Some time later the battalion learned that Major Yates had crashed into a ditch a short distance down the road from the intersection. With his foot broken in two places he lay there several hours before a passing ambulance driver saw him. The medics evacuated him through field hospital channels to England where he could rest until his bones mended.

After a few months in England "Bull" tired of life in a hospital. With his foot in a cast, and on crutches, he went AWOL from the hospital and conned the captain of a ship into giving him a ride across the English Channel. In France the MPs picked him up again and turned him over to a field hospital. From there he went AWOL again, and with a borrowed (?) jeep, drove across France and into Belgium where he rejoined the 51st ECB on December 15, 1944. He was just in time for the Battle of the Bulge.

The Drive into Belgium

During the first two weeks in September the battalion raced across France into Belgium, making three moves. The first and longest covered 152 miles from Gas, France, near Chartes, through Paris, to Perles near Soissons. This was in the general area where major battles, including the Battle of the Marne, were fought in World War I. While digging a small ditch to move rainwater from his pup tent, a soldier from Company A found a rusty American bayonet from the "war fought to end all wars."[16]

The 51st rolled through Paris about 8 days after its August 25 liberation. At that time the citizens were still celebrating. Although there was no food or coal in the city, there was plenty of wine for every American that came through. To show its gratitude the French government paid each Allied soldier the equivalent of about five dollars if he was within a specified radius of Paris during a designated period of time. Members of the 51st collected that amount at the pay table in September.

During the rapid movement across France, the leading Allied units simply outran their supply lines. The emphasis now changed from a war to destroy the German Army to a war of logistics. Everything that was required to keep an Army moving in the field was in short supply, especially gasoline and ammunition. To speed precious supplies to the front, the Army set up the Red Ball Express, a long-distance system of continuous convoy, that sent a steady stream of supplies forward. Each truck assigned to the expressway had a red dot about three inches in diameter painted on its front and rear.[17]

During that period gasoline was so scarce within the 51st that operational assignments could be accomplished only as gas became available. Captain Barnes remembered having to drive a 2½-ton truck 175 miles to the rear to get 1,500 gallons of gasoline for the battalion, and returning on the Red Ball Express highway.

In the new location at Perles the battalion once again sent platoons to the rear to take down Bailey bridges and move them forward to Engineer depots. One platoon, not aware of the Red Ball Express, groped along the highway under blackout conditions heading east late one night with a load of Bailey bridge material. Suddenly there appeared in the east a large glare of light bouncing off the night clouds. Of course, that had to be the German secret weapon about which rumors had circulated for several months. The platoon convoy slowed to a stop and waited for its doom. As the lights got closer, the two headlights of trucks could be seen. These were the first lights that the men had seen on a vehicle at night since leaving the States. As the trucks raced by at break-neck speed, someone yelled, "Better turn on your lights if you don't want to get killed." The men of the 51st had been introduced to the Red Ball Express.

On September 4, the 51st moved from Gas to Perles, France, about 50 miles from the Belgian border. The battalion stayed in Perles for six days, then moved to Rozoy-sur-Serre on September 10. Providing Engineer support to the First Army, and V and VII Corps units, kept the battalion busy. The primary mission of the battalion included maintenance of, and posting signs on the main supply routes as well as operating water points. Special job assignments included filling bomb craters, guarding bridges, repairing an existing bridge to accommodate two-way class 40 (40 tons) traffic over the Aisne River, and the construction of a class 40 Bailey bridge over the Oise-Aisne Canal. In general terms, a class 40 road or bridge can support a vehicle weighing 40 tons. This latter bridge was completed on September 9, 1944.

The day after the battalion moved from Perles to Rozoy, changes were made in the battalion staff because of Major Yates' hospitalization. Captain Huxman was relieved from duty as S-3 and assigned duty as executive officer. Captain Barnes, the assistant division engineer, was assigned as battalion S-3. The battalion mission on arrival in the new area included the posting of route signs and the reconnaissance of roads in the area.

While on a reconnaissance mission in the vicinity of Marche a party of 51st personnel, consisting of Lieutenant Boies, Sergeants Clavan and Turner, and Corporal Lape, encountered a wounded Belgian who pointed out a house in which there were two German SS soldiers. The Germans escaped through the brush before the Americans could surround the house. Shots were fired but apparently no one was hit.

The battalion took down several Bailey bridges and delivered them to Engineer Depot Number E-37 near Recogne, completing the project on September 12. The following day the battalion removed a treadway bridge at Crecy. While at Rozoy, Company B did an excellent repair job of an existing French Bailey truss bridge at Rethel.

On September 13 Company C moved to a new bivouac area near Ortheuville, Belgium, to start construction of a trestle bridge on N-4 over the Ourthe River. The following day, acting on the tip of Belgian civilians, Company C surrounded and captured 58 German enlisted men, one lieutenant, and one medical officer, all from a German paratroop unit. The medical officer and two of the German wounded were turned over to an ambulance convoy. The remainder were turned in to the V Corps POW Collecting Point at Bastogne. The Germans offered some resistance but none of the men from Company C were injured.

After several more days at Rozoy the rest of the battalion, less the already departed Company C, crossed the Belgian border and settled into Martelange, Belgium, on September 17, 1944. By this time, lead elements of the Allied forces had reached the German West Wall (Siegfried Line).

Belgium

The move into Belgium brought about a new type of work. The numerous combat bridges and culverts were now replaced with more permanent structures. Bridge designs were drawn for the various projects and used to provide guidance to the builders. For the next several weeks a number of projects were assigned to the companies by the S-3, Captain Barnes, and efficiently completed.[18]

For example, the timber trestle bridge project on N-4 north of Bastogne near Ortheuville was assigned to Company C. It was begun on September 13 and completed on the 18th. It was a 78-foot long bridge with five spans. In the construction of the bridge the company used I beams as stringers, and did a magnificent job according to the S-3. The steel beams were secured from the Hadir Steel Mill in Luxembourg, from the Providence Steel Mill in Belgium, and from captured stocks.

At the same time new personnel continued to arrive in the battalion. First Lieutenant Paul W. Curtis, assigned to Company A from the 602d

Engineer Camouflage Battalion, arrived on September 16. The next day, Captain Marino Mussomeli, Sergeant James A. Pendergrass, Technician Fifth Elmer C. Stephens, and Private Ernest V. Blankenship came to the battalion from the 3d Replacement Depot. The new battalion surgeon and commanding officer of the medical detachment, Captain T. Reed Maxson, arrived two days later.

On September 17 the battalion headquarters moved to a woods on N4 six miles north of Arlon, Belgium, a distance of over one hundred miles from Rozoy, France. From then until October 1, the battalion completed a large number of road projects in addition to the Company C project at Ortheuville.

Battalion assigned Company B project number 72 at Margut on September 6. It was a timber-style bridge with steel I beams, some 36 feet long and was class 70, one-way, class 40, two-ways. The men finished it in three days. A class 70 one-way bridge can support a tank retriever carrying a medium tank (70 tons).

At Montmedy, France, Company A began project number 71, a bridge over the La Chiers River. This on-site construction called for the lengthening of one span of an existing masonry arch bridge. The result was a 20-foot high, wood trestle bridge with steel I beams up to 36 feet long. It was a class 70, one-way, class 40, two-way bridge. When completed at 1200 hours on September 27, the bridge was 140 feet long with an additional 40 feet for a ramp.

The unit had opened a sawmill nearby to cut bridge timbers for the bridge. The men were able to exceed the normal span length for a standard timber trestle bridge because steel I beams were used. The beams facilitated construction because longer spans required fewer piers for support. Normally a wooden span was 15 to 20 feet long.

The steel I beams used on the bridge were 20 inches high with a flange 10 inches wide, and the web seven-eighths of an inch thick. The beams weighed about 95 pounds per foot. With a span of 36 feet, one beam weighed 3,420 pounds, almost 2 tons. The engineer combat battalion of World War II was never trained or equipped to build a bridge that used this type of beam, but the construction battalions in the Communication Zone were.

A team from H&S Company, with an acetylene and oxygen cutting torch, helped on the beams. When the team members found out they would have to set their tanks on the bank and walk out on the 10-inch wide beams some 20 feet in the air, dragging the acetylene and oxygen rubber hoses behind them, they requested relief from the job. Sergeant Benjamin Ham, a squad leader in Company A, was an old construction stiff before being drafted and had ample experience. He grabbed the torch and hose, went out on the beam, and promptly completed the job. In a draftee army, there was almost always a man with the skill that might be required for a project.

During this period, each company collected several German prisoners who either surrendered or were pointed out to soldiers of the 51st by Belgian civilians. Some of the Germans offered token resistance, but most were anxious to surrender to the Americans. They must have known what it took Adolph Hitler eight more months and a lot more lost lives to realize, that the German Army could not win the war.

Company C continued its work on bridges with Project Number 76, on N44 at Vance, Belgium. This was a class 70, one-way, and class 40, two-way, timber trestle bridge with steel I beams of 18 feet each. Project Number 73 called for the repair of a hole in a masonry arch bridge on N44 at Etalle. Another Company C mission, Project Number 74, was a box culvert of logs, class 70, at Etalle on N44.

At Ell, Luxembourg, Company B constructed a bridge on the existing abutments of a wood trestle bridge using steel I beam stringers. French-made bents were used. It was a class 70 one-way, class 40 two-way bridge, 17 feet wide, with three spans totaling 46 feet in length. Project 81 at Martelange, Belgium called for reinforcing an existing timber trestle bridge so that the 7th Armored Division could pass over it. Posts were added in each bent for reinforcement. The bridge was upgraded from class 40 to class 70. There were eleven spans from 7 to 21 feet in length totaling 131 feet 11 inches. Company B completed this bridge on September 27.

Another bridge completed on the 27th was a wood trestle bridge with steel I beam stringers and a log pier built by Company A at Dampicourt on N381 south of the intersection with N50. It was a 2-way, class 40, 1-way, class 70 bridge, 22 feet wide, with 2 spans of 18 feet each.

Two other projects by Company C included a 22-foot wide class 70, 2-way concrete culvert on the site of a demolished bridge on N48, 5 miles west of Henisch, Belgium. The other project by Company C, 3 miles north of Stockem, Belgium, on N48 was a cinder surface, rock subgrade road, 24 feet wide, designed to change the center line of the road to coincide with the offset center line of the bridge.

Additional road projects included a repair job by Company B at Marville, France, which called for adding one coat of asphalt and gravel to a good subgrade and base course. The base course of sandstone, constructed previously by the French, was about 12 inches deep. Company

COMPLETION OF REINFORCEMENT OF FRENCH-TYPE BRIDGE AT RETHEL, FRANCE.
COMPANY B, 51ST ECB.

Courtesy of National Archives

CONSTRUCTION OF TIMBER TRESTLE BRIDGE AT MONTMEDY, FRANCE.
COMPLETED 1200A SEPT. 27, 44. COMPANY A, 51ST ECB.

Courtesy of National Archives

CONSTRUCTION OF 48' TIMBER TRESTLE BRIDGE ON N44 AT VANCE ON 1200A SEPT. 21, 1944. COMPANY C, SPECIAL JOB ASSIGNMENT 92.

Courtesy of National Archives

SALM RIVER BRIDGE, TROIS PONTS. BUILT BY COMPANY C, 51ST ECB IN LATE SUMMER 1944. BLOWN AFTER PASSAGE OF 7TH ARMORED DIVISION TOWARD ST. VITH IN DECEMBER.

Courtesy of National Archives

TRESTLE BRIDGE, LIENNE RIVER, HABIEMENT, BELGIUM. COMPANY C, 51ST ECB..
Courtesy of National Archives

CAPTAIN JOHN W. BARNES PINS ON SERGEANT VIRGIL H. ROTHRA'S 2D LIEUTENANT BARS IN MARCHE, BELGIUM, JUST AFTER HE WAS GIVEN A BATTLEFIELD PROMOTION. HE WAS ASSIGNED TO THE 104TH INFANTRY DIVISION AND LATER KILLED CROSSING THE ROER. 12 NOV. 1944.
Courtesy of National Archives

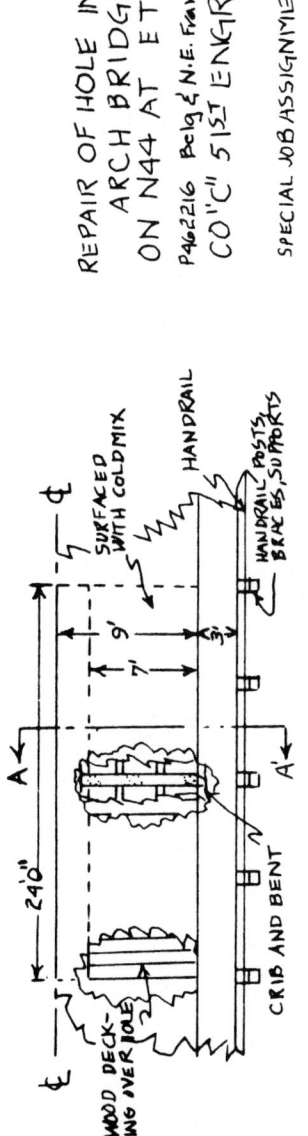
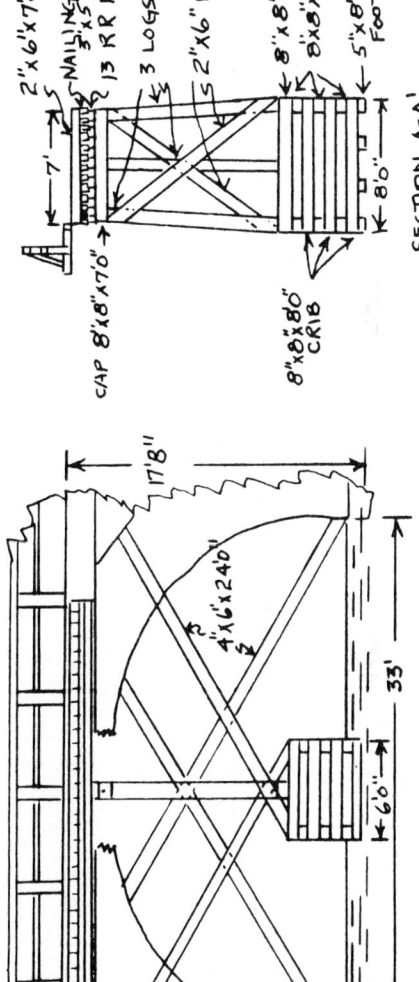

From the collection of John W. Barnes

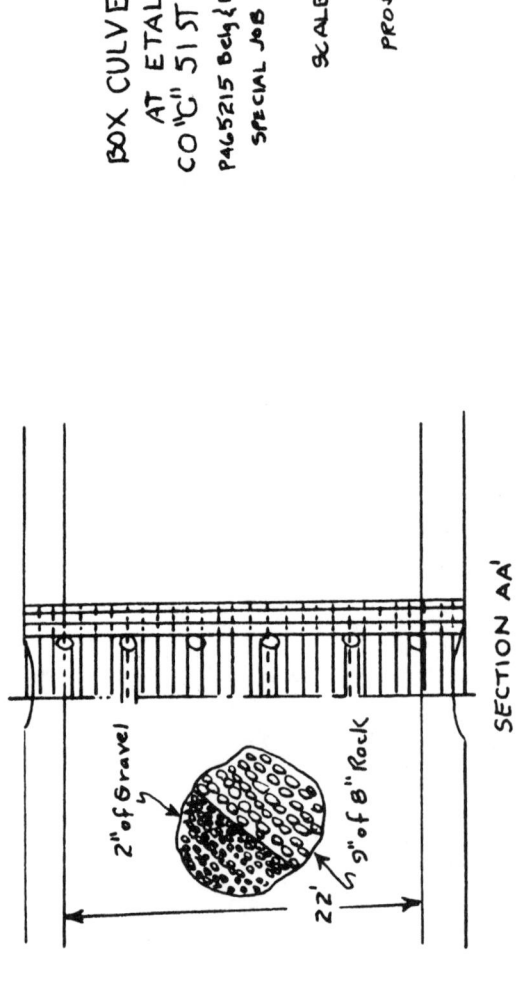
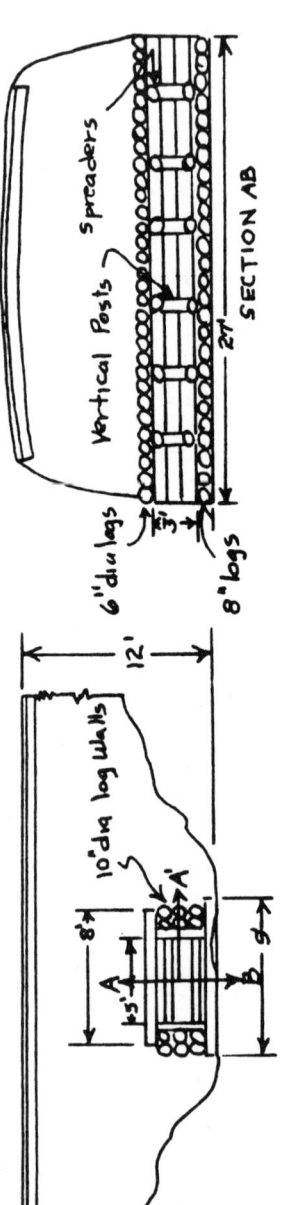

From the collection of John W. Barnes

B laid about 4 inches of Number 2 rock and added about an inch of wearing surface. The width of the road was 24 feet, the length about 400 yards. It was class 70, one-way, and class 40, two-ways. The unit also filled craters and installed culverts on N44 between Etalle and Florenville and on the one-half mile of road south of Gormny. Company C performed the same work on the highway from Etalle to Arlon.

Special Job Assignment No. 86, the construction of a bridge at Montmedy, Belgium, was completed on September 27. That same day Company A completed Special Job Assignment No. 100, construction of a bridge at Dampicourt on N381, south of the intersection of N50 and N831. It was a 36-foot long, 22-foot wide, timber trestle bridge supported in the center with a 10-foot log cribbing filled with rock and sand. A final project, completed on October 1 before the battalion move to Malmedy, was Special Job Assignment No. 107, a bridge over the Attert River on Route N22.

On October 1 the battalion moved into a woods between Malmedy and Eupen. Until the 23d, when the battalion moved again, the 51st entered into a period of rest and training, except for a few jobs filling road craters, and a bridge. During this period Company C put in a "beautiful bridge job" between Trois Ponts and Werbomont on N23. With an already existing one-way class 10 bridge in place, the company put in half the two-way class 70 bridge, keeping the old bridge open to traffic. They then tore down the old bridge and completed the new one on October 14.

During this three-week break the line companies engaged in infantry training and in the care and maintenance of clothing and equipment. They also collected materials with which to fabricate bridges assigned by future projects. By October 17 the battalion had a sufficient stockpile of materials, except for posts and stringers, to construct a 105-foot timber trestle bridge. Material consisted of caps, sills, flooring, curbing, handrails, lag screws, bolts and pins. The concept was to replace the material as it was used, and to maintain a ready source of such material for priority assignments. Posts for trestles and stringers would be fabricated near the bridge site in the interests of efficiency and economy.

Sawmill Operations

On October 23 the battalion moved to a woods near Marche, and a week later into a chateau in town. The battalion devoted this period to the operation of sawmills, and in cutting and hauling logs to feed them. The 51st was tasked to operate enough sawmills in the Ardennes to produce three million board feet of lumber for the Army's winterization program and for use as bridge timbers. It was a big job.

The Army plan called for providing each infantry company with enough lumber for two large heated tents with wood frames and floors, a mess hall so that the soldiers could stay warm while eating their meals and another for drying wet clothing in an effort to reduce the number of trenchfoot cases.

General Omar Bradley, by now Commanding General, 12th Army Group, felt that these tents had a substantial effect on morale and efficiency. Although considered a non-battle injury, trenchfoot took a high toll among riflemen on the line. It was caused by persistent dampness or prolonged immersion of the feet in water and often caused permanent damage to the peripheral blood vessels of the feet. Each casualty sapped the strength of the Army, weakening the offensive. Twelve thousand soldiers, approximately enough for an infantry division, had already been evacuated from American lines. Doctors estimated that most could never again return to combat while many would be incapacitated for life.[19]

At peak production, with the three companies operating 32 sawmills, the 51st produced a total of 80,000 board feet of lumber each day. Sawmill operations stopped on December 17 when the battalion was assigned barrier operations against the German Army's Ardennes Offensive. By that time it had produced 2.6 million board feet of lumber, some 88 percent of the assigned quota. This was clearly a record in First Army.[20]

On December 14 Lieutenant Colonel Harvey R. (Scrappy) Fraser arrived to take command of the battalion. The next day Major "Bull" Yates rejoined the battalion and resumed his duties as executive officer, his foot having healed.

Fraser, an experienced regular army officer, was in command of Company A, 3d Engineer Combat Battalion in Hawaii when the Japanese attacked Pearl Harbor on December 7, 1941. Scheduled to rotate back to the mainland, he stayed on Oahu and continued to command troops there for the next seven months before leaving for Oregon. There he helped train an engineer general service regiment for overseas service. He commanded one of the regiment's battalions, moving it to the east coast and then to England. There Fraser built depots and airfields before going to the continent. Although not in on the Normandy landing, Fraser participated in a combat mission with Brigadier General William M. Hoge during July 1944 for which he won a Bronze Star.[21]

With General Eisenhower's decision to continue the offensive into the Siegfried Line during the winter months of 1944-45, several major projects had to be considered. Backup supply levels had to be increased. The replacement stream of personnel had decreased to a slow trickle and had to be improved. Even though new combat divisions were scheduled to arrive from the States, there were still insufficient personnel to maintain a strategic reserve.

Eisenhower's plans called for major attacks by First Army to the north of the Ardennes, and by Third Army to the south of the Ardennes. In concentrating forces for the offensive, it was necessary to economize forces on some sectors of the front. The natural place to economize was the dense forest and rugged terrain of the Ardennes area. General Bradley believed that the only place in which the Germans could launch a major counterattack was through the Ardennes region. He further believed that unless the enemy overran our large supply dumps, the Germans would soon find themselves in trouble, particularly during clear weather when our air forces could operate efficiently. Bradley traced out on the map the line he estimated the German spearheads could possibly reach. His estimates later proved to be remarkably accurate with a maximum error of five miles or less at any one point.[22]

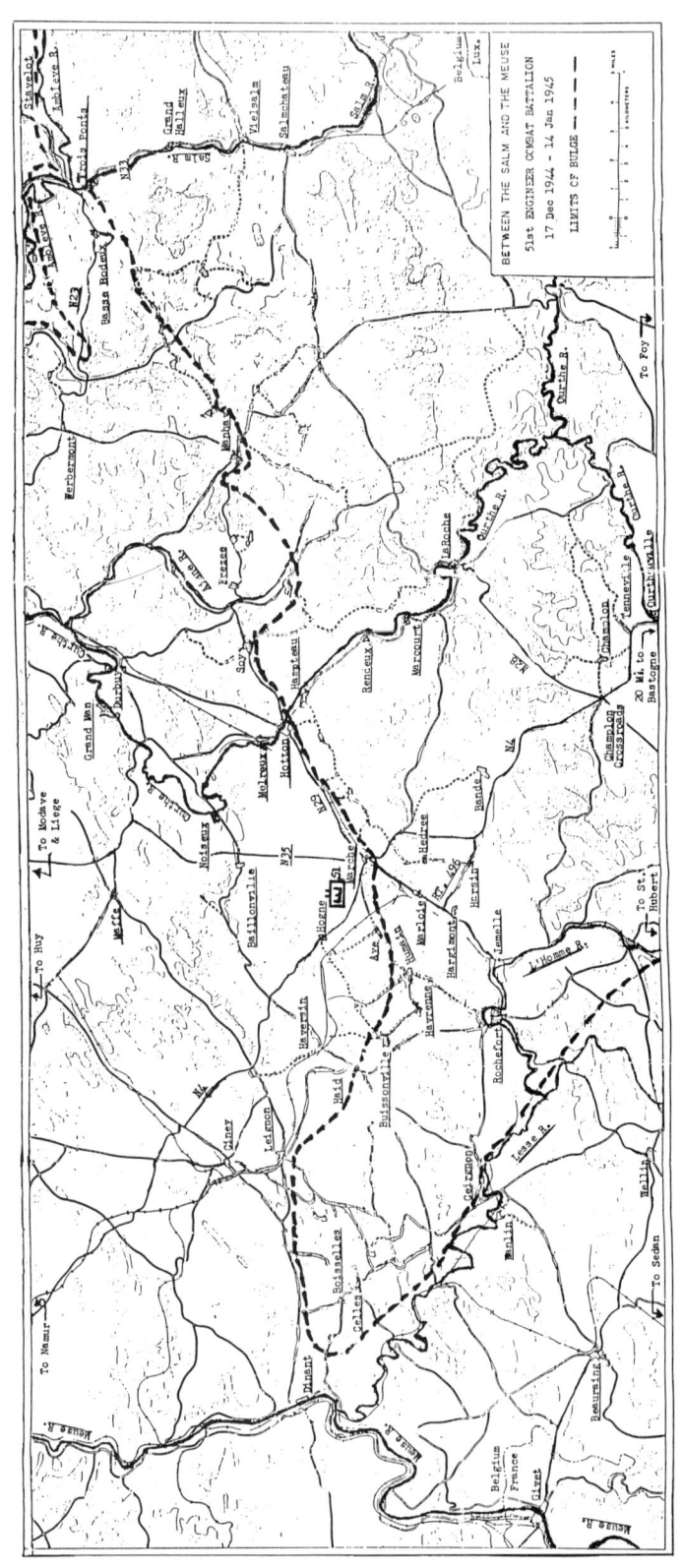

CHAPTER V

THE ARDENNES CAMPAIGN: TROIS PONTS

The 51st Engineer Combat Battalion was located at Marche, Belgium, when Lieutenant Colonel Harvey R. Fraser, assumed command on December 14, 1944. Fraser reported to the battalion by way of the 1111th Engineer Combat Group, taking command under General Orders #15, Headquarters, 51st Engineer Combat Battalion. His assumption of command marked a new era for the battalion. He was a new leader with new ideas on leadership. Shortly Fraser's leadership would be put to the test in combat operations during the Ardennes Offensive. During Reunion I, 51st ECB, in Washington, D.C. in 1986, Fraser and Yates were accorded the greatest tribute leaders can receive from their men. One of the speakers said that "if God ever made the perfect combat commander and executive officer it was Colonel Harvey Fraser," and before the speaker could add Major Yates, the audience sprang to its feet and gave "Scrappy" Fraser a long standing ovation. When the speaker said, "and Major Robert Yates," there was another long ovation.[1]

Fraser had just two days to acquaint himself with the battalion before the Germans attacked. He was impatient to put his personal stamp on the organization. The medical officer was the first of many who felt the impatience of the new commander. Shortly after arrival in the battalion, Fraser visited Dr. T. Reed Maxson's medical detachment aid tent. He examined it for what seemed like a long time then looked Maxson straight in the eyes. "Captain," Fraser said, "I don't like what I see here. I want this medical facility to be a show place of the battalion. Whenever there are visiting brass, here is the first place I am bringing them." Maxson protested feebly that they were in combat and that everything they worked with was clean and that the surgical equipment was sterile.[2]

Fraser brushed aside his protests, telling the doctor he wanted his and his men's boots polished, the shirts to have three pressed lines down the back, and the pants to have a crease down the front. He further stated he wanted the floor of the tent swept frequently and the equipment neatly arranged. Maxson relayed this order to his men and they "liberated" an iron and ironing board. While they were in a barracks situation in Marche, Belgium, they kept three creases in their shirts, their pants pressed, and their shoes shined. Shortly the Germans began their Ardennes Offensive, the colonel became busy, the shoes received less polish, the shirts less creasing, and the pants less pressing. But the medics continued to carry the ironing board and iron with them on the medical detachment truck just in case.[3]

On December 16 Fraser headed out to the line companies and sawmills to meet the officers and men and to observe the battalion at work. That day the battalion produced 50,016 board feet of lumber, bringing the production figures for the battalion to 2,586,667 board feet since they began sawmill operations. It would be the last day in his program of getting acquainted. That day the Germans attacked all along the front and made rapid progress. Now Fraser would see first hand how the unit operated under combat conditions.[4]

The Enemy Objective

During the first two weeks of December 1944, five American divisions and a cavalry group held the 85-mile long Ardennes front. The difficult terrain of the Ardennes and the belief that the German army was near exhaustion had convinced Allied commanders that the Ardennes sector was relatively safe. Three of the divisions were new, only recently arrived on the continent, and manned with green soldiers. The other two were recuperating from heavy losses in the bitter fighting in the Heurtgen forest. In addition, the growing shortage of American troops forced Allied commanders to reduce strengths on portions of the front.[5]

After months of retreat Hitler decided on a bold gamble to regain the initiative in the west. Under the cover of winter weather Hitler and his generals massed some 25 divisions opposite the Americans in the Ardennes. He planned to smash through the thin American line, cross the Meuse River, and drive to Antwerp. If the offensive succeeded it would split the British and American armies and force the British out of the war. Before daybreak on December 16 the German army launched its last desperate offensive, completely surprising the American divisions in the Ardennes.

The German Sixth SS Panzer Army under General Josef "Sepp" Dietrich spearheaded the massive assault. Its objective was to penetrate the American line, cross the Meuse River at Huy, fan out, and create havoc in the American rear. The Sixth SS Panzer Army consisted of two corps with the 1st SS Panzer Division of the I SS Panzer Corps on the south flank.[6]

As the front collapsed, General Eisenhower and his subordinates called up their slender reserves. But while those troops moved into position, the American commanders had to rely on rear-area troops already in the Ardennes. Many of the rear-area troops already available were corps and army engineer combat battalions. Other engineer units were scattered throughout the area in company, platoon, and even squad-sized groups. Engineers who had been engaged in road maintenance and sawmilling suddenly found themselves manning roadblocks and preparing defensive positions in the face of powerful German armored columns snaking their way through the twisted Ardennes road network. These Engineers played a major part in the Battle of the Bulge by delaying a German offensive whose only hope for success lay in crossing the Meuse quickly.

During the initial attack the First Panzer Division was delayed by a poor road network, lack of engineer support, and organized American strong points. Because the road network could not carry the German forces, the division was divided into four march or battle groups (kampfgruppen) with the main group under Lieutenant Colonel Joachim Peiper. By taking circuitous routes his force finally reached Stavelot on the Ambleve River the evening of December 17, but was stopped by a roadblock set up by a platoon from the 291st ECB. At that point Peiper was less than 42 miles from the Meuse. He turned part of his force south in an attempt to cross the Ambleve and Salm Rivers at Trois Ponts. Here on December 18, Peiper was stopped by Company C, 51st ECB.[7]

THE 51ST AGAIN!

Trois Ponts was the headquarters of the 1111th Engineer Combat Group. One of its units, the 291st Engineer Combat Battalion had detachments working throughout the area. When the attack began, the 1111th sent Lieutenant Colonel David E. Pergrin, commander of the 291st ECB to Malmedy to organize its defenses. The group headquarters then ordered the 51st to send its Company C to Trois Ponts to organize its defense and prepare its bridges for destruction. A squad from the 291st assisted.

At the headquarters of the 51st, the missions of road maintenance and repair and the operation of the saw mills ended on December 17. During the late afternoon of that day, the commanding officer of the 158th Engineer Combat Battalion notified the 51st ECB to be on the alert for ground activity in the area. That night the battalion sent Company C with demolition equipment to Trois Ponts. An advance section of about 75 men left Melreux at 2200 hours, arriving at Trois Ponts at 2330 hours where it set up its CP in the railroad station.[8]

Company C's men were spread over a wide area. The 2d Squad, 3d Platoon, under Sergeant John T. Oliver, was near Petit Thier about four miles northeast of Vielsalm, supervising Belgian civilians cutting trees for sawmills. In the late afternoon of December 17, Lieutenant Green came for the squad. He told Oliver, T/5 Frank Simoni, and PFC Edward Gurnsey to stay there and guard a truck-mounted air compressor until he picked them up the next day. The action at Trois Ponts prevented Green's return.[9]

Oliver and his two companions stayed in an old hunting lodge until they saw German paratroopers in the sky and German infantry advancing through the woods. They made a break towards Vielsalm, about six miles south of Trois Ponts, on the Salm River. There they joined with a 105-mm. artillery battery of the 106th Infantry Division and held the Germans at bay for two days.

Late in the afternoon of the 19th, a German officer and two NCOs with a flag of truce approached the farmhouse in which Oliver, Simoni, and Gurnsey had found shelter. The German officer told the group to surrender while they had a chance, because they were surrounded, and in a few hours two panzer divisions would roll through the area. The offer was refused and the Germans returned to their lines. That night the panzer divisions attacked. The artillery officer ducked out the back door followed by Gurnsey. Gurnsey escaped but was seriously wounded and hospitalized. Oliver and Simoni stayed and were captured. The Germans started to take Oliver's wrist watch, but let him keep it when he said it was a gift from his mother who had passed away. The prisoners

51st Engineer Combat Battalion, Company C, Defenses Set on December 19, 1944, Trois Ponts Area

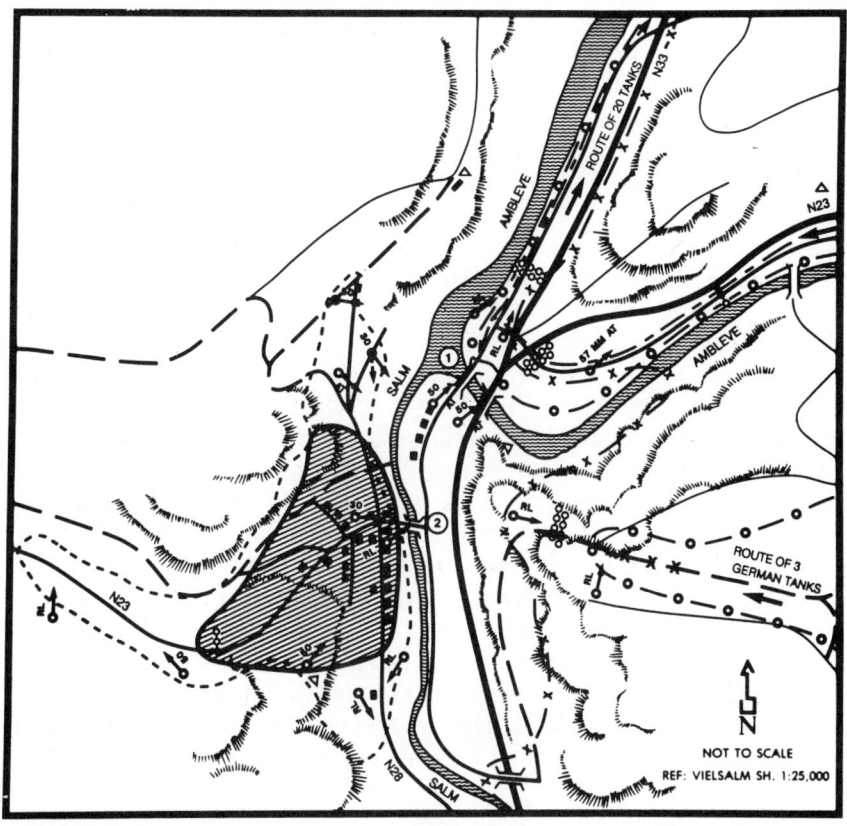

KEY

ROADS, 3-6 METERS	RL ○—→ ROCKET LAUNCHER △ - OP	—x—x— LIMITS OF GERMAN ADVANCE 20 DEC - 21 DEC
SECONDARY ROADS	⦾⦾⦾⦾⦾ DAISY CHAIN	---------- LIMITS OF DAYLIGHT DEFENSE ZONE
EARTH ROADS	←— —← PATH OF GERMAN ADVANCE	▨ LIMITS OF NIGHT DEFENSE
OTHER ROADS & CART TRACKS	—○—○— LIMIT OF GERMAN ADVANCE DEC 19th	
	X 3 GERMAN TANKS	① ② BRIDGES No. 1 & 2 BLOWN IN THAT ORDER

were kept in the basement and interrogated on the location of the British. The next day they were sent to the rear.

Oliver and Simoni stayed together for some time, moving through several POW camps. Then the Germans separated the NCOs from the rest of the men and Oliver lost track of Simoni. Oliver finished the war in a camp near Bremen on the North Sea which contained many political prisoners. When liberated, Oliver went to Camp Lucky Strike, France, where he met his old friend Simoni. They returned to the States together to become civilians.

As Company C moved to Trois Ponts under full blackout conditions the main body of the company followed the advance section at a slow pace, even though the men were familiar with the area. Lieutenant Joseph Milgram was in the first truck. When it reached the Manhay crossroad, a military policeman shined his flashlight into Milgram's face and asked in the most incredulous tone of voice, "Just where the hell do you think you're going"?[10]

He had a point. At this location the unit, with Milgram in the lead, encountered the most unbelievable stream of traffic heading west on the two-lane road Company C was taking east. Although it was pitch black, the men had grown accustomed to seeing tanks, tank destroyers, artillery pieces in tow, command cars, jeeps, and trucks, all coming the other way, bumper to bumper, sliding off the road and having all sorts of trouble moving. According to Milgram, "Here were we idiots, heading east."[11]

Milgram told the MP that they were the 51st Engineers with orders to be in Trois Ponts by morning, and that they were going ahead, come what may. The MP waved them on while shaking his head. After the first few miles, the traffic on the other side of the road disappeared, and Company C settled in to a lonely ride. The men were scared as they groped their way along the road, but they finished the trip without incident.[12]

Trois Ponts

Trois Ponts was well known to Company C. During the fall, officers of the company had visited the many sawmills that the 51st ECB operated in this area of the Ardennes. They knew the roads. Company C had built many of the timber trestle bridges along N23, including the one at Trois Ponts. During the fall Lieutenant Milgram's men regularly reported suspicious sounds in the forest at night such as lights flickering in the trees and evidences of fires in still warm ashes in the mornings. Other traces of the enemy also existed. These findings were regularly reported to higher headquarters, but no one ever investigated.[13]

At Trois Ponts, Company C, commanded by Captain Sam Scheuber, immediately established defensive positions on the west bank of the Ambleve River, located on the eastern edge of town. It prepared two of the bridges across the river for demolition and set up two road blocks. By 0800 hours, December 18, the whole company had arrived at Trois Ponts except the 21 men left behind at Melreux as a rear detachment. To protect the town, the company had eight bazookas, six .50-caliber machine guns, four .30-caliber machine guns, and one 57-mm. antitank gun from the 526th Armored Infantry Battalion. The company, reinforced by a squad each from the 526th Armored Infantry Battalion, and Company A, 291st Engineer Combat Battalion, also picked up some stragglers coming through Trois Ponts.[14]

The 1111th Group began defensive operations at Trois Ponts prior to the arrival of Company C. Colonel Anderson had directed his S-4, Captain Robert N. Jewett to set up a defensive position with a broken-down half-track and a squad of Company B, 526th Armored Infantry Battalion. Jewett emplaced the gun with crew on highway N-23 about a mile down the road toward Stavelot.

Additional support came from Lieutenant Albert J. Walters, a platoon leader in Company A, 291st Engineer Combat Battalion and a squad of his men, who were on their way to assist in preparing a bridge for demolition southeast of Trois Ponts. Lieutenant Colonel James A. Kirkland, Executive Officer of the 1111th Group, discovered Walters on his way to the bridge and assigned him and his squad to Company C. Scheuber sent them to defend the bridge south of town, where they had been heading originally.

Company C held the bridges open long enough to allow a large part of the 7th Armored Division to cross on the way to St. Vith. At some point during the crossing an open-top, self-propelled gun slid off the north side of the bridge and into the Salm River. As the last vehicle of the 7th's convoy crossed the bridge, the crew abandoned the vehicle, dropping thermite grenades into the hatch to deny its use to the enemy should there be a break-through. The vehicle burned furiously.[15]

During that day and night and for some time thereafter the ammunition remaining in the vehicle exploded sporadically but noisily, perhaps leading the enemy to believe there was more firepower available than there was. That unexpected deception, combined with the noise of the 51st trucks going up and down a hill at night, helped considerably to discourage enemy advances toward town.[16]

The initial defense of the town consisted of a platoon of men with two bazookas on high ground covering the approach from Aisomont,

Captain Jewett's group with the antitank gun covering the road from Stavelot, and a rear-guard covering the N23 approach from Werbomont. The remainder of the company deployed with bazookas, machine guns and individual weapons in the buildings of the town along the Salm and Ambleve rivers. Jewett sent two of the 526th's men 250 yards up the road toward Stavelot with a daisy chain of 10 mines. A daisy chain is a number of mines tied together with a rope at about two feet intervals, and is designed to pull a chain of mines across a road in a hurry in order to keep vehicles from passing a point in the road. If a tank approached they were to pull the mines across the road and run back to the roadblock where the antitank gun was located. Lieutenant Richard Green, 3d Platoon Commander, Company C, 51st ECB, and PFC Andrew Salazar, were located just behind the 57-mm. antitank (AT) gun on the opposite side of the road from the half-track. They were under the control of Captain Jewett. Green had three men posted about 200 yards up the Stavelot road from the AT gun. They were to watch the men with the daisy chain and warn the men at the road block if a tank approached them.

Just before noon, tanks were sighted approaching from the direction of Stavelot. Shortly a Tiger Royal tank appeared. The men on the daisy chain pulled their mines across the road, fired on the tankers, then fled toward the road block. The first tank stopped at the daisy chain where it was joined by several other tanks. When this happened the three-man outpost returned to advise Green that tanks were on the way. The lieutenant notified his command post.

Green held his fire on the tanks until he was sure they were German. As a result, the third tank in line got off four rounds before the 57-mm. AT gun got off one round. When the 57-mm. finally returned fire, it immobilized the first tank.

Unfortunately there was not enough ammunition for the antitank gun. It had only seven rounds to start the operation. The crew felt that seven rounds was enough, but the enemy strength turned out to be much greater than expected. Captain Jewett said he could see eight tanks coming around the bend toward his position, but without dismounted infantry. Colónel Anderson, observing at a distance through field glasses, noted a total of 19 tanks that came through the position and then turned right on the road to Stoumont. The defenders started an ammunition line with Jewett throwing the shells across the road to Green, who passed them to Salazar, who then handed them to the gun crew.

The German 88-mm. shells kept hitting closer and closer until finally one of the shells hit the base of the gun, killing the four-man crew, and wounding Salazar in the leg with shell fragments. Meanwhile Company C saw the tanks and blew one of the bridges across the Ambleve. At 1300 hours Colonel Anderson ordered the destruction of a second bridge across the river, cutting the team off from Trois Ponts. The remainder of the crew, headed by Lieutenant Green, loaded onto the halftrack and, followed by the 2½-ton truck, headed toward Stoumont, circling back to Trois Ponts by way of Petit Coo. Captain Jewitt and the rest of the men from the 526th Armored Infantry Battalion returned to the new group command post at Modave.

Stavelot Road

While the battle raged on the Stavelot road, German armor attacked Lieutenant Fred L. Nabors' 2d platoon. Emplaced south of Green on a hill guarding the Aisomont road from the east, Nabors had one bazooka on the road below the hill firing southeast with a good field of fire. He had another just east of it in a good flanking position to the road.

Early on the morning of December 18, three enemy tanks approached Nabors' position. The first tank, with armored plate on the front, was allowed to pass in the hope it would hit a daisy chain across the road. A bazooka engaged the second tank without success. The third tank fired on the platoon and forced it back to the town side of the river on the south side of the Company C line. During the action one of the platoon's bazookas failed to fire and the other was hit by machine gun fire, leaving the men defenseless. Enemy machine gun fire also hit and exploded the daisy chain. None of the tanks attempted to follow Nabors' platoon into Trois Ponts when it disengaged from the action.

At 1300 hours on December 18, the bridge over the Salm River on Highway N23 was blown. So was the bridge over the railroad at the junction of N33 and the Aisomont road. But foot troops could still cross the railroad bridge so Nabors' platoon finished it off the following day. A foot bridge across the Salm was also blown on the 18th. Afterwards Colonel Anderson formed Company C on a 500-yard front to keep the Germans from crossing the river. Shortly thereafter, Anderson put Yates in charge of the defense of Trois Ponts then left for the group's new CP at Modave.[17]

Yates deployed his men along the river, providing flank and rear security for the company. He established positions with good fields of fire for his machine guns and bazookas. Soon an enemy tank, split off from a group of 20 tanks that turned north on the Stoumont road, arrived.

When it reached the junction of N23 and N33, its crew dismounted. At that point Sergeant Evers Gossard's .50-caliber machine gun crew from Company C fired on the Germans. Five of the tank's six-man crew were hit, and three were killed, but the sixth man jumped back into the tank and turned its gun toward the machine gun. Gossard and his crew retired at that point, but the tank stayed for the rest of the day, firing at targets of opportunity. It withdrew that night.[18]

During the day of the 18th, Private first class James M. Snow, Jr., the Company jeep driver was ordered to take Captain A. P. Lundberg, the 1111th Group motor officer, to First Army headquarters to report on the situation at Trois Ponts. Later that day as Lundberg and Snow were returning to Trois Ponts, they ran into a German patrol, and both men were killed.

The men of the company continued sniping at the Germans across the river, but the enemy response indicated a decided German advantage. Yates drew in the company defensive lines at 1700 hours to tighten the perimeter and give all around protection to the town. He then decided to try to deceive the Germans as to the number of Americans in town. Yates had six 2½-ton trucks available at Trois Ponts. After dark he had his men quietly drive them toward Werbomont on N23 under blackout conditions. They then noisily ran them back into Trois Ponts on the same road with their lights on. By this action he hoped the Germans would think he was receiving reinforcements.[19]

Yates also attempted to deceive the Germans about his armored and artillery support. He put chains on a single 4-ton truck and ran the clanking vehicle back and forth through town for the next several days trying to give the impression that he had numerous tanks. In fact, the only heavy weapon the company had was the bazooka. But Yates shifted it around town from place to place after dark, firing it at each stop in an attempt to deceive the enemy into thinking they had some light artillery. Helping in this deception was the M7 tank destroyer which had been set on fire to keep it from falling into the hands of the enemy. As it burned its shells exploded throughout the night of the 18th. Yates also moved small groups of men from place to place in town. At each stop he had them fire hoping to create the impression of many more men than were actually available.

Although Lieutenant Green and his group felt helpless against the German tanks with just rifles and carbines, they did get some help from the Army Air Corps. On the afternoon of December 18, a small scout plane came through the clouds and spotted Peiper's columns heading north to Stoumont along N33. A short time later some P-47s came in and knocked out four or five tanks while strafing and bombing the columns.[20]

With Green's group returned to the fold and Nabors' platoon withdrawn into town, the three platoons were consolidated into two. One group covered the river south of town and Green, with Milgram's 3d platoon, covered the north side of town. Listening posts established 500-600 yards out from the main line of resistance (MLR) during the day were pulled into a tight perimeter defense after dark.

At 0900 hours on the 19th, Lieutenant Green and T/Sgt Matthew R. Carlyle went out on a reconnaissance. They crossed the river and headed up the Stavelot road toward the knocked-out 57-mm. gun. No enemy were found in the railroad underpasses, but further up the road four men in American uniforms were crowded around the 57-mm. gun. They turned out to be Germans who fired at the two Americans. Green and Carlyle withdrew without incident.

In another action just south of the Aisomont road, four or five men in Lieutenant Nabors' platoon engaged the enemy on a hill just south of the Aisomont road. The enemy replied with both small arms and artillery. No casualties resulted, but it taught Company C to keep better hidden and change positions frequently in order to avoid artillery concentrations.

While holding off the enemy, the engineers saw several examples of German inhumanity. Colonels Anderson and Kirkland were watching several enemy tanks approach one of the blown bridges when an elderly couple ran out in front of their house and motioned with their arms. The observers felt they were waving at the tanks or trying to tell them that the bridge was blown. One of the dismounted tankmen shot the woman with his pistol. The man caught her as she fell and was in turn shot. As the two lay on the ground, additional shots were fired into their motionless figures.

In another instance, Major Yates watched a Belgian boy of about twelve running toward the river followed by a German rifleman firing at him. Four or five other German soldiers stood close by laughingly watching the incident. In anger Yates fired several shots at the spectators, dropping one of them before they dispersed. The boy and his tormentor disappeared behind the buildings.

During the day enemy patrols attempted to cross the river but were turned back by rifle and machine gun fire and grenades, for the Germans lacked armor support. Armor could not cross the river because Company C had destroyed all of the bridges and the Germans made no attempt to build a bridge or try an assault crossing.

That evening the enemy arrived from the south and began crossing the bridge on N28 south of town which was defended by Lieutenant Walters' squad from the 291st ECB. With the Germans on the middle of the bridge Sergeant Jean D. Miller touched off the charge. The squad then worked its way back to the Company C defense line at Trois Ponts.

A serious misfortune was averted that evening when a patrol from the 85th Reconnaissance Squadron, consisting of 15 men and 3 M8 assault guns, arrived at Basse Bodeux to the west of Trois Ponts on N23. Company C's rear guard fired on it before identification was made, but no serious damage was done. The next day the 3 assault guns were set up on the high ground on the outskirts of town but they never had an opportunity to engage the enemy.[21]

——— The 505th Parachute Infantry Regiment ———

The following day, December 20, the 505th Parachute Infantry (PI) Regiment, 82d Airborne Division, found out that the engineers held Trois Ponts. The commander, Colonel William E. Ekman, immediately ordered both his 2d and 3d battalions to send three bazooka teams each to assist the engineers of Company C. The rest of the 505th followed, establishing its command post in Trois Ponts at 1300 hours. When Ekman arrived, Yates greeted him with, "I'll bet you guys are glad we're here." Indeed he was. The junction of two rivers with three bridges at Trois Ponts was crucial in defending the American line. The engineers had destroyed or damaged all of the bridges over the two rivers and held the approaches, preventing the Germans from crossing.

With help from Company C, a platoon of engineers from the 307th ECB, 82d Airborne Division, attached to the 505th, partially repaired two of the destroyed bridges, one across the Ambleve and one across the Salm, so the infantry could set up its positions on the east side of the river. A company of the 505th then crossed over the river and set up a defensive line. Another company crossed later in the evening to support the first.

Prior to the arrival of the 505th, the 51st was frequently fired upon by what was obviously American artillery. They were good and the engineers came to respect their accuracy, but the men of Company C were otherwise thoroughly frustrated that nobody seemed to know the 51st ECB was located there. As a result of the firing, they spent a lot of time in the cellars of houses in town.[22]

The paratroopers, when driven to the cellars during a barrage, discovered a store of Belgian beer. The beer was contained in thick ceramic bottles closed with ceramic caps attached to the bottles with wires. Somehow or other, the engineers had missed finding this beer. Milgram claims it was because they were "awfully busy." At any rate, Company C felt they never missed a similar opportunity thereafter.[23]

As the 505th PI passed through the Company C lines, crossed the Salm, and attacked up the hill, the engineers were filled with admiration, even awe. On their way forward, the paratroopers gave away their hand grenades to make room in their baggy uniform pockets for the beer. The bottles were just the right size to fit in the pockets.[24]

Despite the arrival of the 82d, this day proved unfortunate to Company C, not because it was the day of heaviest fighting, but because of the number of casualties taken. Enemy artillery fire intensified along the entire riverfront during the morning. One shell hit Private Carl Strawser's .50-caliber machine gun position, killing him and seriously wounding Sergeant Joseph Gyure. Staff Sergeant William Rankin was killed about 1600 hours when a 20-mm. shell hit his observation post.

At 1100 hours the following day reports showed that the two companies of the 505th were running into trouble across the river. The Germans had launched a strong counterattack and were surrounding the elements of the 505th defending the hill overlooking Trois Ponts from the east. The Germans also directed small arms fire onto the streets and onto possible defensive positions around the town. At 1500 hours, while this action was going on, Major Yates received orders from group to withdraw Company C from Trois Ponts. He ignored the order, responding that he could not do so since he was covering the withdrawal of the 82d Airborne Division.

The engagement across the Salm by the paratroopers was particularly bloody. There were serious losses in dead and wounded but the paratroopers took and held the hill. When the order came to abandon the hill and return to the west bank and the town of Trois Ponts, there was some delay. It was thought the order was being appealed but the order held and the 505th retraced their steps over the Salm.[25]

To a man the paratroopers were angry and bitter. Many of their wounded had to be left on the hill. They told the engineers that the 82d had never before retreated from a position it had taken in an attack. The 505th did not think well of Field Marshal Montgomery and his compulsion to "tidy up" the line.[26]

It was not until 1600 hours that the two companies of airborne infantry began withdrawing under cover of small arms fire from Company C. At the same time, Company C prepared the two "repaired" bridges for demolition. At 1700 hours, once the infantry was across, the bridge

THE 51ST AGAIN!

over the Salm was blown by Company C, on orders from the Commanding Officer, 2d Battalion, 505th. The 505th then took up defensive positions on the west bank of the river relieving Company C, 51st ECB.[27]

When the order came to prepare the two bridges for demolition, Captain Scheuber gave the more difficult bridge, the timber trestle over the Salm, to Lieutenant Milgram. Milgram selected six men, Sergeant Elvin Goldsmith, Corporal Odis C. Faust, T/5 Paul H. Keck, Privates Jessie R. Mock, Maurice S. Walker, and Jose E. Marquez, for the task. He decided to use necklace charges for the stringers with a time fuse and primacord to set them off. He ordered his men to make nine charges.[28]

With the charges prepared, the group headed for the bridge on both sides of the road, attracting small arms and machine gun fire along the way. The enemy fire caused Milgram to change his initial plan of preparing the stringers on the friendly side. It would have involved removal of the decking while under direct fire and possibly a number of casualties. He saw that he could cross the bridge and work in defilade behind the opposite abutment. Milgram's group crossed safely and placed half-pound blocks of TNT in the far abutment under the stringers, but out six or so feet from the shore. Necklace charges were put on the log stringers. All were tied together with primacord and the pattern completed with strong squareknots. When the charges were in place Milgram ordered the rest of the men to leave while he and Keck stayed behind to get the primacord up on the bank where it could be fired. Milgram waded across the 25-foot stream under the bridge to the accompaniment of shots penetrating the flooring and stringers from one or two German .30-caliber machine guns. With the primacord on a wooden roll, Milgram threw it at a low, broken, cyclone wire fence about 10-15 feet above him. Luckily the cord and roll became entangled on the fence and held. At that point Milgram sent Keck back to the unit then returned to the far side of the river to make a final check on the wiring.[29]

After checking the work, Milgram waded downstream behind the shelter of the bank a couple of hundred feet below the bridge then struck out across the stream. Because of the force of the stream he could not keep his feet and fell into the freezing water. When Milgram reported back to Captain Scheuber that the bridge was ready for blowing, he was soaked to the skin. He found a hot radiator and tried to dry himself, his carbine, and his Leica camera but was successful only with the first two.[30]

At 1650 hours Yates gave the order to blow the bridges. The Ambleve bridge presented no problem, but the Salm continued to be difficult. First Lieutenant Johnnie Norton and his platoon gave Milgram and Keck supporting fire as they went down the street and entered a store. They approached the far-side exit located about 50-75 feet from the bridge and on the left side of the street where the primacord had landed. Keck had prepared several fuse lighters with two to three feet lengths of fuses on them. Milgram took these lighters and crawled 60 yards to the primacord. It was still there. He grasped it firmly and attached a fuse. After checking, he pulled it, waited until he saw it burning, then ran down to the corner of the building, passing Keck on the way. Milgram hollered at Keck to get out of the building. They met behind it and in a minute or so the bridge went with a loud bang.[31]

The company finished covering the withdrawal of the 505th's men from the east of the town at 1930 hours. Then and only then did Major Yates order his men to withdraw from Trois Ponts. Company C left town at 2000 hours, rejoining the battalion in Marche at 2330 hours, December 21, 1944.[32]

By December 20 German headquarters had determined that the Sixth SS Panzer Army had been stopped at Trois Ponts and the surrounding area. It then assigned the main task of exploitation to the Fifth Panzer Army in the center of the German line. How had the Sixth Panzer Army been stopped? Hugh M. Cole in his *The Ardennes: Battle of the Bulge* states that the initial American defense had been stronger than anticipated. It had denied the Germans free use of the road net in the salient. The American reaction to the threat had been more rapid than expected. Reserves had poured in to buttress the line. Company C, was one of those units that denied the use of roads to the Germans, leading to Sixth Panzer Army's failure to adhere to its timetable. As Peiper later said:

> "We proceeded at top speed towards Trois Ponts in an effort to seize the bridge there. . . . If we had captured the bridge at Trois Ponts intact and had had enough fuel, it would have been a simple matter to drive through to the Meuse River early that day."[33]

But on that day, December 18, 1944, Company C, 51st Engineer Combat Battalion, occupied Trois Ponts and held off Peiper's much larger and more heavily armed kampfgruppe. The company held off repeated German tank attacks, set up road blocks, and prepared two bridges for destruction. In so doing, Company C played a major role in keeping the 1st SS Panzer Division from splitting the Allies and reaching the Meuse.

For his leadership and gallantry at Trois Ponts during the Battle of the Bulge, Captain Scheuber of Company C, earned the Silver Star. Lieutenant Milgram also earned the Silver Star and Major Yates the Bronze Star for their actions at Trois Ponts.

THE 51ST AGAIN!

With the exploitation mission transferred to the Fifth Panzer Army further to the southwest, Company C rejoined the 51st ECB in time to help the rest of the battalion stop the Germans at other crucial strong points.[34]

MAJOR GENERAL MATTHEW B. RIDGEWAY, COMMANDING THE 18TH AIRBORNE CORPS, CONGRATULATES CAPTAIN SCHEUBER AFTER PRESENTING HIM WITH THE SILVER STAR.
Courtesy of National Archives

CHAPTER VI

THE ARDENNES CAMPAIGN: HOLDING THE LINE

After Company C left for Trois Ponts late on December 17, Colonel Fraser ordered the commanders of Companies A and B to prepare their units to move and then to report to battalion headquarters. The two companies loaded their combat allowance of ammunition, demolitions, and pioneer tools, and issued each man one day's C and K rations. Excess equipment and kitchens were to be left at their command posts, but the kitchens were to be ready to move on a moment's notice.[1]

The company commanders reported promptly to battalion headquarters for further directions, bringing radios, field phones, and maps in anticipation of immediate action. Fraser cancelled all previous missions and made new assignments, ordering Company A to Hargimont and Company B to Hogne; they were to move by motor column and arrive at their respective destinations by 0500 hours the next morning. At the end of the meeting, the company commanders joined their units to await movement orders.

51st Engineer Combat Battalion Defenses, Hotton Area, 21 December 1944

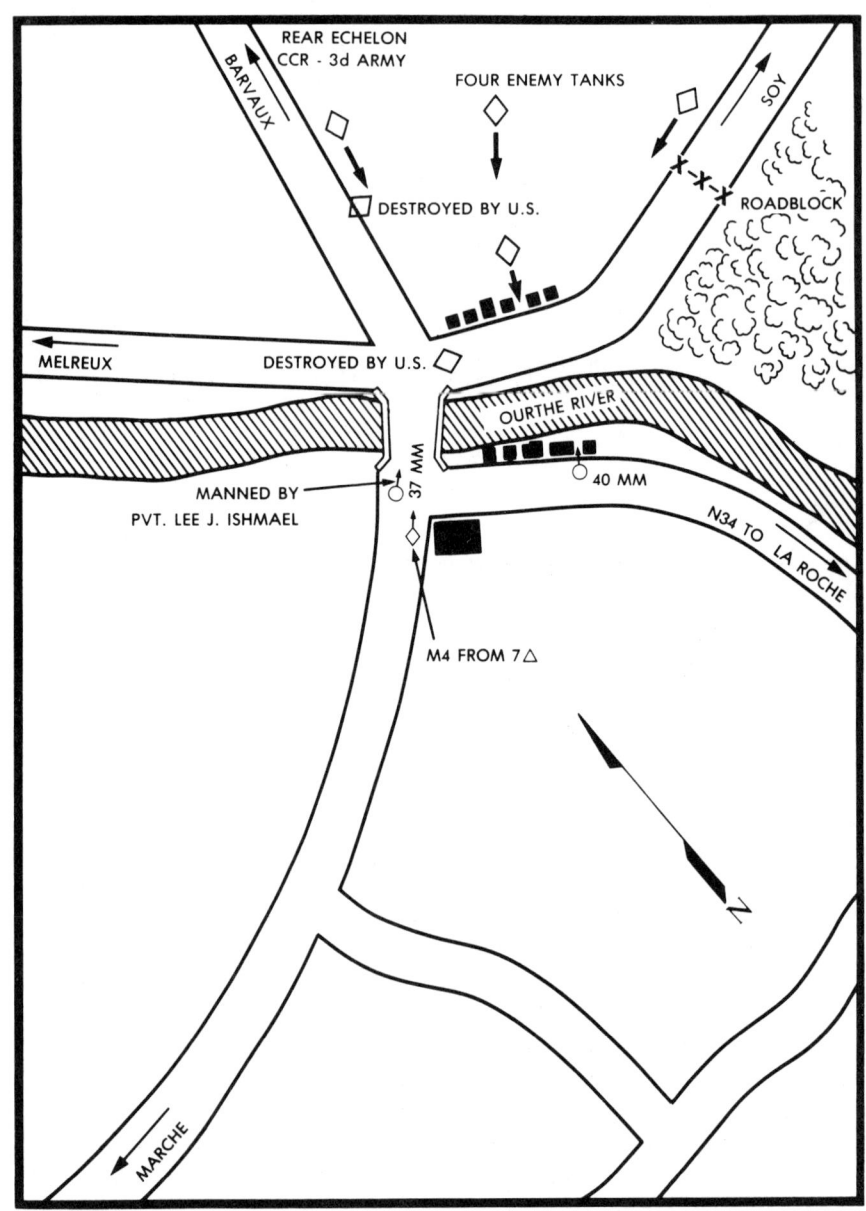

BRIDGE AT HOTTON, BELGIUM, 1944.
Courtesy of National Archives

Preparing the Defense

By this time operational control of the 51st had been transferred from the Area 2 Defense Commander to the 1111th Engineer Combat Group. The 1111th, located near Trois Ponts, assigned the 51st ECB to prepare for demolition all crossings of the Ourthe River from Durbuy to La Roche. The battalion then allocated this mission to Companies A and B, ordering them to establish obstacles such as minefields, and abatis on the roads near the river, and plant demolitions on bridges and culverts. The key point for the battalion in the defensive line was the Ourthe River bridge at Hotton.[2]

By 0700 hours, December 19, the battalion had prepared all crossings for demolition. Two antitank minefields were laid just 200 yards downstream from the Hotton bridge, and one in the ford under the railroad bridge in Melreux. Below La Roche, at the extreme south of the barrier line, the Canadian 9th Forestry Company prepared the crossings on the Ourthe River for demolition.

Although the situation in the area was unclear, there was no doubt as to the need to keep the roads clear. Refugees clogging the roads presented a real problem. So did the hundreds of shell-shocked U.S. troops racing to the rear. If the bridge had not been held by the 51st, all the refugees would have been cut off by the Germans. Fraser saw whole artillery battalions racing rearward and tried to get them and others to help the 51st fight at Hotton, but only a few stragglers wanted to stay. Many of the troops were from the 106th Infantry Division. The roads were a mess. The American Army in retreat was not a pretty sight.[3]

Doc Maxson remembered Fraser and the other officers in the battalion trying to stop the retreating units. He recalled how "Scrappy" Fraser told those units that he had orders from First United States Army to put all retreating groups in a line along the Ourthe River. Some of the stragglers stopped and augmented the defenses of the 51st ECB, but most just kept going.[4]

Rumors of enemy parachutists behind the American lines kept everyone in a turmoil. As a result Colonel Fraser instituted a rigid civilian check system. At the 51st's Hotton check point, 21 civilians were found to have American clothing, cigarettes, and rations in their baggage. All except one spoke German and one had a German officer's pass book. They were turned over to the interrogation camp at Namur. In a separate incident one civilian detainee was detected wearing a German uniform under his civilian clothes while directing traffic. At Humain eight civilians were picked up and searched. Discovered in the search were four Mausers, a pistol, and some German grenades. They were turned over to the military police at Marche.

At one point there were no officers or men available to man a checkpoint for refugees on the highway in front of the 51st ECB command post. Fraser looked at Doc Maxson, and said, "Take off that helmet with the red cross on it and put on side arms and man that road block with one of your aid men." Doc responded immediately but soon got into trouble. Four motorcyclists drove up to the checkpoint, showed their credentials, and were allowed to pass. As soon as the motorcycles were gone some civilians ran up yelling, "La Boche, La Boche." One of the group that spoke English informed Doc Maxson that those were German soldiers he had just let through the checkpoint. The word got through to Scrappy Fraser that all was not well at the checkpoint, and the medics were soon relieved of duty.[5]

THE ARDENNES CAMPAIGN: HOLDING THE LINE

To keep the German infiltrators from getting at ammunition and fuel supplies, the battalion took control of a reserve Belgian emergency supply of gasoline, oil, and kerosene in the area. The storage points, such as the one at Marloie where American gas was stored and the ammunition supply point at Jamelle, were moved to new and safer locations.

On December 20, Company B continued to set up and maintain barriers along the line of the Ourthe River. A bridge southwest of Durbuy was prepared for demolition. Further to the southwest, a detachment with a bazooka and .30-caliber machine gun defended a weak bridge at Grand Man. At Noiseux, the piers of a destroyed bridge were wired for demolition, and a team with a .50-caliber machine gun and a bazooka guarded the crossing. The railroad bridge near Melreux was also prepared for demolition and the ford beneath it mined. Another ford 200 yards downstream from the Hotton bridge was mined and the Hotton bridge on N29 set for demolition. A team from the 440 Antiaircraft Artillery (AAA) Battalion helped the 51st defend the bridge at Hotton.

Second Lieutenant Spearmin of the 440th AAA Battalion came into the 51st ECB Command Post on December 20 and said he wanted to fight with the engineers. Most people, he noted, were running to the rear, but he had come to fight and win the war and wanted to do so now. His 95 men made up 8 sections, each consisting of a 40-mm. gun, a .50-caliber machine gun, and a bazooka. Six of these sections were spread out along the line, and two were assigned to the Hotton bridges. Fraser later regretted that he did not recommend Lieutenant Spearmin for a Silver Star.[6]

Company A prepared a footbridge in Hampteau for demolition and defended it with two .50-caliber and one .30-caliber machine guns. A refugee and straggler post was set up just to the southeast in cooperation with Belgian officials. A short distance down the road in that direction, two footbridges were prepared for demolition and a guard set. A weak, class 10 bridge at Marcourt was also prepared for destruction. It was defended by a half-track, and men armed with a bazooka, two .50-caliber machine guns, and one .30-caliber machine gun. One squad, with a .50-caliber machine gun and a bazooka, defended the road junction at N34 and 488.

Company A also prepared other road blocks. Abatis was placed on N4 near Tenneville with 30 mines installed after the trees were blown. Further north at an intersection called Champlon Crossroads on N4 and route 28, a platoon of Canadian Foresters, 13 men from the 158th ECB, 13 men from the 51st, and 12 from the 440th AAA Battalion defended the intersection. Armaments included one 40-mm. gun, one .50-caliber machine gun, and one bazooka. On N4 near Champlon, a tank retriever, an 81-mm. mortar, and a .50-caliber machine gun guarded a masonry culvert. Further north on N4 near Bande a masonry bridge was prepared for demolition. This was defended by 13 men and a .50-caliber machine gun. South of Marche where N4 crossed the Hadree, the intersection was defended by a 40-mm. gun belonging to the 440th AAA Battalion. In the event of an enemy attack all men and equipment south and east of this roadblock were to fall back to that point and make a stand.

Additional roadblocks included a bridge at Rochefort prepared for demolition by Company B, and defended by a 40-mm. gun, a bazooka, one .50-caliber machine gun, and one .30-caliber machine gun. The road net from Marche-Aye-Humain-Rochefort, and N35 from Marche to Rochefort was effectively blocked to the enemy advance northwestward from the southeast.

Further north, debris blocked the intersection at N35 and 29 near Baillonville, and on N35 near Hasard abatis and mines blocked the road. At Hogne west of N35 on N4 a culvert was wired with explosives.

During the day a continuous reconnaissance was made on N4 toward Bastogne. Enemy armor and infantry coming up N4 temporarily stopped at Ortheuville, 2000 meters southeast of Tenneville. The battalion called for all possible roadblocks that could be established on N4 northwest of Ortheuville. Shortly after receiving word of the enemy at Ortheuville, the 158th ECB said that N4 was cleared all the way to Bastogne. The enemy ground troops had been routed and some armor destroyed. Even so, the battalion had two squads of the 3d Platoon, Company A ready to put in road blocks if necessary.

The Battle of Hotton

On December 21, 1944, at approximately 0700 hours, 25 German infantry men crossed the Ourthe River at Hampteau and drove off two squads of Company A, 51st ECB. These were the first probing fingers of the 116th Panzer Division which had already lost 24 hours in a countermarch maneuver on the 19th. Now, without rest since the 16th and dead tired, they were attempting to break the 51st's line. But on this day the Fifth Panzer Army's advance would be carried by forward patrols of the 2d Panzer Division and the 116th Panzer Division only. These patrols were separated by the Ourthe River so they fought two distinctly separate battles.[7]

The Hampteau defense had been organized by the leader of the 1st platoon, Lieutenant Floyd D. Wright. On the road to Soy, about 30 yards northeast of the foot-bridge across the river, his men laid a hasty minefield. Private Stanley A. Driggs guarded it with his M-1 rifle. On the southwest side of the river, about 30-40 yards from the footbridge, a bazooka team of three men had a detonator set to blow the bridge. Along the Hotton-LaRoche road, two bazooka teams some 700 yards apart, were protected by daisy chains of mines. Half a squad of riflemen, two .50-caliber machine guns, and two tanks waited west of the Hotton-La Roche road.[8]

Just prior to the battle of Hotton, jeep patrols from the 820th Tank Destroyer Battalion (TD) received fire near La Roche. They relayed the information to 2d platoon, Company A, at Marcourt. The 2d platoon subsequently blew their bridge. Wright had tried to talk the 820th TD Battalion into reinforcing the 2d platoon's roadblock at Marcourt, but failed. He sent his platoon sergeant, Staff Sergeant Donald A. Bonifay, along with Sergeant Benjamin Ham's squad to Marcourt; they arrived in an M8 armored car at 2d platoon at 0130 hours December 21 and reported to First Lieutenant Paul W. Curtis Jr., the platoon leader. Curtis put them on line to defend the town. There had been a brief fire fight between two German half-tracks approaching the bridge and his own .50-caliber machine guns, but no casualties. But when the 51st ECB guards tried to halt an American patrol at Marcourt, Cpl Jerry Stephens, was killed and T/5 Clifton M. Pratt wounded, all because of mistaken identity.[9]

Bonifay left Sergeant Ham's squad at Marcourt and returned to Hampteau in time for the fighting there. At 0510 hours, Driggs ran back across the bridge to report the approach of a German armored car from the northeast. The armored car began shelling the town while the rest of the men from the car started firing at the bazooka teams. An attempt was made to blow the bridge but the wires had been cut. By this time Hampteau was on fire and the Battle of Hotton had started. Lieutenant Colonel Fraser ordered Wright to reinforce Company B at Hotton. At 0900 hours Bonifay took one last look at the burning but deserted town of Hampteau and made his way back to Hotton on foot. At Hampteau T/5 Floyd Johnston exposed himself to observed enemy small arms fire and 47-mm. HE fire in order to remove his vehicle after enemy infantry had entered town.[10]

About 0730, firing broke out in Hotton near the critical class-70 bridge, and a half hour later a small-scale battle was in full swing. Fraser put Captain Hodges in charge of the defense at the bridge. Hodges had one squad from Bruce W. Jamison's 1st platoon, Company B; the 1st Platoon, Company A, commanded by Wright; a squad of 23d Armored Engineers, 3d Armored Division (AD), with a 37-mm. anti-tank gun; two

40-mm. Bofors AAA guns; several bazooka teams; and some .50-caliber machine guns. These formed the opposition to the Germans. Captain Barnes later reinforced Hodges with a ten-man patrol from battalion headquarters. Hodges put most of these personnel and equipment in defensive positions on the southwest side of the Hotton bridge.

On the northeast side of the bridge were personnel of the 3d Armored Division Trains and some heavy equipment. Additional 3d Armored Division personnel southwest of Hotton fought off German infantry and tanks located on the heights on the east bank of the Ourthe River.

Early in the battle, Fraser was in constant telephone contact with Lieutenants Jamison and Wright, getting eyewitness descriptions of the fighting. The Army telephone lines between Hotton and Marche did not work but the Belgian civilian telephone system was still usable.

The situation in Hotton soon deteriorated and Fraser urgently requested help from the 84th Infantry Division. Part of that division had arrived in Marche but had no mission yet. When his appeal was dismissed, Fraser put the Hotton phone next to the Marche phone so the sounds of battle could be heard. The commanding general, Major General Alexander R. Bolling, personally refused aid until the facts of the matter could be brought to his attention. Eye-witness reports from officers were called rumors without factual basis.

At 0833 the telephone connection went out, so Fraser left his command post in Marche and drove to the scene of the battle at Hotton. While there, Private Lee J. Ishmael, Fraser's driver, seeing that the crew manning the 37-mm. gun was hesitant about putting the piece into action, decided to man the gun himself. With the assistance of the men on the crew, Ishmael disabled one of the German tanks, causing its crew to abandon it.

While the battle progressed, Lieutenants Jamison and Wright found an M4 tank armed with a 76-mm. cannon in an ordnance detachment on the outskirts of Hotton. They tried to talk the tank commander into supporting Company B at the bridge in Hotton. But the tanker was reluctant to move his tank to a defensive position without a crew and support. He insisted that he would need three men inside the tank to man the cannon and at least fifteen riflemen deployed around the tank for protection. On being assured that these men would be provided, he moved the tank to a firing position on the southwest side of the bridge. Three men from the 51st went inside the tank and about twelve men deployed outside to protect the tank. One of the men deployed outside the M-4 was Wright's driver, T/5 Floyd Johnston.[11]

This tank became part of an unorthodox but effective combined arms team, along with the 37-mm. AT gun, the 40-mm. Bofors, and the bazooka teams. Between them they put four German heavy tanks out of action. By 0900 hours two tanks from the 3d Armored Division trains, one medium and one light, occupying Hotton northeast of the bridge, also engaged the enemy. A German Mark VI tank approaching the bridge from the Soy road quickly knocked out the light tank. The M-4 knocked out one German tank. Shortly thereafter a German round barely missed the M-4. Johnston ran over to the sergeant in charge of the tank and told him that he and another man saw a flash from the shrubbery between two buildings across the river. The sergeant fired one shot that was too high. Johnston ran back and told the sergeant to lower his sights into the bushes. The second shot was a direct hit, sending a cloud of black smoke into the sky. Another of the German tanks was knocked out by the 37-mm. cannon.[12]

Captain Barnes, having sent his squad of volunteers from H&S Company to Hotton, went down N4 to the outskirts of Marche where an M10 three-inch gun motor carriage backed up a 51st roadblock. Barnes brought the M10 back through Marche toward Hotton for reinforcement, but was stopped by General Bolling of the 84th Division. Barnes explained the situation at Hotton to General Bolling but the general would not take his word for it. Finally, about an hour later at 1000 hours, an officer of the 84th accompanied the Battalion S-2 to Hotton. When they arrived at 1030 hours, the town was being heavily shelled. While there the representative from the 84th received additional reports as to the gravity of the situation but remained unconvinced. Still he did promise help.

During the battle that continued into the afternoon, the Germans shot out the wiring on the demolition charges on the bridge. Jamison and Wright jumped into the shoulder-deep, freezing water and, while under enemy small arms fire, repaired the wiring. With the appearance of the relief force from the 84th, most of the 51st withdrew toward Marche, having succeeded in defending the bridge at Hotton. One half-squad was left behind to blow the bridge if necessary.

The first platoon of the 84th task force arrived around 1500 hours, some six hours after the first request for assistance. Additional reports of enemy action led the 84th to send two additional companies to reinforce the platoon. By the time they arrived the fighting was about over. Hodges, with the aid of a full-strength platoon and a tank destroyer, and assisted by some personnel of the 3d Armored's Trains fighting on the northeast side of the river, had already saved the bridge from the Germans. The tank destroyer had knocked out two more German tanks, making a total of four. Hodges looked into one of the burning German tanks and noticed that the personnel were wearing American uniforms.

By the time the 84th arrived to take over the town, the 3d Armored Division had assumed responsibility for the east bank of the river and chased 5 German half-tracks with some 50 men, 4 large German personnel carriers loaded with about 100 men, and a German heavy tank. Those enemy units had evacuated the Hotton area and were heading for Erezee in a northeasterly direction.

The stiff defense by the Engineers at Hotton convinced the LVIII Panzer Corps commander that a continued effort in that area would lead nowhere. Krueger then ordered the 116th Panzer Division to disengage on the Soy-Hotton road, pull back, and cross the Ourthe at La Roche. The 560th Volks Grenadier Division continued its attack to the northwest.[13]

Aided by a few men from the 3d Armored Division, and the 1st Platoon, Company A, the embattled engineers of Company B, in a seven hour battle, had defeated the enemy attempt to take the bridge at Hotton. Their actions had preserved a key link in the Allied supply lines to forward units and had denied the German 116th Panzer Division an opening to the Meuse River. That feat of arms was subsequently acknowledged by the German corps and army commanders. Later the bridge would play a key role in the American offensive that followed. Captain Hodges was awarded the Silver Star for his heroic achievements at Hotton.[14]

A separate action that afternoon took the life of Lieutenant Curtis. He led a patrol of about ten men and a half-track from company headquarters to the Ourthe River near Rendeux to destroy a footbridge. The men who had been guarding the bridge had been pulled off and sent on another mission. At the bridge site Curtis, Saunders, Wimberly, Ochson, and Kelly moved forward and found the wires leading to the demolition charges had been cut. The severed wires plainly indicated that the Germans had been there. They were still there. A hail of small arms fire broke out and Curtis was mortally wounded.[15]

Although heavy fighting occurred at Hotton on December 21, only two members of the 51st sustained injuries: Captain Hodges was hit by a shell fragment in the leg, and Private Ishmael was wounded in the hand.

—— Delaying Action on N4: Ortheuville to Marche ——

While Company B held off the 116th Panzer at Hotton, Colonel Fraser sent Captain Radford, H&S Company, with two of his men to

Champlon Crossroads to support Company A and a Canadian Forestry unit. When they arrived in the late afternoon, they found the Canadians but no one from Company A. The Canadian unit commander agreed to deploy in the woods southwest of the crossroads while Radford set up his .50-caliber machine gun in the woods northwest of the crossroads.[16]

Within a short period of time, a battle could be heard in progress to the southeast toward Ortheuville. The roar of tanks, bursting shells, small arms fire, and the screams of wounded men were easily distinguishable. It did not take long for the Canadian Forestry commander to decide that he had urgent business to the rear: he abandoned Radford and his two men. Fraser then sent Radford seven miles northwest to 496 and N4 to set up a checkpoint. The three men spent the night at the checkpoint without incident. The next morning, December 22, they spotted a group of over 20 civilians coming down the road, headed west. Harold Self and Wilson Roberts were manning the machine gun some 25-30 yards away. Radford had no way of covering this group of civilians, some of whom were obviously soldiers in civilian clothes judging from the way they carried themselves. Without enough men to search the group, all Radford could do was force them to turn around and go back to Bastogne.

Later that day, Radford created a roadblock. He convinced a sergeant on a 7th Armored Division tank retriever to stay and help push four carloads of gravel across the road. Radford wanted to get them into position to blow later. No traffic came through the checkpoint for the rest of the day so the tanker decided he had to go west on urgent business. Radford convinced him and his two crewmen to stay by threatening to shoot them.

That night Radford decided that the gravel car obstacle had to be set up and blown. At the roadblock were the two H&S men, the three 7th AD tank retriever men, and two mechanics and five cooks from Company A, 51st ECB. The tank retriever pushed the cars across the road, effectively blocking it, then took off. TNT was put under the wheels and set off. The explosion tore up the ends of the gravel cars without knocking off the wheels, blocking the road with quite a pile of twisted metal and spilled gravel. The explosion also brought down the power lines along the road and created a spectacular electrical display. If nothing else, perhaps the downed wires would electrocute a few Germans. Radford and his men then headed for Marche.

On the morning of the 23d, while Fraser and some of the 84th personnel discussed the probable location of the Germans, Colonel Ander-

THE 51ST AGAIN!

son sent Radford to N4 to determine the answer. He and Sergeant Kelly took off in a jeep driven by Private Finn. Radford thought he knew about where the Germans were from the night before. The blown N4 culvert should have slowed them down a little. As his jeep swerved around a curve at about 25 miles an hour they were surprised to see the muzzle of a tank pointing in their direction. Finn stopped the jeep about 125 yards from the tank, threw it in reverse, then zigzagged back to the curve some 400 straight yards behind them. The Germans had just captured a sedan full of Canadians and only noticed Radford's group when they saw the jeep backing away. Radford "watched the jerry gunner slink into his turret" and could "almost feel the shell whistling through the jeep," but made it safely around the curve. Finn then turned the jeep around and high-tailed it back to Marche. They had run into the Germans less than a mile from the junction of 496 and N4. The masonry bridge near the junction was still intact.

Meanwhile, Wright's platoon of Company A, fresh from the fighting at Hotton, reported to battalion headquarters in Marche. Here two or three extra demolition men were attached to the platoon. He also picked up extra blocks of TNT with supporting devices, anti-tank mines, and an additional portable radio. Wright was given orders to proceed down a designated road with his platoon until he ran into the Germans. He was then to "do something to slow them down." In its simplicity this was an astonishing order.[17]

The platoon moved out about noon on December 22 in an "approach to contact" formation. Wright's jeep led with T/5 Floyd Johnston driving and PFC Clinton L. Jordan operating the radio. The squad trucks followed at about 200-foot intervals between vehicles. Staff Sergeant Bonifay was in the last vehicle with the extra radio.

Out in the countryside, Jordan tried to radio Bonifay but could not make contact. The antenna cable had jarred loose and fallen to the ground some distance back. The tension was already acute, and loss of radio contact with the rear of the column only increased anxiety. Wright told Jordan to force his bayonet into the connection where the antenna was supposed to be and try to contact Bonifay again. Of course that did not work.

After sneaking and peeking over each hill, and around each curve, then driving as fast as possible to the next hill or curve, the platoon reached a "Y" in the road near the town of Jemelle. The road came in from the east, then split, with one leg going to the northwest and one to the southwest. The platoon came in from the northwest and at the "Y", learned from some civilians that a German tank column had just passed and was moving down the southwest leg of the "Y". Tread marks on the road confirmed this story.

The platoon then retraced its own tracks to find a suitable place to establish an obstacle. Within sight of the "Y", on the side of a steep hill, was a stretch of road with large trees on each side. Two squads, minus their demolition men, were deployed for security while the rest of the platoon attached TNT to trees that were to be dropped across the road to form an abatis. They also placed anti-tank mines throughout the area. When all was prepared the platoon withdrew to the other side of the hill to blow the charges. The demolition men had done an outstanding job. The huge trees shivered and shook, then each one fell criss-cross over the road to form an impassable obstacle. There was no moon and the night was extremely dark as the platoon headed back to Marche. There was also no rest. Wright and his platoon were ordered to Rochefort to blow another bridge.

Captain Karl Pedersen, Company A, with his 3d Platoon led by Lieutenant Raymond A. Trafford and Staff Sergeant George M. Sherwood, had established and continued to maintain a chain of road blocks along N4 southeast of Marche. The nearest, of ten men and one 40-mm. gun, was established south of Marche near Au Gris Molin. Further south at the junction of N4 and route 496 were 13 men with a .50-caliber machine gun, an 81-mm. mortar, and a tank retriever. Still further, near Bande on N4, 13 men and a .50-caliber machine gun covered a masonry bridge that was prepared for demolition. About four miles beyond them a masonry culvert was wired for demolition. At the Champlon crossroad of N4 and 28 were 13 men armed with a 40-mm. gun, a .50-caliber machine gun, and a bazooka, all from Company A, and 13 men from the 158th ECB. The 10-man defensive force about 2000 meters further south on N4 had already laid 30 mines and prepared abatis.

This obstacle was some three miles north of Ortheuville, a town the Colonel Meinrad von Lauchert's 2d Panzer advance guard had taken from the 158th the night of December 20. A few German patrols probed the roadblock but took no serious action because Lauchert's tanks were waiting for gasoline and could not move. Besides, his men were tired. But they were only 16 miles from Marche and less than 40 miles from the Meuse. The 22d passed with little activity but on the morning of the 23d, the 2d Panzer Division began to move.[18]

─────────── Champlon Crossroads ───────────

The 2d Panzer Division had Marche as its first objective, a short distance from Ortheuville. But they were delayed for several hours by the fortified road blocks established and manned by Company A, 51st ECB. At 1530, two enemy tanks were seen about 2,000 meters further east on N4 and the abatis was blown by Trafford and his ten men. The men returned to the roadblock at the Champlon crossroads at N4 and 28. Captain Pedersen consolidated his position near this crossroad with all available weapons and men. At 1700 enemy infantry troops set up a skirmish line along route N28 towards La Roche.

At 1730 the enemy fired a few rounds of 88-mm. shells. Company A returned the fire with .50-caliber machine guns, the 40-mm. gun, and rifles. Then Pedersen ordered his men back about 1.5 miles to blow a masonry culvert. They then retired to the next obstacle at N4 and 496. At 1930 battalion ordered all personnel to return to Marche, leaving the road to Bastogne in German hands. But the company had held its roadblocks long enough to allow the 7th Armored Division trains to escape from La Roche and reach Marche safely. Pedersen's delaying action on N4 also gave the 84th Infantry valuable time to prepare for the defense of the Marche area and permitted the 2d Armored Division to assemble northwest of Marche.[19]

As Company A retired from the vicinity of the road block at the junction of N4 and N28, Trafford, with several of his men, pushed a railroad car across the road to slow down the German advance. Later Trafford had to go back to the road junction to remove the obstacle. These orders were probably the result of a VII Corps counterattack planned for December 24.

About three miles north of road junction N4 and 496, Trafford encountered American soldiers laying a mine field. He was sitting on the passenger side of a 2½-ton truck that had several men in the rear cargo area. The truck was being guided through what was supposed to be a safe lane when it struck a mine. The cab of the vehicle burst into flames and the clothing of both men caught fire. Trafford grabbed the driver and pulled him out and into a ditch partially filled with water. He then rolled himself and the driver over and over in the ditch to extinguish the flames. At this point Trafford passed out. The next thing he remembered was awakening in the 39th Field Hospital with second- and third-degree burns and shrapnel wounds. Private Houston M. Fairchild and "Pop" Johnson were also injured and evacuated to the hospital.[20]

The truck was demolished. It had been carrying three extra 5-gallon cans of gasoline. Trafford ended up in a hospital at Rheims, France. To avoid being sent to a replacement depot he slipped out of the hospital and returned to Company A on January 22, 1945.

Not until early afternoon on December 23 did the leading battalion of the 304th Panzer Grenadier Regiment overrun the 4th Cavalry outpost at Harsin about four miles south of Marche. It was dark when the German battalion finally fought its way into Hargimont, severing the road from Marche to Rochefort.

The Battle of Rochefort

As dawn broke on December 22, the main task for General Bolling's 84th Division was finding the enemy. Major General J. Lawton Collins, commanding VII Corps, feared that the Germans might move in from the south and west, the general direction of Rochefort and Marche, and interfere with the concentration of VII Corps troops. The 51st shared his concern. Major General Matthew B. Ridgeway, CG, XVIII Airborne Corps, dispatched Combat Command A, 3d Armored Division to set up a screen on the west bank of the Ourthe River between LaRoche and St. Hubert. That force ran into the Germans just outside of Marche. The 51st sent Lieutenant Attardo to Rochefort, followed by the 1st Platoon, Company A, under Lieutenant Wright, to blow the bridge in town. That bridge had been prepared for demolition by Company B, but the men had been pulled off and sent on another mission.[21]

Driving from Marche to Rochefort under blackout conditions, the 1st Platoon entered the town of Humain, about halfway between the two cities. There Wright found the 24th Cavalry Squadron. He asked the commanding officer where the Germans were and for support while on his mission to blow the bridge. The commander neither knew the location of the Germans nor honored his request for support, saying he was told to move into the area and wait for further orders.

Wright moved on to Rochefort, not knowing if the Germans were there. He stopped his vehicles on the edge of town and the platoon went in on foot to locate the bridge. No battle noises could be heard; the night was still and very dark. As the men moved quietly through the streets, they knocked on several doors to ask the inhabitants if they had heard or seen any Germans. None had. The platoon moved on to the river and found the bridge.

Wright left his platoon in an alley under cover and with Bonifay approached the bridge to set off the demolition. They found the fuse, pulled the fuse lighter, and then "ran like hell" down the cobblestone street, sounding like a "herd of elephants." They had no choice but to make a noisy exit for they did not know how much time it would take before the TNT ignited. Diving into an alley for cover, they waited for an explosion. When, after two or three minutes, nothing happened they realized that something had gone wrong with the fuse. They also realized that after all the noise they had made, if there were Germans in town, they would be waiting for them.

After furtively returning to the bridge, Wright and Bonifay discovered that the fuse lighter had not worked. Wright used his pocketknife to skin back the cover of the time fuse and expose the black powder. Bonifay then lit the fuse with his cigarette lighter as Wright continued to hold it until it started to spit fire. With the fuse burning, Wright laid it down and the two once again ran down the street and dove into the alley. In a few seconds a tremendous explosion shook the ground. Cobblestones rained around the area for several seconds.

Once again the two men returned to the bridge, this time to check their work. Standing on the abutment of the bridge they could see, even though it was dark, that the roadway of the bridge was laying on the river bed. They headed for the edge of town where they had left their vehicles, then returned to Marche a distance of about seven miles.

It was still dark early in the morning of December 23 when Wright arrived at battalion headquarters in Marche. He reported that his mission had been completed; the bridge in Rochefort had been destroyed. Much to his amazement, Wright was ordered to return to Rochefort and rebuild the bridge. Like Trafford with his roadblock, Wright had to undo his work.

Possibly the battalion had gained information about a planned counterattack that would require a bridge in Rochefort. Generals Montgomery and Hodges had agreed on December 22 that VII Corps would counterattack on Sunday the 24th. The 2d Armored Division would be on the right wing, the 84th Infantry in the center, and the 3d Armored Division on the left wing, and the 75th Infantry Division in reserve. In actuality the counter-attack did not begin until January 3.[22]

Shortly after daybreak on December 23, Wright and his platoon returned to Rochefort. The weather was cold, the sky overcast; it had been like that since the beginning of the Battle of the Bulge. Wright and Bonifay discovered they had done their job very well. They had to measure the span on the completely demolished bridge and obtain Bailey bridge material to replace it. Looking upstream a few hundred feet, Wright was surprised to see a wooden vehicular bridge crossing the L'Homme River. Because of the darkness he had not seen this bridge a few hours earlier when he had destroyed the stone arch bridge. The wooden bridge was unusual in that the wood deck for the roadway was only two or three feet above the water.

Wright and his driver crossed the bridge to reconnoiter the far side. As they drove into the town square of Rochefort, they were amazed to find American soldiers and vehicles on the streets. Wright learned that an infantry battalion headquarters was billeted in the basement of the Grand Hotel de l'Etoile located on one side of the town square. He reported to the commander of the unit, Major Gordon A. Bahe, 3d Battalion, 335th Infantry Regiment, 84th Infantry Division. Major Bahe had arrived early that morning with two companies to join his Company I, already located there.

The day before, on December 22, the 84th was trying to locate the Germans on their exposed south and southwest flanks, where they feared a possible penetration. General Bolling, after conferring with General Collins, had sent Company I to Rochefort where it arrived late in the afternoon. The 51st was not aware of this action. At the same time Lieutenant Attardo, battalion S-3 section, went to Rochefort to blow the bridge. Late that night when Wright reported in after establishing a road block near Jamelle, Attardo had not returned. Wright's platoon was then sent to Rochefort.

Wright asked Bahe if he had heard a loud explosion during the night. He replied that he had but thought it was a German V2 rocket that had fallen short. Wright then advised Bahe that he had created the noise when he destroyed the L'Homme River bridge to his rear. He also hastened to inform him of the wooden bridge that crossed the river and assured him that he still had a bridge he could use. Wright then promised Bahe that he would replace the one he destroyed as soon as he could get the Bailey material.

When Wright rejoined his platoon at the near shore abutment, a lieutenant from the 300th ECB claimed that he had orders to relieve Wright's platoon in that area. Wright said he would have to receive the orders from battalion. He was going there to order bridge materials so he invited the lieutenant to follow him. Marche was about a 15-minute drive in daylight.[23]

With Johnston driving and PFC Jordan in the rear of the jeep, Wright set off for Marche. The lieutenant from the 300th led the way in his jeep, sometimes reaching speeds of 50 to 60 MPH. Wright wanted his driver to pass the other jeep because he doubted the lieutenant knew the location of the 51st headquarters. After two attempts, it was plain that it was too risky. Wright fell in behind him.

The two jeeps were soon out of town and into farm country when a German armored vehicle approached from around a curve in the road. It immediately opened fire with machine guns at a range of about 200 feet. It may have been part of the 2d Panzer Division which was nine miles northwest of Rochefort that night. Enemy fire hit the lead jeep and it stopped in the middle of the road. Johnston turned his jeep into a ditch beside the road. As it hit the ditch the horn started blowing. Wright dove into the ditch, while Johnston and Jordan raced to a nearby farm building for cover. The horn on the jeep continued to blow. The Germans stopped firing and backed out of sight around a curve. Evidently they thought there were other elements following and the horn was a signal.

With the Germans out of sight, Wright got back into his jeep. As he turned the steering wheel the horn stopped blowing. A bullet had struck the steering wheel shaft and shorted the horn wires. Wright's crew went to the lead jeep and carried out the wounded lieutenant and his driver. The radio operator in the back of the jeep was dead. They put the wounded lieutenant and his driver in the jeep and sped back to Rochefort.

Wright told Bonifay to take the wounded men to an aid station. He then sent Sergeant Kroen's third squad south along the west bank of the L'Homme River to a railroad bridge where it was to slow down any German movement from that direction. Sergeant John Stiftinger, 2d Squad, was put in charge of the platoon. Wright then crossed to the east side of the river to advise Major Bahe that he had German armor to his rear and needed to get some tank destroyers or anti-tank guns to stop them.

As Kroen and his men approached the railroad bridge to the south, they noticed that the bridge passed over the road that ran parallel to the river on the west bank. He deployed his squad on the bridge in such a fashion that they could arm and drop bazooka ammunition on any German vehicles or tanks that passed under them on the road below. Having lost their bazookas in previous action the men determined to make the best use of the ammunition they were carrying.[24]

In the meantime Bonifay found a medical unit on the Meuse River where he left the wounded men from the 300th ECB. He then tried to return to Rochefort but was turned back by road blocks manned by the 2d Armored Division.

At that time American forces in Rochefort consisted of Major Bahe's 3d Battalion (minus Company L), 335th Infantry; a platoon each from the 638th Tank Destroyer Battalion, 309th ECB, and 29th Infantry; and two platoons of the regimental anti-tank company, besides the platoon of the 51st ECB. By late afternoon on December 23, the Germans had begun to shell Rochefort. A couple of hours after midnight, Panzer Lehr began its main attack from the south.[25]

In just a few minutes the situation deteriorated. Major Bahe could do nothing more than try and hold on. In his basement headquarters at the hotel, runners and radio messages from his companies advised that his outpost had been overrun and that the Germans had circled the town. With that news, Wright realized that he could not get out to rejoin his platoon. The platoon already realized it had been cut off and had withdrawn to a pre-arranged assembly point in Givet. The 51st used this procedure so that people would have a known place to assemble.

The infantry wounded were brought into the battalion command post. Major Bahe repeatedly asked regiment on the radio for permission to withdraw. He was told to hold Rochefort. The situation continued to get worse. At one point regiment told him to attack to the north and tie up with friendly forces. He replied that he could not hold on to what he had and that it was impossible to attack in any direction. He again requested permission to withdraw but was refused.

There was very little food in the basement of the hotel, and supplies could not be brought into town. But a large pile of Irish potatoes and several racks of baked cinnamon rolls were found in the storage bins in the basement which enabled the men to keep their stomachs full.

Throughout the night the rifle companies fought fiercely, but were slowly pushed back toward the square in the center of town. By noon the Germans controlled the streets around the square. From a street-level window of the basement of the hotel Wright could see a .50-caliber machine gun crew force a German tank to back out of sight behind a building. Perhaps the machine gun broke the glass in the driver's peep hole or the fire was so intense that it heated the armor plate so that the driver could not hold his face close to it.

Finally, early on December 24, Major Bahe received permission to leave. Bahe called his company commanders to the basement command post and told them of his intent to withdraw. He noted that there were a few vehicles parked in an alley nearby that the Germans had not reached. They would accommodate only the people in the CP. With the help of smoke grenades and a heavy volume of fire Bahe felt they could run across the street and reach the vehicles. The wounded would have to be left behind with an aid man.[26]

At this point, a soldier sitting in a corner of the room with a bullet hole in his upper lip that was large enough to stick your finger into, got to his feet and in a gurgling voice said, "I'll be damned if you are going to leave me here." Each company was to disengage and withdraw to the west on foot avoiding main roads. Military historian Hugh M. Cole described the situation very well: "Driven back into a small area around the battalion command post where bullet and mortar fire made the streets a 'living inferno', the surrounded garrison made ready for a break."[27]

With smoke and heavy covering fire, Wright and the others dashed across the street one-by-one as bullets ricocheted around them. The wounded who could run did so. Those who could not remained in the basement with a medic. Once in the alley, Wright hopped into a jeep that had a machine gun mounted on it. When the vehicles were loaded, the men drove them out of the alley with all weapons firing as rapidly as possible. The men shot at every door and window in sight. It was like the old Wild West movies when the bandits shot up the town as they made their getaway.

The column headed east then turned south and then west. On this route it did not cross the L'Homme River, which loops around the northern part of Rochefort, then joins the Lesse River which flows to the northwest and joins the Meuse River near Dinant. To the complete surprise of the men in the column, after passing the first three or four city blocks, they did not encounter a single German or receive any fire. They did not see any other American forces either. Once in the countryside the men stopped briefly. An elderly lady from a nearby farm house passed out a platter full of fried potatoes as if giving out Christmas gifts. After the men paused to enjoy the food, the column headed for Givet.

That afternoon was unforgettable. It was the first clear sky and sunshine since the Battle of the Bulge began. The sky became even more beautiful as it filled with fighters and bombers headed east to bomb and strafe the German armored columns. By that time, Wright's platoon had the dubious distinction of being shot at by both sides of a pincer movement around Rochefort; to the north enroute to Marche by the German 2d Panzer Division and in Rochefort by Panzer Lehr.

As the column approached the bridge over the Meuse at Givet the men knew they were safe. British tanks in firing positions lined both sides of the road. Major Bahe rounded up several 2½-ton trucks to go back east to find his companies that were coming out on foot. Wright had operated sawmills in the area and knew most of the back roads and logging trails between Givet and Rochefort. He offered to guide Bahe along the roads that his companies would most likely be following.

It was a slow process. They stopped on the top of each hill to look for the soldiers and for Germans: they did not know whom they would encounter first. As late afternoon approached the blue sky changed to gray. It was Christmas Eve, 1944, and still no men in sight. As Bahe and Wright inched their way to the crest of yet another hill and looked to the valley below they saw two columns of U.S. infantrymen, one on each side of the road.

The jeep raced down the hill toward the two columns. The Army 2½-ton truck of WW II with its front wheel drive seemed to need two acres to turn around. On this day those trucks turned around on a dime, never leaving the gravel surface of the trail they were on. There was much jubilation from the troops, with cheers and applause, but it quickly ceased for the whereabouts of the German panzer division was unknown. Both columns loaded into the trucks and headed for Givet. Christmas came early for some members of the 3d Battalion, 335th Infantry Regiment, 84th Infantry Division. Back in Givet Wright found his platoon right where they were supposed to be. It was a joyous reunion.

Several hours after dark on December 24, Wright sent Bonifay and two men back to the chateau near Ciergnon on the Lesse River, where Company A had had its CP on December 17, 1944. All non-essential items of equipment and baggage had been left at the chateau for a week under the guard of Corporal Loyd E. Sweatt. Bonifay's orders were to pick up Sweatt and all the baggage he could and return to Givet. He took the half-track driven by Sergeant Weil and assigned Sergeant Kroen to man the .50-caliber machine gun mounted on it.[28]

Ciergnon lay about 13 miles east of Givet. Having no knowledge of the location of the Germans, Bonifay proceeded cautiously. The night was cold and clear with several inches of snow on the ground. The half-track could be heard for miles. The group passed through Beauraing without incident, then headed northeast toward Ciergnon. There Bonifay was challenged by a small detachment of combat engineers under the command of a lieutenant. After establishing their identity, the lieutenant told Bonifay that the bridge over the Lesse River was prepared for demolition and would be blown shortly. The lieutenant gave Bonifay 30 minutes to cross the bridge, get to the chateau, about a quarter mile from the bridge, and return.[29]

Corporal Sweatt, having been put on guard duty by the Company Commander, Captain Pedersen, was reluctant to leave his post without orders from the captain. Some firm persuasion from Bonifay convinced Sweatt to leave. Loading all the barracks bags and equipment that the half-track could hold, the crew headed for the bridge. Shortly after crossing, a loud explosion was heard as the engineers blew the bridge. Bonifay and his crew returned to Givet less cautiously than when they went to Ciergnon.[30]

After a good night's sleep, the first in over a week, the men of First Platoon, Company A, 51st ECB, headed north on the west bank of the Meuse River on Christmas Day. Their objective was battalion headquarters, which they thought was still in Marche. Along the west bank of the Meuse River they passed several large quartermaster supply depots. Around noon, they stopped at one of them, and after explaining to the commander what the platoon had been doing, received an invitation to get into the chow line for a full Christmas dinner with turkey and all the trimmings. They were probably the only element of the 51st Engineer Combat Battalion that had their turkey on schedule on Christmas Day.

Late in the afternoon of December 26, 1944, Wright reported to Fraser at battalion headquarters. Fraser had not heard from Wright's platoon for over two days and was preparing to report the entire platoon as missing in action. Fraser was happy to see them and learn that the platoon had not taken any casualties. After taking the report, Fraser instructed Captain Pedersen not to give the 1st Platoon any new assignments for two or three days. The men were grateful for the rest.

> The defense of Rochefort had not been too costly: fifteen wounded men, under the care of a volunteer medic were left in the town and another 25 killed or captured. But the Panzer Lehr commander, General Bayerlein, who had fought in both Bastogne and Rochefort, later rated the American defense in Rochefort as comparable in courage and in significance to that of Bastogne.[31]

Standing Firm

While Wright was at Rochefort, the rest of the battalion was also busy. On December 22 a barrier line was installed from Hamoir to Hotton along the Ourthe River, then through Marche and southwest to Rochefort. It consisted of prepared demolitions in culverts, mines in roads at critical intersections, bazooka teams, and 40-mm. AAA guns from the 440th AAA AW Battalion. Company B sent out patrols in the vicinity of Grandham north of Noiseux, and one squad encountered some mortar fire. The patrol retreated to a footbridge and set up guard. Defensive positions were also maintained at points along route 29 north of Marche. Bridges and culverts were mined, minefields installed, and craters established. Abatis were also placed.

At 1500 hours, Company C, having just returned from its defense of Trois Ponts, sent an officer group to reconnoiter N4 and to set up road blocks to the south of Marche. The lead vehicles of an enemy armored column, made up of five tanks, two half-tracks filled with infantry, and unseen armor, located on N4 north of 496, fired on the reconnaissance group and cut off their escape. The officers escaped by running through fields, and later returned safely, but Major Yates was captured by the Germans.

Yates had just returned from the hospital a week earlier where he had been confined with a broken ankle. He had not been able to run so he hid in a bush for several hours before being discovered and taken prisoner by the Germans. While guarded by a German soldier, Yates dove into the stream beside them and, under a hail of bullets, worked his way downstream under three feet of water. Yates later said the Germans who shot at him could not tell his rear end from the logs that were floating downstream from a bridge blown upstream.[32]

The battalion had just about given up on finding Yates when it got a call from the duty officer, 84th Infantry Division who said he had a major down there with his clothes frozen stiff, and who claimed to be part of the 51st ECB. One of our units picked him up by a creek. Send someone down and get him. Fraser raced down to the 84th to get him. Yates was shivering like an aspen leaf in the wind. Fraser said, "We thawed him out and he was ready to go the next day. We always thought he had nine lives. He was very upset because the Germans had taken his pistol."

On December 23, the battalion headquarters moved to a new CP in Maffe, north of Marche. Company A moved to Haversin, Company B to Borion, and Company C to Nettinne. Company C was relieved from protecting the 84th Infantry Division's headquarters at 0800 hours and given the mission of establishing roadblocks, mining bridges, and preparing abatis in its new area. Several roadblocks were established in conjunction with elements of the 309th ECB.

At 1230 hours, small arms fire was heard south of Haversin. Two patrols of three men each went south and west of Haversin to investigate. One patrol encountered three German tanks with about ten infantrymen on each tank. The patrol was not fired on and it quickly reported back to the company CP. Company A then moved back to the battalion headquarters at Maffe and established a new CP.

At 1710 hours Lieutenant Henry advised the battalion CP that his patrol had not found the Germans reported in the vicinity of Maffe. Around 2100 hours three enlisted men from Company B brought in six male civilians from the vicinity of Grand Han where earlier in the day a ferryman was mysteriously shot. The suspects were taken to the 2d Armored Division for interrogation.

On December 24, Company A sent out two full squads to Noisseux to prepare the treadway bridge and its existing piers for demolition. Another squad went to prepare four railroad bridges for destruction, two in Marche and two just southwest of the town. At this point, Company A was fully committed. To relieve the battalion situation slightly, the

THE 51ST AGAIN!

1110th Engineer Combat Group and the 275th ECB took over some of Company B's defensive positions, and Company B went into reserve. Company C still maintained its positions along the highway, gaining some support from the 61st ECB, but also remained completely committed.

During the day action took place all along the line. At 1000 hours the 84th notified the battalion that a firefight was in progress in Marloie, with the enemy using small arms and mortars. Actually the Germans were wearing American uniforms but using German weapons. At Faviet at 1005 hours, Lieutenant Middleton, Company B reported that he was fired on by German 88s. At 1600 hours, Lieutenant Kelly reported hearing small arms fire in the vicinity of Halleux. At 1700 hours Colonel Fraser reported 150 enemy infantry without armored support attacking in the vicinity of Marenne. A few hours later Major Gee, the assistant area security officer for VII Corps, arrived in the area and asked the battalion to investigate a rumor concerning enemy agents signalling from the church tower in Maffe.

On Christmas Day, the battalion established its rear CP at Clavier. Company A, in order to complete its preparation of four railroad bridges for demolition, organized one platoon into four sections with one section at each site. A hasty minefield was installed at the intersection of N4 and the railroad in Marche. One platoon had the responsibility for guarding the treadway bridge at Noisseux that had been prepared for demolition. Six men were in Hotton, prepared to destroy that bridge on orders. At this point both Companies A and C were fully committed, the latter having taken over two bridges from the 291st ECB and one from the 61st ECB.

With the confusion arising from the German attack in the Ardennes area, it was inevitable that some friendly fire would be taken by American troops. It came on Christmas morning 1944. After breakfast T/4 George Verrall, Company B, was standing in the middle of a field over a helmet of warm water, in snow up to his keister, with only his boots on. He was trying to remove several days' worth of grime when in came a P-38. It had just mistakenly dropped two 250-pound "eggs" on an American artillery emplacement in the field next to Company B before it started to strafe them. It laid down two tracks of .50-caliber fire, one on each side of Verrall. Moments later, after Captain Hodges had fired a flare to warn the aircraft that this was a friendly unit, Verrall spotted one of his compatriots climbing out of the slit-trench latrine in what had been his last set of clean clothes. He was now in worse shape than when he had changed into them.[33]

The next day the battalion continued its defense of railroad bridges, minefields, and roadblocks. After noontime, the division area was put on alert for fifteen minutes, but it was soon extended to one hour. Heavy fighting had been reported between Hotton and Marche, but the battalion did not become involved. That evening VII Corps alerted the battalion for an expected parachute attack sometime during the night but nothing happened.

The following day the battalion rear CP reported a German had parachuted in during the night. A parachute with German jump hook had been found but nothing more. That night another two paratroopers were reported to have come down.

The 51st continued to maintain the barrier line through the end of the year. While supporting the infantry on December 29, T/5 Oliver M. Connelly, Company A, took his tractor into a mined area to dig in a tank destroyer. As he was led through the minefield by a guide, the tractor struck a mine, knocking several plates off the track, and throwing Connelly from the seat. As he lay on the ground a soldier came over and shook him and asked: "Are you dead, are you dead?" When Connelly came to he said: "Hell no I'm not dead." The soldier said: "Run and catch that dozer because it's heading for the German lines." Connelly got up, caught the dozer, turned it around, and completed his work. He was then taken to the battalion aid station where Doc Maxson took 27 pieces of shrapnel out of him.[34]

For his actions, Connelly was awarded the Silver Star for gallantry. Colonel Fraser said later that he had recommended Connelly for the Bronze Star but the Army Board had raised it to a Silver Star. It was the only time Fraser had had an award raised in degree.[35]

Until January 2, 1945, the battalion continued maintaining the roads, and roadblocks in their area of responsibility. Some sporadic German shelling continued in the Hotton area, and suspicious persons continued to be picked up and turned over to the military police and intelligence, but there was no heavy fighting.

The German offensive had come to a halt. The 51st Engineer Combat Battalion, spread thinly along the Ourthe River, had played a primary role in keeping the German onslaught from splitting the Allied lines and racing to the Meuse River. It was an action of which each man in the 51st could be justly proud. Its country was proud also, presenting the 51st Engineer Combat Battalion with the Presidential Unit Citation for its heroic role in the Battle of the Bulge. The French also honored the 51st ECB with the French Croix de Guerre with Silver Star.[36]

Each of the companies of the 51st had made significant contributions to the successful effort in stopping the German attack. Company

THE 51ST AGAIN!

C at Trois Ponts initially, and later on the barrier line in the Marche area, Company B at Hotton, Company A at La Roche, Hotton, Champlon Crossroads, and at Rochefort, and tiny parts of all three companies as well as H&S Company, at roadblocks scattered throughout the area, had stopped the Germans cold with their active defense.

When the tide of battle finally turned and the American Army went on the offensive, the 51st Engineer Combat Battalion had been relieved by units from five divisions, four American and one British. Elements of the 82d Airborne Division relieved Company C at Trois Ponts, and units of the American 84th Infantry Division, the 2d and 3d Armored Divisions, and the British 53d Division relieved the 51st ECB in the Hotton-Marche-Rochefort area. This was probably a first in Engineer history.[37]

On January 3, 1945, the American Army went on the counteroffensive. The 51st Engineer Combat Battalion, in the forefront during the Battle of the Bulge, continued to lead during the campaign which followed.

CHAPTER VII

THE AMERICAN COUNTER-OFFENSIVE: FROM THE ARDENNES TO THE RHINE

On December 28, 1944, General Eisenhower met with Field Marshal Montgomery to plot the role of the First United States Army in the coming counteroffensive. First Army's task was to link with the Third United States Army at Houffalize, nine miles northeast of Bastogne, then drive on St. Vith. The attack would begin shortly after the New Year. In actuality, Third Army's commander, Lieutenant General George S. Patton began his opening moves several days before the end of the year. First Army began its attack on January 3, 1945.

First Army's XVIII Airborne Corps, under Major General Matthew B. Ridgeway, held a portion of the line from Waimes, through Malmedy, to Stavelot, then along the Amblève to Trois Ponts. From there the line went across country to Bra. Where the line crossed the Lienne River near Bra, on the southwestern flank of XVIII Airborne Corps, the VII Corps took over. It would carry the burden of First Army's attack. Two of its infantry divisions, the 75th and 84th, held a 14-mile front extending from Bra southwestward to the Ourthe near Hotton. Those divisions, along with the 83d Infantry Division, and the 2d and 3d Armored Divisions, were scheduled to trap the Germans at the point of the bulge. Major General James M. Gavin's 82d Airborne Division would protect the left flank of the VII Corps.[1]

The terrain in the area in which this fighting took place was difficult and made worse by the weather. Only one major road led directly to any part of the objective leaving a network of secondary roads, connecting the villages of the area, to serve as main avenues of advance even though encumbered by numerous bridges, defiles, and hairpin curves. The roads were an especially difficult problem because two armored divisions would be attacking over them. When the operation began on January 3, the fog was so heavy that not one tactical plane could support the attack. Poor visibility over the next two weeks limited tactical aircraft operations to one day only. Much of the time snow flurries and light rain caused icing problems for the infantry and armor. On January 7, a heavy snowfall added more snow to that already on the ground, building drifts in some areas up to three to four feet.[2]

Support to the Divisions

At the beginning of the new year, the 1111th Engineer Combat Group committed the 51st Engineer Combat Battalion to keeping the Germans from breaking through the Marche-Pessoux-Maffe-Hotton area by maintaining road blocks and a barrier line. Shortly thereafter, on January 4, 1945, the battalion moved to Moldave, Belgium, to begin a long promised rest. The respite lasted just six hours. The group assigned the 51st a new mission, this time, close engineer support to the 82d Airborne Division. From January 5-10, 1945, the battalion operated in close association with the 307th Engineers of the 82d Airborne Division, then provided close support to the 275th ECB of the 75th Infantry Division when the 75th relieved the 82d on line from January 11 to 19.[3]

The battalion's new assignment began on the night of January 2, 1945, while the 1st Platoon, Company A, was guarding a double-double Bailey bridge at Noiseux, Belgium. The bridge had been prepared for demolition. About midnight Colonel Fraser asked if the bridge could support the movement of an armored division. The question could not be answered immediately, a situation which always raised the hackles of the battalion commander when he was looking for an instant answer.

The builders of the bridge had exceeded the recommended length of a double-double Bailey bridge for a class 40 (40-ton) load. They had used good engineering design by constructing a 20-foot pier as a center support, thus creating two connecting short spans, instead of a single long span. However, any load on the bridge caused the lower chord of the bridge to deflect downward until it contacted the pier. In addition, the pier was neither level nor plumb, and many pieces of timber were not properly joined. Had these irregularities not been present, the platoon officer could easily have determined the load capacity of the bridge.[4]

When he heard all of this, Scrappy ordered, "go out and get a tank and drive it over the bridge to see if it will hold up." The tone of his voice made it very clear that any idiot should have arrived at this solution already. He made it plain that at daybreak an armored division was scheduled to pass over the bridge. Conditions were abominable. The night was pitch black, the temperature below zero, and the roads covered with a thick sheet of ice, built up from several weeks of snow, rain, and freezing weather. We had to find a tank commander, either drunk or crazy, who would drive his tank over a high-level bridge to see if it would support the tank.

Technician Fifth Grade Johnston was a wizard at driving his jeep under such poor road conditions. He and his platoon leader, Lieutenant Wright, headed down the road toward the rear of the division area. Within a few miles they found several tents grouped together that turned out to be a tank field maintenance detachment. About six tanks were parked around the tents. Entering one of the tents, Wright saw that just about everyone was "dog drunk" or well on their way to becoming so. Some of the men were waiting for their tanks to be repaired, while others were waiting for daylight so they could return to their units. A civilian pot-belly stove in the middle of the tent made that small area a "heaven on earth" that few men were willing to vacate. Wright explained his problem to the men present, asking for volunteers to help him out.

After listening to the lieutenant's tale, not one man of the group stepped forward. Finally, after a little more discussion about the pending attack at daybreak and winning the war, a sergeant staggered forward and said, "Let's go, sir." Wright was not encouraged with the sergeant's bravado for he had serious doubts as to his ability to function, considering the adverse conditions of the road, driving at night, and his physical condition. As Wright considered the situation, the driver of the tank, who was cold sober, got up and said that he would go with the sergeant.

With the jeep leading, the group moved off toward the bridge at a snail's pace and under blackout conditions. The tank followed, driven by the sergeant (who insisted on driving), with the regular, but sober,

THE 51ST AGAIN!

driver in the turret. A short distance down the road the jeep passed a Signal Corps half-ton truck parked on the shoulder of the road. A few seconds later Wright and Johnston heard a loud crunching sound. Johnston stopped the jeep, and Wright hurried back. The tank had completely leveled that half of the truck nearest the roadbed. Fortunately the two linemen with the truck were several hundred yards away looking for a break in the telephone lines. The sergeant quickly decided that the driver should take over and switched places.

It was still pitch dark when the small convoy finally reached the Bailey bridge. Walking out onto the bridge with a flashlight, Wright explained to the sergeant and driver that he would walk in front and guide the tank to the center of the bridge where the driver would stop it. The lieutenant would then inspect the center pier after which the tank would proceed on across the bridge.

This stopping on the center span violated all standard operating procedures (SOPs) for crossing military bridges. At every bridge built by combat engineers, a sign prohibited stopping or changing gears on the bridge because of the increased stress these actions caused. However, on this night Wright intended to stop the tank in the middle of the bridge so that the center pier could be inspected under load. Additionally, the stopping created more stress on the bridge than could reasonably be expected from moving tanks, thus ensuring the capability of the bridge to stand up under an armored crossing.

After hearing the crossing procedure explained, the sergeant either sobered up or found his senses. He emphatically stated that he would not drive his tank across the bridge. No amount of persuasion was going to change his mind. Finally, the tank driver agreed to drive it across. From that point on the sergeant kept repeating to Wright that he, Wright, would be completely responsible for the tank if anything happened to it.

The sergeant stood on the abutment of the bridge while the tank crossed to the center. There the tank stopped while the center support was examined. Then it completed the crossing. Once across, the tank turned around, recrossed, picked up the sergeant, and vanished into the darkness. Because nobody thought to ask, the names of the sergeant and driver have been lost to posterity.

Wright then told Fraser the bridge would support a tank. About two hours later, at daybreak on January 3, 1945, the 2d Armored Division raced across the bridge without a hitch. About noon that same day, two officers from a British Army pioneer company arrived at the bridge to relieve the 1st Platoon. Their first question was, "Where is the Officers Mess?" Wright pointed to an open case of C Rations sitting in the corner of the room and invited them to help themselves.

During the first part of the Allied offensive, the 51st ECB kept the division main supply routes open in spite of the snow. It also maintained a barrier line along the Lienne, a river which flowed north into the Ambleve near Stoumont. The weather made the battalion's mission all the more difficult, for the winter of 1944-1945 proved to be very severe. The extreme cold, accompanied by heavy snow, added greatly to the difficulties and hazards of constructing bridges, removing mines, and clearing snow from the roads. Without the engineers to perform these missions, the infantry could not advance.

The 51st and 238th Engineer Combat Battalions, the 501st Engineer Light Ponton Company, the 629th Engineer Light Equipment Company and the 994th Engineer Treadway Bridge Company all joined or re-joined the 1111th Engineer Combat Group, First Army by January 4, 1945. It marked the first time that the 51st, 238th, and 1111th operated as a unit since training days in Plattsburg. The 51st and 238th were the original battalions of the 51st Engineer Combat Regiment before reorganization and the activation of the 1111th Engineer Combat Group.[5]

AN ABATIS NEAR FORGES, ONE OF THE MANNED BLOCKS ALONG THE AMBLEVE RIVER NEAR STOUMONT. CO B, 51ST ECB. THE G.I. HAS FINISHED PLACING THE CHARGES AND IS READY TO EXPLODE THEM TO MAKE AN ABATIS OUT OF THE TREES.

Courtesy of National Archives

COMPANY C ROAD BLOCK. BRIDGE PREPARED FOR DEMOLITION NEAR TARGNAN. JANUARY 1945.

Courtesy of National Archives

EIGHTY-FOOT CLASS 40, DOUBLE-SINGLE BAILEY BRIDGE AT GRAND HALLEUX, BELGIUM, OVER THE SALM RIVER. CONSTRUCTED BY CO A, ON NIGHT OF JANUARY 14-15, 1945.

Courtesy of National Archives

The 300th ECB was already part of the 1111th Group at the time these units were attached. That brought together Lieutenant Colonels Jay P. Dawley, 238th ECB, and Riel S. Crandall, 300th ECB, along with Harvey Fraser, all classmates at the United States Military Academy. Upon graduation from the academy, all three of them had been assigned to the 3d Engineer Regiment in Hawaii. Bachelors at the time, they were known as "The Three Musketeers."

That same day the 1111th tasked the 51st, now located at Xhoris, Belgium, to provide close engineer support for the 82d Airborne Division. Company A, also at Xhoris, was to maintain the roads in the Army net within its company area. One platoon was attached to Company B to assist in road maintenance, and one squad, still at Noiseux, continued guarding treadway and Bailey bridges. Company B, located in La Levee, Belgium, maintained 10 roadblocks along the Lienne on highway 432 between N23 and N33. The rest of the company maintained roads in their company area. Company C, located at Niaster, Belgium, maintained the road network within its company area.

Probably the most difficult duty for the 51st during the period was removal of the numerous minefields and barriers emplaced by various units, both enemy and friendly, during the recent German breakthrough. Records of the minefields were vague and sometimes did not exist. Even so, it fell to the engineers to find and either mark or remove those minefields and demolitions. The 51st was one of those Engineer units expected to accomplish this job despite snow and extreme cold.[6]

On January 8 the battalion established a new command post at Stoumont, co-located with Company A. Company B moved to Chevron, and Company C to Lorce, west of battalion headquarters, and north of Company B. In addition to the maintenance of roads in the new area, Company A also had to clear a minefield near Trois Ponts, construct a culvert in Basse Bodeux, and maintain and guard a class 10 bridge near Fosse. It completed the culvert the following day at noontime, and finished removal of the minefield at 1900 hours on January 9.

Company B continued its barrier line maintenance, but turned over the northern half of the line to Company C. It then took over the duty of guarding bridges and maintaining roads in its new area. Company C, in addition to its barrier line duties, was assigned the duty of clearing a liaison aircraft landing strip west of La Gleize which it completed the following day. It also began work on a steel culvert at Reharmont, southwest of Basse Bodeux. The construction of the culvert released two treadway bridges for use on the front lines. The company completed the mission at 2300 hours, January 12.

On January 11 the general mission of the 51st changed from close support of the 307th to close support of the 275th ECB, 75th Infantry Division. The 51st was to be prepared to build bridges in support of division operations. From January 15 to 18, 1945, the 51st constructed five bridges in the division area around Stoumont.[7]

─────────── Bridging at Grand Halleux ───────────

One of the five bridges was a class 40 double-single Bailey bridge put across the Salm River at Grand Halleux by the 1st Platoon of Company A. The small village of Grand Halleux was located about six miles south of Trois Ponts and four miles north of Vielsalm. The platoon moved into Grand Halleux on January 11, to prepare for the eventual construction of the bridge.[8]

The Salm River, running south to north, essentially divided the village in half. From the river, moving either east or west, the terrain rose gently over snow-covered farmland for about 1,000 feet before turning to heavy forest on the ridgeline overlooking the river and the village. Located in the west half of the town was an infantry battalion of the 75th Division. One of its rifle companies had crossed the easily fordable river and occupied a line along the eastern edge of the village. From there the infantry could observe across the open farmland to the forested ridgeline.

The Germans controlled this ridgeline, which gave them direct observation for mortar and artillery fire on the bridge site as well as on the road leading into the village from the west. If more than one truck or jeep at a time used the road, the Germans shelled it. For this reason the platoon moved into Grand Halleux by infiltrating one vehicle at a time. The infantry battalion command post was in a building located on the north side of the main road about 200 feet from the bridge site. The 1st Platoon moved into a building on the south side of the road about 100 feet from the bridge site.

They brought bridge material in at night one truckload at a time. After each truck was unloaded it went to the rear. This was done as quietly as possible, so as not to attract the attention of the Germans. During this effort to move material into town the 3d squad truck, driven by Private First Class Earnest F. Minyard, was hit by an 88 shell. Eight pieces of shrapnel tore into the back of the cab and destroyed a tire. Nobody was wounded by the shrapnel, but Minyard's ears were damaged by the concussion. The area was covered with several inches of snow and the soldiers used bed sheets from the empty buildings to cover the bridge material, hiding it from the Germans. By January 12 all bridge material was at the site, camouflaged, and ready for construction.

Staff Sergeant Bonifay, with the 1st squad, led by Sergeant Benjamin C. Ham, laid out the bridge site. Tracing tape strung from bank to bank established the centerline of the bridge. The ground was levelled from this line to receive plain rollers and four rocking rollers. Shortly after the layout crew left the bridge site, a German mortar shell exploded on the centerline tape on the near shore, breaking the tape. The implication of this deadly accuracy was clear. The Germans had zeroed in on the bridge site. The centerline tape was not reinstalled.

Bridge construction was delayed until the night before the division's scheduled attack. For four forlorn days the platoon waited for the order. The weather was miserable—rain, snow, freezing temperatures, and then snow again. Most of the time the temperature stayed well below freezing. The Company A mess sergeant, Staff Sergeant Robert L. Hardcastle, managed to visit Grand Halleux once a day so that the 1st Platoon could have at least one hot meal. On one such occasion, German artillery broke up the repast and chased the mess truck out of the valley.

The Germans bombarded the village several times each day. The timing of the shelling was unpredictable. When the shells came in everyone dove for the cellars of the buildings. On January 13, the third day of the wait, Private First Class Emile B. Doucet, while racing for the cellar during one such shelling, was struck in the left elbow by a piece of shrapnel coming through a window. Doucet was evacuated, eventually receiving a medical discharge from the army. His left arm remained stiff for the rest of his life.

On the fourth day the phone call ordering construction of the bridge finally came from the division G-3 at 2200 hours. Fraser was notified immediately. The night was pitch dark and cold, with the temperature some 15 to 20 degrees below zero. The panel crew, consisting of Ham's 1st Squad and Sergeant Charles G. Kroen's 3d Squad, began work immediately. The transom crew was given to Sergeant John J. Stiftinger's 2d Squad.

As the first two panels and a stringer were placed on the steel rollers a problem appeared. Three days of rain, snow, and freezing weather had left a layer of ice about an eighth to a quarter of an inch thick on the bridge parts. The ice prevented the assembly of the bridge. Clamps would not reach to hold the stringers in place and bolts and pins could not be placed.

The men used hacksaw blades to scrape the ice at critical points so the bridge could be assembled. It worked well, but it was slow. The bitter cold prevented the men from working more than short periods of time. When their hands became numb they were unable to hold either the hacksaw blades or any other tool. To keep the job going the engineers rotated into the platoon building to warm their hands enough for them to go back to work.

Shortly after construction started, Colonel Fraser arrived. The night was still dark and he wanted to know why he could hear so much scraping. He listened patiently to the explanation then said "get some torches to melt the ice." He felt it was taking too long to scrape it off. Scrappy was told about the 88-mm. shells landing in the village, and about the direct mortar hit on the centerline tape, but he brushed those concerns off. The bridge would not be ready for the 75th when needed.

The men broke out the blow torches and got to work. The first torch had been lit for about one minute when all hell broke loose. German artillery rounds began pouring in. At first the rounds landed well behind the bridge site. Then the Germans began walking them toward the bridge. As they exploded the men hit the ground and tried their best to disappear into holes in the ice and snow. When the shelling was over and all was quiet the men stood up and, without an order being issued, began scraping ice again with hacksaw blades. Miraculously, no one was injured from the shelling.

Construction continued slowly. As the stringers were placed on the lower chord of the panels, the men always rotated the stringer toward the near shore. This way every man knew which way to move the stringer. It also helped reduce the number of smashed fingers.

In the darkness Stiftinger saw that one man was trying to rotate the stringer in the wrong direction. Stiffy, known for his ability to chew out a man when he did something wrong, started in on the errant engineer and warmed the night air with his tirade. Not until first light the next morning did Stiftinger learn that the man he had chastised was the battalion commander. During the night Scrappy had noticed that the stringer crew could use another hand, so he stepped in to help in order to speed the construction of the bridge. By first light it was also noticed that the back of Scrappy's field jacket had been torn to shreds by the shelling during the night. Fortunately not one piece of shrapnel touched his skin. Because of the cold, he wore a coat liner, a sweat shirt, a wool shirt, and a wool undershirt under his field jacket.

At 0800 hours the morning of January 15, the division launched the attack with a hail of small arms fire, mortar fire, and artillery. The bridge was ready. The first tank across started down the approach ramp on the far shore and took a direct hit from an 88 shell. The disabled tank effectively blocked the bridge from further use. The follow-on tanks

COMPANY C, CLEARING MOUNTAIN TRAIL FOR ADVANCING 82D AIRBORNE DIVISION NEAR HOLZHEIM, BELGIUM.
Courtesy of National Archives

YOU CAN FEEL THE COLD IN THIS PHOTO TAKEN IN FEBRUARY 1945 WHEN THE 1ST PLT, CO A, 51ST ECB WAS ATTACHED TO THE 32D CAV SQDN. From left around clockwise: PFCS GORDON L. BRADFORD, ROY G. FENT, AND RAY FRANKHOUSER, T/5 WILLIAM E. ROBINSON, AND PFC JOHN F. SHELETSKY.
From the collection of Al Bolha

THE 51ST AGAIN!

SUPPER IN THE SNOW, STOUMONT, BELGIUM. JANUARY 19, 1945. SGT BENJAMIN C. HAM, PFC ERVIN H. ANDERSON, PFC SIDNEY L. WOOD, T/5 RAYMOND MITCHELL. 1ST PLT, CO A.
From the collection of Al Bolha

veered to the left, forded the river, and continued the attack. After the assault wave had passed the tank was removed, permitting normal use of the bridge. The platoon had spent five days in Grand Halleux, built a bridge under adverse conditions, and had only one casualty—Doucet.

On the day of the attack, Company B began construction of a 60-foot, class 40, double-single Bailey bridge south of Vielsalm on N28 at Salmchateau. The Germans, still on the far shore, harassed the construction crew with artillery, mortar, and small arms fire all during construction. Although there were no casualties, two vehicles were destroyed. The greatest hazard in building the bridge proved to be the weather. Parts coated with ice made assembly difficult and hazardous. But the construction crew worked steadily through the bitter cold and completed it the next morning.[9]

That same day, Company C built a 130-foot, class 40, double-double Bailey bridge at La Tour. Company A constructed another bridge, a class 40, 48-foot treadway, south of Trois Ponts on N28. At Vielsalm, Company B built a 50-foot, class 60 double-single, Bailey bridge. A large number of booby traps and mines had to be removed at that location. The extreme cold, along with the ice and snow, made conditions extremely difficult for the men.

THE AMERICAN COUNTER-OFFENSIVE:

For the most part the battalion continued its road maintenance, snow clearance, and mine sweeping throughout the rest of the month. Company A started construction of a culvert near Fosse at the class 10 bridge site on January 25 in order to be able to take down another bridge. They completed the culvert the next night.

On January 27 the 1111th Group tasked the battalion to provide close engineer support to the 504th and 508th Regiments, 82d Airborne Division. That work included clearance of snow and maintenance of mountain trails and firebreaks used as supply routes in the division zone of advance. In performing this mission, the 51st worked side by side with the 307th Engineers.

The snow was so deep that the infantry could only advance behind dozers. The men had difficulty finding the mines so the dozer operators plowed ahead, often running over mines and disabling their vehicles. For several days the battalion picked up a new dozer every day from the engineer depot. When a dozer was disabled it was reported to the ordnance people, who picked it up for repair when the snow melted. The dozers had been outfitted with armored cabs for protection of the operators. But the men soon learned that when an operator hit a mine he would be blown into the top and either killed or hurt. So they kept the top open. The operator would be blown out of the dozer and land in the snow with only minor injury.[10]

From January 29 to February 4, 1945 the 82d Airborne Division advanced much faster than the unit on its right flank, the 87th Infantry Division. This latter division formed the left flank of Patton's Third Army. The result was an unprotected gap of about 20 miles on First Army's southern flank. The 32d Cavalry Reconnaissance Squadron had to cover that gap. The 1st Platoon, Company A provided engineering support. That support consisted of removing obstacles and mines so that the 32d could move forward, make contact with the Germans, and keep that contact until the 87th Infantry Division could move up and close the gap.[11]

While moving on a trail in a very dense part of the forest a troop (company) of the 32d ran into a roadblock defended by several German infantrymen and an anti-tank gun. The roadblock consisted of log posts and cribs filled with rock and dirt. The obstacle, along with about 10 inches of snow on the ground and dense woods on each side of the trail, effectively blocked any forward movement. Early in the afternoon the squadron commander decided to eliminate the roadblock with the forces at his disposal and not wait for the 87th to move up. He brought up two more troops and the attached platoon of the 51st.

His plan of attack was simple. One of the troops would move by foot through the forest and come in on the right flank of the roadblock. Another troop would do the same on the left flank. The third troop was to be in reserve. The engineer platoon was given the mission of leading the frontal attack, sweeping for mines as it advanced down the trail. In support of the engineer platoon, and ten feet to its rear, was an assault tank which was to fire on the roadblock as the attack progressed. The plan called for the two troops on the flanks to move into position close to the roadblock and report in by radio when in position. If radio contact could not be made they were to fire a green flare to show they were in position. The engineers put two mine detector crews in front to sweep the trail, one squad in column in the ditch on each side of the trail, and one squad in reserve behind the assault tank.

With about one hour of daylight left, and a heavy snow falling, the squadron commander, having received neither word nor signal from the two troops on the flanks, decided to launch the attack without them. With darkness closing in, the engineers clamorously opposed the order: they would be leading an exposed frontal assault with no apparent assistance or support from the flanks, and only the assault tank from the 32d in the rear immediately behind them. This was a no-win situation for the engineers. But, on command from the squadron commander, they shut up and launched the attack.

As they moved down the trail, each man fired his M-1 rifle into the roadblock while the assault tank behind them fired its howitzer and machine guns as rapidly as possible, adding to the firepower directed on the obstacle. The assault tank personnel did not like being out there either.

The assault had advanced about 200 feet when, through the falling snow, several men could be seen standing in front of the roadblock waving their arms back and forth over their heads. The platoon leader gave the order to cease fire and the assault force moved rapidly forward to the roadblock. To the complete and happy surprise of all, they found that the Germans had withdrawn and one of the cavalry flank troops had moved into the position. Poor marksmanship must have been the order of the day for no casualties were reported from the fiasco. Once the exposed flank was closed by the 87th the 1st Platoon rejoined Company A on February 4.

During the first week of February, the battalion continued to work with the 82d in the Ardennes. In that wooded sector northeast of St. Vith, Belgium, and north of the Luxembourg border, there were no paved roads and the task of opening up forest trails, firebreaks, and an unimproved dirt road to take the pounding of division traffic fell to the 51st. The battalion accomplished this task despite many difficulties. In numerous instances, dozer operators took their dozers ahead of the infantry to complete required tasks, leaving themselves open to enemy attack.

Road maintenance and clearance now became harder because of the warm thaw during the first week in February. The thaw, which followed January's unusually heavy freeze, rendered even good roads impassable in some instances. The paved highway from St. Vith to Schonberg and Manderfeld, on which the 82d Division had running rights, required concerted maintenance to keep it passable. Company B worked steadily on this road to keep it open the first two days of February. The work included the construction of a 24-inch concrete culvert on the road between Schonberg and Andler.

On February 5 the 51st built two culverts, one at Schonberg, and one at St. Vith. The former was a 40-foot tile culvert with a creek bottom foundation and a two-foot water gap. The latter was a wooden box culvert. It replaced a masonry arch bridge that had been destroyed.[12]

Germany and the Roer Crossing

On February 4 rumors had the battalion making another move. The next day advance information from group indicated that sometime during the night of February 6-7, the battalion would leave for an assembly area northeast of Eupen, Belgium. At 1945 hours the battalion, less Company B, left Medendorf, Belgium, and headed to an assembly area west of Kornelimunster, Germany.

At the end of the Corps offensive in the Ardennes, the battalion, still attached to the XVIII Corps and in direct engineer support of the 82d Airborne, moved with the Corps to the general sector just south of Aachen, Germany. The 51st made the movement under strict security. All shoulder patches and vehicle bumper markings were removed to conceal the identity of the unit, radio silence was imposed, and the movement took place under total blackout conditions. The battalion arrived in the assembly area the following morning at approximately 0400 hours and spent the rest of the day setting up security, and performing maintenance of individual and organizational equipment. Company B followed on February 9.

The 51st would now be involved in the crossing of the Roer River. It was a difficult period of the war for First Army. There were seven dams located on the Roer and the Allies feared that the Germans might destroy the Urft and Schwemmanauel Dams, sending tons of water cascading down river and flooding the Roer valley. The Germans destroyed only the machinery and valves at the Urft Dam rather than the dam itself, resulting in a steady flow of water which created a long-lasting flood in the valley. It also raised the level of the river and prevented use of assault boats and floating footbridges for many days. When the current subsided sufficiently for the construction of footbridges and the use of assault boats, crossing still proved to be hazardous.[13]

With the 51st now just inside Germany, a doctor from the 82d who was waiting to deliver a baby for a German farm woman came to Doc Maxson for help. Because his unit was moving out he wanted Doc to do the job. Doc agreed and sat with her all night. Finally, about 0900 hours the next morning, she delivered. In limited German, with some sign language tossed in, the father asked Doc his name for he had decided to name the child after Doc. When he found out his name he decided to name it Max if it was a boy and Maxine if a girl. It was a girl. He asked Doc what he could pay him for delivering his child, and together they decided on a bottle of the German's best schnapps. The German then took a pick out into the yard and came back later with a bottle of schnapps. He told Doc that if he had left his schnapps where the German soldiers could have gotten it, they would have drunk it all, so he buried his supply at various locations around the farm. Because it was quite cold, with the ground frozen hard, he had needed a pick to dig up the reward. Headquarters Company sent this account to the *Stars and Stripes*, stating that this was the first baby in Germany delivered by an American doctor since the war began. The paper subsequently printed Doc's news.[14]

A recent thaw had made roads there almost impassable. The volume of troop and vehicle traffic had literally destroyed the roads. The 1111th ECG appointed the 51st Engineer Combat Battalion to make the roads in the Eupen-Rotgen-Kornelimunster area passable. In response, on February 10, Company C installed corduroy on the road between Raeren, Belgium, and Rotgen, Germany.

When the battalion first crossed the Siegfried line and moved into Germany, Captain Pappy Radford of Headquarters Company, decided to organize a deer hunt for a change of menu. Doc Maxson volunteered to help. Radford suggested that Doc get a plain helmet because the red cross on his steel pot (helmet) might cause the deer to jump up and run before they got close enough to shoot them. Even with that wild story, Doc suspected nothing amiss. As the "hunting party" went down the hill to the west of the camp, they found several places where Germans had been sleeping. Doc was impressed with the caution that Pappy used in approaching these areas. All of a sudden, Doc realized that the mission of the hunting party was to secure the camp against retreating German soldiers, not to enhance the diet. Although, in the long run Doc felt the mission was a worthy one, he was angry because he was bamboozled.[15]

On February 11 at 1800 hours, Company B completed an 80-foot, class 40, double-single Bailey bridge over the Kall River north of Rollesbroich, Germany. The 51st had to clear the road of abatis, mines, and booby traps before their trucks could move to the bridge site. That same day the battalion got 425 infantry men from the 48th Armored Infantry Regiment to help with the road work. They were attached to Company A for work on February 12, and to Company C the following day. The men proved willing and cooperative. They accomplished a great amount of work with picks and shovels, clearing the choked ditches along the roads so that standing water could properly drain off.

In preparation for the crossing of the Roer River, Company B began training on constructing assault bridging and footbridging on a lake near Rotgen on February 12. Company A set up a similar program the next day on the Inde River near the autobahn. Both companies put up the triple-treadway expedient assault boat bridge. Although more difficult to construct than other bridges that could span the river, it was much sturdier and stronger. On February 14 the 1111th loaned the light equipment platoon of the 501st Light Ponton Company to the 51st to assist in the crossing of the Roer River.

In addition to training for the river crossing the 51st continued to maintain the main supply route for the 82d Airborne Division during the second half of February, when it moved into the Hurtgen Forest south of Zweifall. The segment of the route from Lanschoss through Germeter to Hurtgen was in terrible shape, and every company worked on it full strength for almost the entire two week period. Only constant work from dawn to dusk on the part of all officers and men kept this critical road passable.

During the battle of the Huertgen Forest, the same ground changed hands many times. Both sides suffered terrible casualties. The forest itself, a place of densely planted stately evergreens, had been shattered by the artillery fire of months of close combat. Minefields and tripwires to booby traps were everywhere. Worst of all, these and the ground between the trees had been covered with the tops of trees which had been severed either by air bursts or, as some thought, by the use of the new

ETQ HQ 45 13830 17 FEB PHOTOG T/5 EDWARD A. NORBUTH
IN ORDER TO CONCEAL FORTHCOMING MOVEMENTS FROM THE ENEMY NEAR GERMETER, GERMANY, US ARMY ENGINEERS OF THE 51ST ECB HAVE ERECTED CAMOUFLAGE NETTING ALONG THIS ROAD. HERE THEY EFFECT REPAIRS TO THE ROAD CONCEALED BY THE NET.

Courtesy of National Archives

PIERCED STEEL PLANK AIRSTRIP BEING INSTALLED BY COMPANY B, 51ST ECB, FOR THE 9TH INFANTRY DIVISION ARTILLERY NEAR GERMETER, GERMANY.
Courtesy of National Archives

MEN OF COMPANY B, OPERATING A FLYING FERRY MADE FROM FOUR ASSAULT BOATS FASTENED TOGETHER AND PULLED ACROSS THE ROER RIVER BY BLOCK AND TACKLE. ZERKALL, GERMANY. FEBRUARY 1945.
Courtesy of National Archives

MEN OF COMPANY B, WIRING DUCK BOARDS TO FLAT FLOATS DURING THE CROSSING OF THE ROER RIVER. ZERKALL, GERMANY. FEB. 27, 1945.

Courtesy of National Archives

MEN OF THE 9TH ID CROSSING THE ROER RIVER ON AN ASSAULT BRIDGE PUT UP BY MEN FROM CO B. THE FIRST MEN ACROSS THE BRIDGE ARE WALKING THROUGH TAPED LANES WHICH ENGINEERS HAVE CLEARED OF MINES. SMOKE USED TO CONCEAL OPERATIONS FROM ENEMY OBSERVATION. ZERKALL, GERMANY. FEB. 27, 1945.

Courtesy of National Archives

U.S. proximity fuse. It was not really a forest that remained, it was a tangle of stalks where the stench of enemy dead made it even more grim.[16]

Company C had to keep the only road through the forest open so that the infantry and field artillery holding the line on the west bank of the Roer could be supplied, and the buildup for the river crossing could continue. The trucks rolled by incessantly, but every day the bulldozers of Company C pulled increasing numbers of them out of the mire.

It seemed like a losing cause to the men. They had no suitable building materials. Every day the road became muddier as whatever foundation it had continued to sink into the mud. The unit was desperate for a solution. There was only one answer: Schmidt.

The town of Schmidt lay in the middle of the forest. It had already been demolished in earlier battles. The houses of Schmidt had been built of bricks and it was in their rubble that the unit found the answer to keeping that road open. By the time of the Roer crossing, often working under the firing of American artillery—Milgram says his ears ring to this very day—the men threw, bulldozed, and trucked just about every brick of the whole town of Schmidt into that quagmire of a road. But the 51st kept it open.

One time while loading rubble from a bombed out building for a road bed, the Chief of Staff of the 9th Infantry Division came out of the cellar hollering. "Hey, you guys are hauling away my CP," Colonel William C. Westmoreland, complained. He later became Chief of Staff of the United States Army. The 51st moved to another rubble pile.[17]

On the 15th, while Company C was working its stretch of road, one of the men tripped a wire leading to a harmless looking Riegel Mine. It exploded, killing two Americans, Private Gerald C. Brown and Private First Class David L. Wotton, and wounding four, one seriously. The mine had been laying on the surface of the ground in front of a house in which American troops had been living for several days, but no one had bothered with it until then.

On February 16, a platoon from Company A constructed a footbridge and assault boat bridge (triple treadway) over the Kall River at the request of Major General James M. Gavin, commanding general of the 82d Airborne. He wanted his men to practice a real bridge crossing on available equipment before trying to cross the Roer River. The current on the narrow Kall, about six miles an hour, gave the engineers valuable experience in floating bridge construction.

They also gained more experience under fire as German mortar rounds exploded behind them on the training site. On one visit to the site, General Gavin told the engineers that the 82d was going to cross the Roer River even if he had to drive every division vehicle into the river and have his men crawl over the top of them.

During this period, the 307th Engineer Airborne Battalion drew up detailed plans for crossing the Roer. The plans called for the 51st to construct footbridges, supply assault boats and the men to paddle them, and build Bailey bridges at specified sites. In anticipation of building a Bailey bridge which might require a "broken back," that is, a bridge not perfectly horizontal, the 51st had obtained parts of the Intermediate Floating Crib, Type A. These included male and female span junction posts, span junction links, span junction bearings, and junction chesses. Training on assembling this junction showed that the "broken-backed" bridge was thoroughly practical and could be used in any situation where called for. One would soon be built.

While the 51st planned for the crossing of the Roer, it also completed other tasks. On February 17 Company A installed an airstrip for the 408th Field Artillery near Schmidt. Company B dug gun pits for the field artillery in the vicinity of Germeter, Germany. Then, on February 18, the 51st began providing support to the 9th Infantry Division under III Corps. On February 21, a squad of Company C cleared and levelled a field for a 40 by 900-foot pierced steel plank airstrip for the 9th Infantry Division field artillery. It was completed at noon on the 24th.

Meanwhile, the crossing of the Roer, originally scheduled for the 16th, was postponed to the 19th, then to the 22d. Each time the 51st was prepared to cross the river. On the 16th, the assault boats were hidden on the bluffs above the river. That night the men carted the boats down to the river and then struggled to get them back up and hidden before daybreak. On the third attempt, February 22, General Gavin called Fraser and Edwin A. Bedell, the 82d Division Engineer, together and said: "We are going to get across tonight and if all others fail Harvey, you and I and Bedell are going across on a log." The third attempt was also aborted. Gavin and Fraser surmised that the First Army plan called for the 1st Division to make the main crossing of the Roer north of the 82d area, and meant our crossing to be a strong feint to keep the enemy from moving troops to oppose the main crossing. On February 17 the 9th Infantry Division relieved the 82d Airborne, and the 51st was attached to III Corps and placed in direct support of the 9th Division.[18]

Although the general crossing plan did not change under the 9th Infantry Division, changes in the detailed plan did occur. The 9th's plan called for a M-2 steel treadway bridge on pneumatic floats to bridge the Roer. As a result, on February 21, one platoon of Company B began training with the treadway bridge on the Inde River. But once again the date for the crossing was postponed, this time to the 25th.

On the night of February 24, the 51st was again ready to bridge the Roer. Just southwest of Zerkall, 110 feet of triple-single Bailey bridge stood waiting on trucks. Near Schmidt the battalion had another 110 feet of triple-single Bailey ready to move to Bruck-Hetzingen for construction. In an assembly area northeast of Schmidt, trucks loaded with 216 feet of treadway bridge and inflated pontons were ready to move to a site south of Bruck-Hetzingen. A 216-foot footbridge was in Zerkall ready for installation with an equal amount in a draw near Hetzingerhof. Early in the evening III Corps cancelled the planned assault crossing. This was the fourth cancellation. At least the men of the 51st did not have to carry the assault boats down to the water this time. The battalion carried the assault boats throughout the entire war, but this was the closest they ever came to using them in action.

To take the place of the assault crossing, the corps staff planned a hook to the north using the 1st Infantry Division bridgehead. Once the 9th Infantry Division cleared the high ground east of Zerkall and Bruck-Hetzingen, the battalion was to be ready to put in any or all of the proposed bridges. Part of the 9th would cross the Roer in the 1st Infantry Division area and attack south in an effort to clear the high ground opposite the 9th Division area.

On the morning of February 27, the rest of the 9th Division crossed the Roer River. Company B of the 51st built a 96-foot floating footbridge at Zerkall that afternoon in 30 minutes. Heavy anchors and float cables held the footbridge in place. The downstream end of each float was weighed down by a filled sandbag, elevating the upstream ends and counteracting a tendency for the bridge to overturn in the swift current. The engineers did not have any difficulty in keeping the bridge intact during the crossing of several infantry battalions.

Company B started a 120-foot class 40 double-single Bailey bridge nearby. Much preliminary work was required in constructing 3 × 12 foot cribbing to support the bearing plates on both approaches, because the road was only eleven feet wide. The bridge was supported by an intermediate concrete pier, making the 120-foot structure a class 40 double-single bridge. Approach work required the removal of a building so the bridge could be launched, and the widening of road curves in the town of Zerkall, so equipment could be moved on site. The bridge was completed early the next morning.

On the afternoon of the 27th, Captain Sam Scheuber reconnoitered the site at Bruck-Hetzingen for a Roer River bridge. Knowing that the river and the long approach were under enemy observation, Scheuber reluctantly followed orders. He selected First Lieutenant Richard I. Green to assist him. Green, just as reluctant as Scheuber, went with him. Along the way they passed a dug-in infantry unit. The infantry lieutenant tried to dissuade them from going beyond further. But Scheuber had been ordered to make the recon and that was that. With only the two of them crossing the observed area, they felt the Germans would not waste mortar or artillery fire on them. It turned out to be true. They were able to see the blown-out bridge, the middle pier, and the far shore among the shelled buildings from covered positions in the town some one hundred yards away. Scheuber's preliminary reconnaissance of the bridge at Bruck-Hetzingen, where a single-span Bailey bridge was planned, called for a bridge whose curvature in a vertical plane might require a two-span, broken-backed Bailey bridge.[19]

Later that night Scheuber and Green came back with dozers and bridging equipment. Company C started construction of the 110-foot double-single Bruck-Hetzingen Bailey bridge under cover of darkness. The men constructed and maintained the bridge while under constant artillery and mortar fire and sporadic small arms and automatic weapons fire as well. The high ground opposite Bruck-Hetzingen had not been cleared. Fraser and Yates were both at Bruck-Hetzingen, and they knew it was hot. They had a radio man with them, and the mortar fire seemed to follow them wherever they went. Yates hollered at the operator to shut off the radio. About the same time, the radio man dove for the prone position and broke the radio, so it was quiet. Yates was sure that the Germans had somehow zeroed in on the radio.[20]

Company A provided security for the operation. During construction it turned out that Scheuber had two choices. He would either have to reduce the height of the center pier about one foot and build a heavier bridge, or he would have to reduce the length of the span by one half and get by with a double. Scheuber chose the latter. He used the center pier to support two spans each of which was only half the total length. Double capacity, half the work. What was wrong with that?

Scheuber went to work. The slight curvature of the existing bridge imparted a small angle from the horizontal to each span where the bridge was supported on the far shore intermediate pier. The near shore span was intact, the center span half demolished, and the far shore span completely demolished. To accommodate this small angle, the top panel pin of each of the four panels was extracted and the bridge was strengthened to take shear at the section by the addition of heavy wood uprights between top and bottom panel chords. The intermediate support of the bridge gave it a Class 40 classification, though it was 110 feet in length. They completed the bridge before dawn on the 28th.

The next morning, after an infantry division and its artillery had crossed over the bridge, some staff officer from the 1111th Group came by and noticed one center pin was missing from the upper truss over the center pier. He reported the fact to the battalion commander and to Colonel Anderson. Anderson later chewed out Scheuber and Fraser for poor engineering. But, as Scheuber said, he was only a registered professional engineer in the state of Texas. And after all, a division did cross the bridge without any trouble.

On March 1, 1945, the battalion moved to its new command post at Rotgen, Germany, where it continued its missions of reconnaissance of roads and bridges and of maintenance. On March 5 Company A constructed a 70-foot, class 40, double-single Bailey bridge across the Erft River in Klein Vernich, completing it at 1800 hours. The next day the battalion came under the control of the 1159th Engineer Combat Group, commanded by Colonel Kenneth E. Fields, but continued its missions of maintaining roads and building bridges in the area.

Company A built a 33-foot Armco steel culvert, 48 inches in diameter on March 7 in Lommersum. It also assembled a 70-foot, double-single, Bailey bridge at the same location. On the same day the First Platoon, Company A, was clearing what was left of a log crib obstacle in the drainage ditch on the side of a road. The area had been swept and cleared of all metallic mines. However, the mine detector could not detect a wooden box mine buried in the ground. While digging with a pick-mattock, Private First Class Ray Haywood struck the mine and it exploded, sending mud and stones for fifty feet in all directions. Haywood was fatally wounded. Privates First Class Earlie Kennedy and Gordon G. Morgan were seriously wounded, but recovered.[21]

The next day the 51st was relieved of its direct support of the 9th Infantry Division and moved to Esch, Germany. The following day it moved to Neuenahr, Germany, in preparation for constructing a heavy ponton bridge across the Rhine River. The Rhine, sometimes called the gateway to Germany, would be the most important river crossing to date for the battalion. The "51st Again" would soon provide one of the first two bridges to span the Rhine River barrier, allowing American troops to pour into Germany weeks earlier than planned.

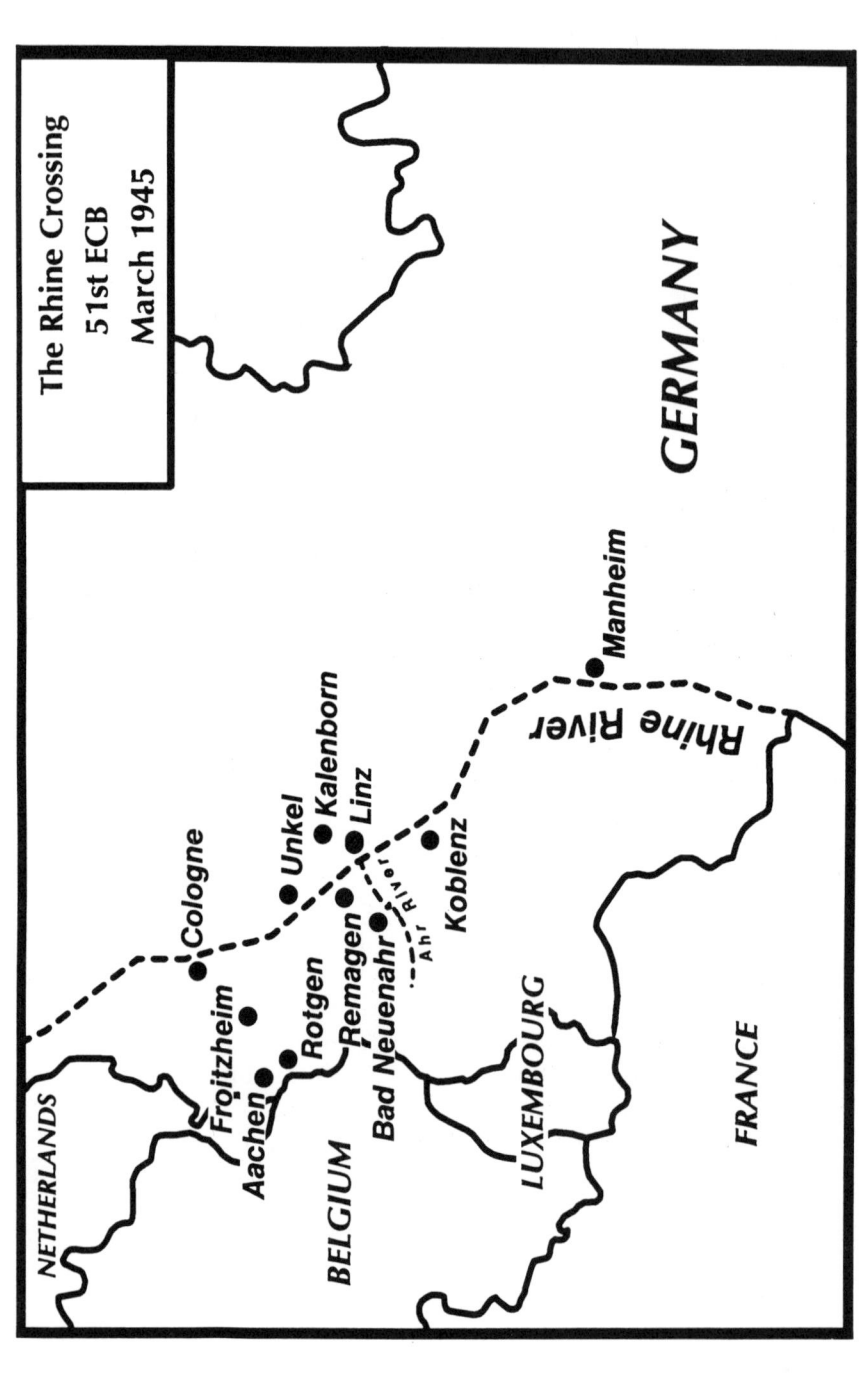

CHAPTER VIII

THE RHINE CROSSING AND THE REDUCTION OF THE RUHR POCKET

Following the failure of the German winter offensive, only the Rhine River stood between the Allies and the heart of Nazi Germany. The Allies began their offensive to the Rhine in February 1945. In the First Army area, Brigadier General William M. Hoge's Combat Command B (CCB), 9th Armored Division, advanced in two columns. Hoge, a former engineer who built the Alaska Highway in 1942, pursued the fleeing Germans toward the Ahr River while a part of his force headed east to the Rhine at Remagen. The latter group discovered the Ludendorff bridge still intact and told Hoge, who immediately turned toward Remagen. When Hoge saw the bridge still standing he seized the unexpected opportunity and ordered his task force commander, Lieutenant Colonel Leonard E. Engeman, to "go down and grab that bridge."[1]

On March 7, while Engeman prepared to cross the Rhine, a German prisoner warned that the bridge was about to be blown. Hoge told Engeman to get across immediately. Just then the Germans blew a big

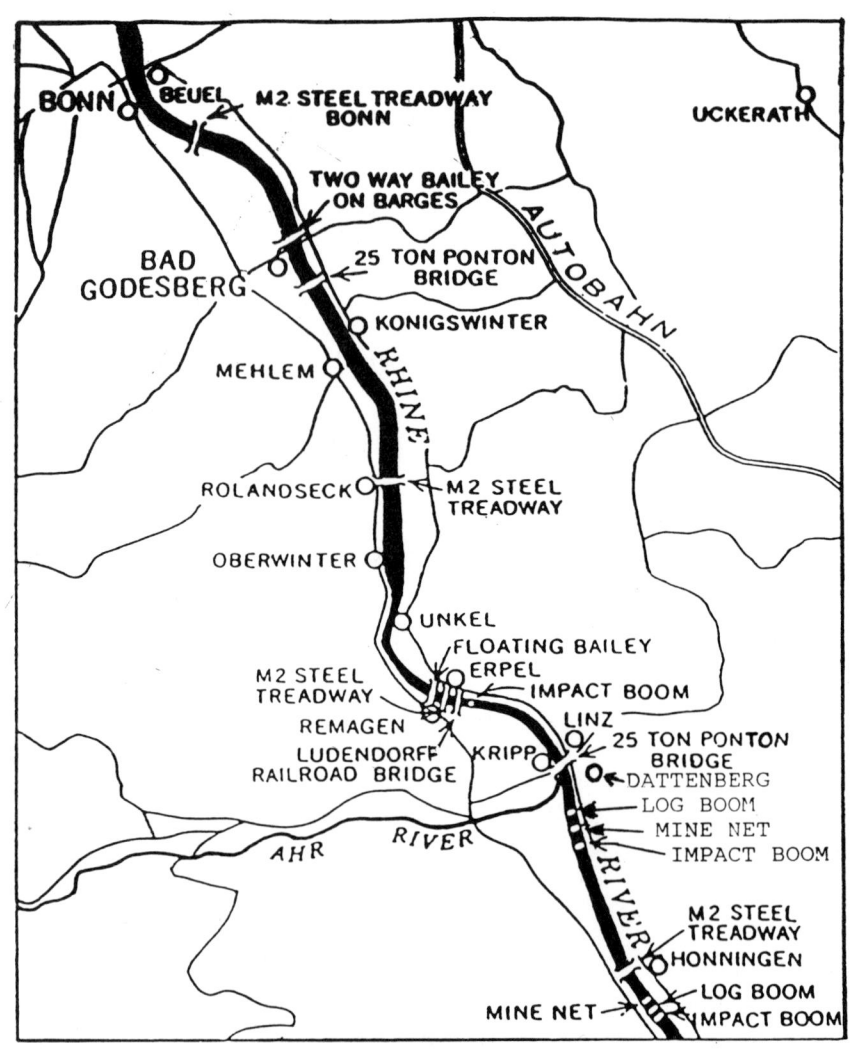

**FIRST ARMY CROSSINGS ON THE RHINE.
ONLY THE 25-TON BRIDGE WAS BUILT BY THE 51ST.**

crater in the west side approach. Engeman's tanks had just gotten around the crater and onto the bridge when another explosion blew out a big panel joint about midstream on the bridge, leaving a hole about 20-30 feet in diameter. However, some of the charges failed to go off, and the bridge continued to stand. Evidently some wires had been cut by artillery fire.[2]

Hoge then sent the infantry across. Along with them, he sent a squad of Engineers to remove demolitions from the bridge. They discovered about 1,000 pounds of explosives, which they cut loose and dropped into the river below.[3]

While crossing, CCB received orders to head south to Koblenz on the west bank of the Rhine. With half his force already across the river, Hoge decided to wait. He wanted to see if the bridge would stand up under heavy traffic. It did, so he disobeyed his last order. Hoge called his division commander, Major General John Leonard, to advise him of the situation. Leonard approved the crossing at Remagen. Word went back up the line through III Corps, First Army, and Twelfth Army Group, to the Supreme Commander: Hoge had a bridge.[4]

Hoge, although an armor general, still acted and thought as an engineer. He did not for a minute miss the significance of the still-standing Ludendorff. He also knew enough to call for tactical bridges to support the crossing.[5]

Hoge had good support for this effort. Colonel F. Russel Lyons, III Corps Engineer, and his deputy, Lieutenant Colonel Eugene J. Stann, both had worked for Hoge on the Alaska Highway. Lyons also knew the neighborhood. He had been present at the dedication ceremonies for the Ludendorff Bridge in 1918. Later, as local commander of the Army of Occupation, he had actually controlled the operation of the bridge. When Lyons learned that Hoge had captured the Ludendorff, he rushed equipment and materials to the bridgehead. In twelve hours, aided by his memory and a nighttime reconnaissance, he had a plan ready for the crossing, and field work began.[6]

General Dwight D. Eisenhower ordered General Omar Bradley to put at least five divisions onto the far bank. Bradley had already begun exploiting the bridgehead. By March 9 an armored command held a lodgment some three miles deep. The 9th and 78th Infantry Divisions quickly supported the 9th Armored Division in the enlarged and strengthened bridgehead, rendering its elimination by the Germans almost impossible.[7]

────── Planning for Bridging the Rhine ──────

As a result of the decision to exploit the bridgehead, the engineers made an effort to restore the Ludendorff Bridge. By daylight, March 8, large quantities of heavy equipment were arriving on the west bank of the Rhine. Plans called for additional crossings so the Ludendorff Bridge could be closed for much needed repair. Those plans called for three heavy ponton ferries, one M-2 steel treadway bridge, and one reinforced heavy ponton bridge in the bridgehead area near the Ludendorff Bridge.[8]

When Colonel Fraser heard that the Ludendorff Bridge had been captured, he called his friend, Colonel Stann, and reminded him that the 51st was available to build a bridge across the Rhine. Stann said he thought there would be a job for the 51st, and there was.[9]

Several engineer units were disengaged from their tasks and immediately sent to the proposed crossings. The corps engineer assigned the task of building a M-2 steel treadway bridge downstream from the Ludendorff Bridge to the 291st ECB with support from the 998th and 988th Engineer Treadway Bridge Companies. It then assigned the 51st, supported by the 181st and 552d Engineer Heavy Ponton Battalions, the task of building a heavy ponton bridge across the Rhine at Kripp, upstream from the Ludendorff Bridge.[10]

At 2200 hours, March 8, the 51st, some 40 miles west of Remagen at Esch and five miles south of Lammersdorf, was alerted for the new assignment and attached to the 1159th Engineer Combat Group. It was told, "You are to build a ponton bridge across the Rhine from Kripp to Linz and are to move to the Kripp area tomorrow." None of the battalion officers had any idea of the tactical situation at that time.[11]

The 552d and 181st Heavy Ponton Battalions were attached to the 51st ECB and started moving from Zulpich. At 0600 hours, March 9, Fraser and his company commanders met with the 1159th Engineer Combat Group (ECG) Commander, Lieutenant Colonel Kenneth E. Fields, at Kripp about 1.5 miles south of Remagen. They looked around for bridge sites, taking into consideration the approaches and the available road net, and found an ideal site with good access to both shores. It also had a good road net to handle the traffic.[12]

Fraser told Companies A and C to construct the pontons and Company B to prepare the approaches. When the 51st reached the site, it discovered that the high hill across the river northeast of Dattenberg had not been cleared of Germans. They could actually be seen moving around on the hill. The Germans were also sending in a little sniper fire. Colonel Fraser tried to get artillery fire delivered on the Dattenberg area, but his request was refused because there were too many friendly troops in the vicinity.

As a result of the excellent enemy observation on the proposed bridge site, Fraser told Fields that it was not practical to build a bridge there until the German snipers across the river were eliminated. But III Corps directed that the bridge be built regardless, and that construction should begin at 1800 hours, on March 9. Accordingly, Second Lieutenant Hervie Middleton took a dozer and a platoon of Company B across the Ludendorff Bridge and up the river to prepare the far approach. They discovered that the Germans had retreated a few hundred yards to a hill overlooking the bridge site. The engineers were met by small arms fire when they started their task, but took no casualties.

During the afternoon the 51st learned that III Corps had ordered all work on the bridge to stop until further notice. Company B's platoon stopped its preparation of the approach and holed up in the basement of a warehouse in Linz where the men discovered a large supply of pink champagne.

That night, the platoon set up two .50-caliber machine guns for security at the bridge site on the east shore. After dark, a company of the 78th Infantry Division, supported by two tanks, made a reconnaissance across the river in an effort to clear out the Germans. They started to make good headway, but panzerfausts knocked out both tanks before they reached Dattenberg. Middleton's platoon covered the withdrawal of the American infantry. Captain Hodges suggested to Middleton he should consider retreating. Middleton was appalled. He did not want to "leave all this booze," so the platoon stayed in their warehouse. About midnight the Germans attacked the Company B platoon and Middleton was hit in the arms and hips by a burp gun. Four others in the platoon were wounded, but the German attack was repulsed.

Soon enemy small-arms and mortar fire intensified in the Kripp area driving the .50-caliber machine guns out of their position. By this time, Colonel Fraser demanded artillery fire. "It took two or three hours to get an FO (Forward Observer) up there," he said, "but the artillery laid in several effective barrages."

On the next day, March 10, a task force of the 9th Armored Division pushed down and took Dattenberg. At that time Middleton was evacuated by ambulance. On his way to the hospital he had the ambulance stop at the Company B CP so he could pick up his monthly Class VI ration (a fifth of scotch and a fifth of gin). His part in the war was over, but he fully recovered from his wounds. The platoon sergeant, S/Sgt Russell E. Watson, took over Middleton's command on the far shore.[13]

——————— Building the Bridge ———————

Around noon and after on March 10, the men of the 51st ECB could see elements of the 9th Armored Division entering Dattenberg. "We got into a huddle and decided we should get going," said Colonel Fraser. However III Corps had not given the go ahead so Fraser headed for the 1159th ECG headquarters and there found that corps had just ordered the 51st and the ponton battalions to move to Unkel several miles down stream where the tactical situation was allegedly better suited to building a bridge. Fraser was not happy with this decision. It meant moving 60 heavy ponton trailers and 50 vehicles through the bumper-to-bumper traffic jam that had formed in an effort to cross the Ludendorff Bridge. In addition the 51st had already staked out the site and had accomplished a considerable amount of approach work at Kripp and Linz.

In light of this new situation Fraser sent a reconnaissance party up to Unkel to survey the proposed site. In the meantime he received Fields' permission to see the corps engineer. He set out for Colonel Lyons' CP near the Ludendorff Bridge. He knew it would be impossible to go by vehicle because of the heavy traffic, so he went on foot. Fraser found Lyons at the 291st ECB treadway bridge site and told him the far shore had been reasonably cleared of Germans and that for obvious reasons, including the heavy traffic problem, they did not want to move. The corps engineer did not know that Dattenberg had been cleared, thus making the Kripp site feasible. When he heard Fraser's plea, Lyons said, "Harvey, if you think you can build the bridge there go ahead." Fraser started back along the river on the dead run but the artillery fire was so intense that he had to "hole-up" several times. It took him an hour to go about a mile and one half despite the fact that he was a fine runner and had lettered in track and cross country at West Point. When he finally arrived at the Kripp site around 1600 hours he said to Major Yates, "let's get going." Yates had everything well organized and was champing at the bit. With approval granted, the men aggressively started work from both shores.

The decision by Fraser to hold to the Kripp to Linz area was significant to the success of the Remagen bridgehead operations. A move to the new site through the traffic jam could have delayed completion of his bridge by two or three days. It might not have been available when the Ludendorff Bridge fell in the Rhine.

Yates was already covering the area with smoke pots. He told Fraser that the S-4, Captain Coats, had "two and one-half tons of smoke pots on a ¾-ton truck." The wind was perfect for laying smoke and six pots were kept smoking steadily during daylight hours while the bridge was being built. When Company B lit their smoke pots, they received considerable mortar fire in the area, but there were no casualties. The net effect of the smoke, according to Major Yates, was very good.

THE RHINE CROSSING AND THE REDUCTION OF THE RUHR POCKET

In building the bridge, the abutment was put in first, then the trestle or cross beam approaches. Because of the shallow water on the west side of the river, five trestles were put in on that side and two on the east side or far bank. These trestles were placed fifteen feet apart. Their placement delayed the completion of the bridge for about three hours.

Just as work on the bridge began, six rounds of enemy heavy artillery fire came in. Two landed on the far shore, but three landed on the center line of the bridge site, indicating that the enemy was zeroing in. The possibility of the artillery coming in kept everyone on edge after the first six rounds. The men thought that the enemy might wait until the bridge had been completed, and then open up. Major Yates felt that they had it, but soon friendly forces forced the enemy gun to withdraw.

The speed of the current was also a problem. At the point of construction the current was extremely swift because the Ahr River entered the Rhine just above the bridge site, and because of a bend in the river. Fraser estimated the speed at 10 feet per second, the maximum speed for ponton anchors to hold.

In spite of those problems, construction progressed rapidly until about 1700 hours when enemy planes began to come over in pairs. The planes did little damage around the heavy ponton site. They appeared more interested in the Ludendorff Bridge a mile down river.

Interestingly, early in the evening of March 10, civilians in the Kripp area started moving out of town. When questioned they said that the German underground had informed them that Kripp would be leveled that night. That was not encouraging news for the bridge builders. Colonel Fraser contacted the town burgomaster and threatened dire consequences if the exodus did not stop. It stopped!

The bridge was built in parts, with four groups working simultaneously on four-boat rafts, most of which were put together after dark by feel. The parts were together by 0400 hours the next morning. The bridge consisted of 14 four-boat rafts, and 75 feet of trestle. When the rafts were in place, they were reinforced with pneumatic floats between the ponton boats so the bridge would take the weight of 36-ton Sherman tanks. A total of 60 pontons and 57 pneumatic rubber floats were used.

As the bridge parts were maneuvered into position with power boats, the river rose and the current became stronger. Maneuvering single-screw power boats was hazardous. If a boat turned crosswise in the stream it would swamp and sink in seconds, even before the engineers could grab their rifles. Although the men were careful, one of these power boats did turn crosswise and sink. Another developed

THE AMERICAN ARMY ROLLS OVER THE RHINE INTO GERMANY ON THE 969 FOOT HEAVY PONTON BRIDGE WHICH THE 51ST AND TWO SUPPORTING ENGINEER BATTALIONS BUILT BETWEEN LINZ AND KRIPP, MARCH 12, 1945.

Courtesy of National Archives

THE 51ST'S RHINE BRIDGE LOOKING TOWARDS THE HILL WHERE THE GERMAN SNIPERS COULD SEE WHAT THE MEN WERE DOING. MARCH 12, 1945.

Courtesy of National Archives

ENGINEERS PUMPING OUT A PONTON ON THE RHINE BRIDGE, PART OF THE CONSTANT MAINTENANCE THE BRIDGE NEEDED. MARCH 1945.

Courtesy of National Archives

THIS CAN TRUTHFULLY BE CALLED "WATCH ON THE RHINE." PFC ELDER D. CANNON, CO A, 51ST ECB. KRIPP, GERMANY. 2100 HOURS, MARCH 1945.

From the collection of Al Bolha

CONSTRUCTION CREWS, CO A, 51ST ECB, ARE SHOWN AT WORK ASSEMBLING A 110-FOOT, CLASS 40, DOUBLE-SINGLE, BAILEY BRIDGE AT NUTTLAR, GERMANY. APRIL 9, 1945.
Courtesy of National Archives

EIGHTY-EIGHT FOOT TIMBER TRESTLE BRIDGE NW OF BIGGE, GERMANY. CONSTRUCTED BY CO A, 51ST ECB. COMPLETED AT 2300 HOURS APRIL 11, 1945.
Courtesy of National Archives

COMMANDERS AND STAFF OF 51ST ECB.
Front row — left to right: CPT MARINO MUSSOMELI, S-3; CPT ALFRED E. RADFORD, CO, H&S CO; LTC HARVEY R. FRASER, BN CO; CPT KARL G. PEDERSEN, EXO; CPT PRESTON C. HODGES, CO, B CO: CPT SAM C. SCHUBER, CO, C CO; 1LT FLOYD D. WRIGHT, CO, A CO.
Back row: CPT MAURICE COATS, S-4: CPT THEODORE MAXSON, BN SURGEON; 1LT WILLIAM R. MUELLER, BN S-1; 1LT RICHARD I. GREEN, BN L.O.; 1LT CHARLES ATTARDO, ASST BN S-3; AND CWO WILFRED G. MORIN, ASST BN ADJ.

From the collection of Maurice E. Coats

PALM SUNDAY. HOLY COMMUNION, MARCH 1945. NEAR KRETZHAUS, GERMANY. 51ST ECB. CHAPLAIN HAROLD E. BERGER, 1111TH ECG.

From the collection of Al Bolha

WOJG JULIUS J. HORECKA, H&S CO, RECEIVES BRONZE STAR MEDAL FOR MERITORIOUS SERVICE AS AN OUTSTANDING MOTOR OFFICER FOR THE 51ST ECB FROM COL F. RUSSEL LYONS, III CORPS ENGINEER. LOOKING ON ARE COL H. WALLIS ANDERSON, 1111TH ECG COMMANDER, AND LTC HARVEY R. FRASER.

Courtesy of National Archives

AWARDING OF PRESIDENTIAL UNIT CITATION BY COL F. RUSSEL LYONS, III CORPS ENGINEER, TO LTC HARVEY R. FRASER, AT HEISTER, GERMANY, FOR ACTION BY THE 51ST ECB IN THE BATTLE OF THE BULGE. MARCH 23, 1945.

Courtesy of National Archives

THIS SKETCH MEMORIALIZES THE THREE ENGINEERS KILLED DURING THIS BRIDGING OF THE RHINE. IT SHOWS A HEAVY PONTON BRIDGE AT KRIPP. *From the collection of Floyd Wright*

motor trouble. This stymied the operation until additional boats were obtained from one of the neighboring treadway bridge companies that was trying unsuccessfully to operate a ferry. Depot stocks for power boats were exhausted because many had been swamped on the Roer River.

The 51st discovered that the Navy had some landing craft vehicle and personnel (LCVPs) in the area, and called for their assistance. At 1300 hours 10 LCVPs arrived from LCVP Unit No 1, U.S. Navy, and saved the day for the 51st ECB. By this time, approximately 700 feet of bridge had been constructed on the near side and 200 feet on the far side. Suddenly the anchors began pulling up. The battalion solved that problem by using triple anchors. Shortly thereafter one of the LCVPs on the upstream side of the bridge turned crosswise in the current and was swept down river where it slammed into the 200-foot section of the bridge on the far side of the river. It either broke or pulled up all the anchors, breaking a section loose from the far shore and starting it floating down the river.

Several LCVPs took off downstream after the 200-foot section. They caught up to it, stopped it, and pushed it back upstream where it was anchored in place again. During that operation the far end of the 700-foot section bent precariously but three other LCVPs moved downstream of the bridge and held it in place until the engineers could strengthen the anchors. The successful maneuvering of the LCVPs kept the bridge from being swept downstream and taking out the treadway bridge under construction by the 291st ECB just below the railroad bridge.

Up to that point, experienced men from the heavy ponton battalions had been advising the men of the 51st on the technical details. That relationship had led to some confusion as to who was in charge of which projects. Colonel Fraser ordered Major Yates to take full charge of connections, anchors, and the lead section. Fraser, who had overall charge of the construction, took direct control of the abutments on both shores. Now Fraser and Yates were in charge of all aspects of construction, making it easier to construct the bridge now that there were fewer bosses giving orders.

Yates hit on the idea that it would be expedient to anchor the bridge onto a barge tied to the shore on the east bank. They installed more triple anchors, and used ropes to pull the 200-foot section back into place. Construction of the bridge then continued.

Finally, at 1900 hours on March 11, 27 hours after starting construction, the 51st completed the 969-foot heavy ponton bridge except for putting on a few frills like luminous buttons, tread planking, and of course, straightening. The bridge was cleared for Class 12 or lighter loads when completed. Later, with improved rigging and anchorage, it took a Class 24 maximum load. The swiftness of the current would allow none greater. Traffic started at 2300 hours with 1 vehicle crossing every 2 minutes for 7 days. The total traffic during that week amounted to 2,500 vehicles including tanks.

The First Army Engineer, Colonel William C. Carter, arrived during the early morning of March 12 and saw immediately that there was trouble with the anchors. Fraser told him that they needed 1,200 feet of one-inch cable. Carter, driving his own pick-up truck, left, and in an hour returned with the cable. The battalion pulled it across the river, anchored it at both ends, and hooked the bridge anchor lines to the cable. The result was a perfectly straight bridge. Carter never revealed where he got the cable.

With the bridge completed, the 51st moved to Bad Neuenhauer for much needed rest and recovery. The 552d Heavy Ponton Battalion had the task of providing maintenance and security on the bridge and Company C of the 51st was attached to provide security guards on each end. Artillery fire and aerial bombing continued after the bridge had been completed. On March 12 a round hit the bridge, knocking out five pontons, and puncturing three rubber pneumatic boats. These were yanked out, patched and replaced, by Company C, with the help of the 552d. Later, one of the booms upstream broke loose and cracked into the bridge, puncturing two pneumatic pontons. The 552d got a crane and lifted the boom out. The only delay was a traffic stall for about two hours.

During the Rhine River operation at Kripp-Linz, several men were wounded and six were killed. Those killed were: Major William F. Tompkins, Commanding Officer, 552d Heavy Ponton Bridge Battalion; Private First Class George A. Rozich, 181st Heavy Ponton Bridge Battalion; and Private First Class Cecil C. Blackburn, Company C, 51st Engineer Combat Battalion. When the Germans dropped a 500 pound bomb on a barge which Yates had used as an anchor, three men from Company B, 51st ECB were killed: Sergeant L. D. Conley, and Privates First Class Raligh Tillman and Edgar L. Mathis.

Eight or nine additional air attacks followed within twenty minutes. When the barge sank with the anchor ropes still intact, Yates rightfully noted, "A sunken barge is a better anchor than a floating one."

When the bridge was finished Major General John Millikin, CG, III Corps was proud of his engineers. "I feel," he said, referring to the bridges just completed by the 51st and 291st ECBs, "that one of the most outstanding accomplishments of the entire operation was the building of the two additional bridges under artillery and small arms fire. They [the engineers] started building even before we were able to clear the area of small arms fire which was our first objective. They also did a grand job of protecting the bridges and sweeping the river with search lights." Colonel F. Russel Lyons, III Corps Engineer said, "The importance of these bridges is the fact that they are the longest tactical bridges ever constructed; and also the first tactical bridges ever built over what we have always considered to be a major obstacle to the progress of an American Army."

When the battalion first moved into the Remagen area, Doc Maxson was in England. Scrappy Fraser had given him a week's leave. On his return he found the aid station in a two-story house on the main street leading down to the ponton bridge. It was there that he heard his first jet airplane. The noise it made as it flew over was "horrible." Doc was just going out to the bridge to conduct a routine health inspection on a platoon working on the bridge when a German jet came down the river and dropped a bomb. It sailed over the heads of the platoon, exploding downstream about a mile. Obviously the pilot was short on jet experience, but Doc did not want to give him a second chance. He decided that it was not necessary to go out on the bridge under the circumstances. He penciled in his report, stating that the platoon was okay. It had passed what was commonly called the "graphite" test.[14]

During the building of the bridge, the Germans fired several V-1 rockets at the site from launchers in Holland. That was the only time that V-1s were ever fired at German soil. On March 14, the men of the 51st crossed their own bridge and moved deeper into Germany.

────── Germany and the Ruhr Pocket ──────

Once the bridge over the Rhine was completed, the battalion improved and maintained the approaches to the bridge and guarded the anchorage barges from enemy attempts at destruction. Company A took over the operation of the ferries at site Number 2. Those members of the battalion not directly involved in the operation and repair of roads, bridges, and ferries, turned to the care and maintenance of their individual and organizational equipment.

On March 21, 1945, III Corps returned the 51st to the 1111th Engineer Combat Group from the 1159th Group. The 51st then resumed direct support of the 9th Infantry Division on the east side of the Rhine. While the battalion prepared to move, the companies reconnoitered the road network in the new area. On March 22, the battalion moved by convoy to the vicinity of Kalenborn, Germany, where it established a new CP. The companies began work on repairing and maintaining the roads in the area, and sweeping the roads and shoulders 20 feet on each side for mines.

The next day the 1111th ECG told the 51st ECB to build a bridge over the Wied River. The battalion S-3 assigned Company B the job of building the bridge, and tasked Company C with repairing the road leading up to the site. Work started on the bridge at 1315 hours, and at 1830 hours Company B completed construction on the 110-foot, class 40, triple-single Bailey bridge.

Three days later, on March 25, 1945, Company C began and completed three Bailey bridges within a 24-hour period. Approach work for a bridge near Neustadt, Germany, began at 0500 hours, and actual construction for the 50-foot, class 60 bridge at 0800 hours. Company C completed the first bridge, a double-single Bailey bridge, at 1100 hours. Approach work started for another bridge shortly before 1100 hours. Company C completed this second bridge, a 110-foot class 40, triple-single Bailey bridge at 1745 hours. It began construction on a third bridge, a 50-foot, class 60, double-single bridge, at 1715 hours, completing it in less than three hours.

The 51st ECB moved to a new CP in Gullesheim, Germany, on March 27, and continued repairing and maintaining roads and guarding bridges. In addition to sweeping for mines, the battalion removed destroyed vehicles and road blocks from the roadways and filled in craters. The next day, the 1111th ECG attached the 998th Treadway Bridge Company to the battalion to remove a treadway bridge. Work began at 0830 hours and ended at 1600 hours. On the 29th, the battalion established a new CP in Langenhahn, Germany, and on the last day of the month moved on to Rodenhausen, Germany.

From April 1-4 the battalion worked on the III Corps main supply route (MSR) "D" from Burg to Marburg. The condition of the road was excellent, but because of unusually heavy traffic, the 51st had to continuously repair the shoulders and drainage ditches. The battalion also maintained a 24-hour patrol along the road to keep it clear of wreckage caused by bombing and strafing and by accidents. The road and an area 20 feet on each side was swept for mines and signs posted indicating the mine-free areas. In maintaining the road, the battalion used 190 cubic yards of crushed rock, 4,650 gallons of gasoline, and 125 gallons of motor oil. Six hundred dump-truck hours were expended during the four-day period.

THE 51ST AGAIN!

On April 5, group ordered the battalion into close support of the 9th Infantry Division. The 51st stayed with the 9th for a week, removing vehicles, tanks, and enemy road blocks from the roads, and maintaining the divisional MSR. At 0800 hours, April 9, Company A began a 110-foot, class 40, double-single, Bailey bridge at Nuttlar. They built the bridge over a partially demolished, four-span stone and masonry-arch bridge. The Germans had dropped three of the four spans during their retreat. The intact span and the three stone piers were used to make one complete bridge. Company A completed the work in seven hours.

The next morning, Company A began construction of an 88-foot timber trestle bridge at the site of a demolished two-span stone and masonry-arch bridge near Bigge. It was class 70, one-way, and class 40, two-ways. No part of the wrecked bridge could be used and the parts the enemy had left standing had to be cleared away before actual construction work could begin. Actually only one span of the bridge was partially damaged, but the handrail was bent and interfered with the repair work. Major Yates was in charge of the work and he put a couple of blocks of TNT on the handrail to remove it. When the charge blew, the whole bridge fell down and a small job became a large one. Only odd-sized lumber and timber was available and the engineers of Company A consumed much time in hand-cutting and hand-trimming the material at the bridge site. But they completed the bridge the next night.

On April 13 the 1111th Engineer Combat Group returned the 51st to maintaining roads and destroying abandoned enemy ammunition in III Corps' rear area. The battalion worked at this assignment for four days. But on April 17 work was suspended because of the sudden collapse of the Ruhr Pocket in the III Corps sector. All available trucks in III Corps were detailed to haul the great number of prisoners taken from the Ruhr to the First Army prisoner of war (POW) enclosure at Brilon. Each line company in the battalion furnished ten 2½-ton trucks with one officer, ten drivers, and ten assistant drivers. H&S Company supplied four 2½-ton trucks, and one weapons carrier with drivers and assistant drivers, one maintenance warrant officer, and two mechanics. The 51st received its orders at 0230 hours, and the battalion detail arrived at Brilon at 0800 hours, ready to haul prisoners.

The 17th of April was indeed a sad day for the 51st Engineer Combat Battalion. Major Robert B. Yates, battalion executive officer, was assigned as commanding officer, 1262d Engineer Combat Battalion. Yates had served the 51st and Scrappy Fraser well, especially through the difficult days of the Ardennes offensive. Fraser assigned Captain Karl G. Pedersen, commanding officer, Company A, 51st ECB, as the new executive officer, and appointed First Lieutenant Floyd D. Wright commanding officer of Company A. One other change occurred that day. Captain John D. Barnes, battalion S-3, was hospitalized and Captain Marino Mussomeli, liaison officer, took his place.

At an officer's call that same day, Captain Sam Scheuber told Doc Maxson about the estate he was using for Company C headquarters. He mentioned that he had found a wine cellar that was stocked with Canadian Club whiskey and invited Doc over for dinner. Things had been rather quiet in the area for about a week so Doc agreed. The cocktail hour extended much longer than it should have—maybe they drank too many toasts to Bull Yates—and dinner was late. When Scrappy Fraser came in to talk to Scheuber about plans for a battalion movement the next morning at 0400 hours, Doc tried to stand but was unsuccessful. The next day, after the convoy arrived at its destination, Fraser let him have it. He said that he had only one medical officer and that he had been completely unable to function the previous evening. Fraser said: Haven't I done a lot for you? I gave you a leave and this is how you repay me and the unit. He said that the incident would go on his permanent record in Washington. Doc felt bad in more ways than one at that point, but did learn from his experience.[15]

Later, after the German surrender, Doc Maxson was reassigned to command an ambulance company. He was sad to leave. Colonel Fraser called Doc into his office, said a few nice words about his work in the unit, then handed him the reprimand, stating that he had decided not to send it to Washington for inclusion in his files. That made the sad parting for Doc a much happier experience.[16]

It was at 2230 hours on April 17 that Fraser was ordered to the 1111th ECG headquarters regarding a battalion move. There he learned for the first time that the entire III Corps, with all attached units, was to leave First Army for an assembly area in the vicinity of Ochenfurt, Germany. From there they would move several hundred miles away for an assignment with Lieutenant General George S. Patton's Third Army.

CHAPTER IX

THIRD ARMY AND THE DRIVE TO BAVARIA

After the collapse of the Ruhr Pocket, many people thought that Nazi Germany might fall back to a last ditch position in the Alpine region of southern Germany and western Austria, an area called either the Alpine Redoubt or National Redoubt. The intelligence staff at Supreme Headquarters, Allied Expeditionary Forces, could find no positive evidence of a German plan based on a National Redoubt strategy. However, if the German armed forces did continue to resist, the most logical place would be the Alps. So it was prudent for the Allied forces to cut off this area.

At this point in the war, III Corps, with six divisions, found itself without an area of operations or an objective. As fate would have it, far to the south in the Third Army area, VIII Corps, with five divisions, was reassigned to First United States Army. To compensate for this loss, higher headquarters assigned III Corps, with all attached units including the 51st Engineer Combat Battalion, to General Patton's Third Army.[1]

The Long March

As part of this movement, the "51st Again" began its longest motor march of the war at 0200 hours, April 19, 1945. It completed the trip of 255 miles to the south at 2200 hours that same day. During those 20 hours the battalion moved from Kustleburg in the Ruhr Valley, to Wulkersdorf, Germany, some 28 miles northwest of Nurenberg.

The order of march was H&S, A, B, and C Companies, with Colonel Fraser in the lead. The heavy equipment of the battalion followed the companies by 30 minutes. Leaving the initial point at Wallau at 0200 hours, the convoy arrived at the refueling point, Bad Homburg, by 0600 hours that morning. The convoy was intact until it reached a point approximately seven miles from Wurzburg. Here, because of a main road intersection at which convoys were converging, control became difficult. Trucks from other units broke into the 51st column, splitting it up. The convoy was delayed at that intersection for approximately four hours.[2]

Private First Class Carleton E. Moore, Company A's motorcycle driver, remembered the gridlock well. With the convoy unable to move, Colonel Fraser left his jeep short of the intersection and headed for the front of the convoy. Straddling the back of Moore's motorcycle, Fraser directed him to drive forward to find out why the column was stopped. Even on a motorcycle Moore could only get to within 100 feet of the intersection, for all four directions were blocked with halted, bumper-to-bumper vehicles. Moore could see, but did not hear, the conversation between Fraser and the military police lieutenant who was attempting to straighten out the mess. As the lieutenant braced himself, Moore claimed "that he saw sparks and blue flames gushing from Fraser's mouth." Without any further delay, the "51st Again" moved briskly through the intersection. The delay did provide time for the troops to eat lunch. On the outskirts of Wurzburg, Fraser halted the convoy to reform it. During that break everyone ate supper.[3]

In the course of the trip, only one major breakdown occurred. A 2½-ton truck broke its steering gear. Lieutenant Henry's battalion motor pool mechanics quickly repaired the truck and had it back in the convoy. Other breakdowns were negligible, mostly flat tires. Colonel Fraser praised the drivers and mechanics for their well-disciplined driving, their efficient repair and maintenance, and for their cooperative spirit during the entire movement. This was an habitual trait of Scrappy Fraser. When the men did something good, he was the first to let them know it loud and clear. This kept *esprit de corps* high, and gave the soldiers a strong desire to do even better with the next assigned mission.

By 2130 hours, the convoy had cleared Wurzburg and headed toward Neustadt. Captain Radford of H&S Company met the convoy there and

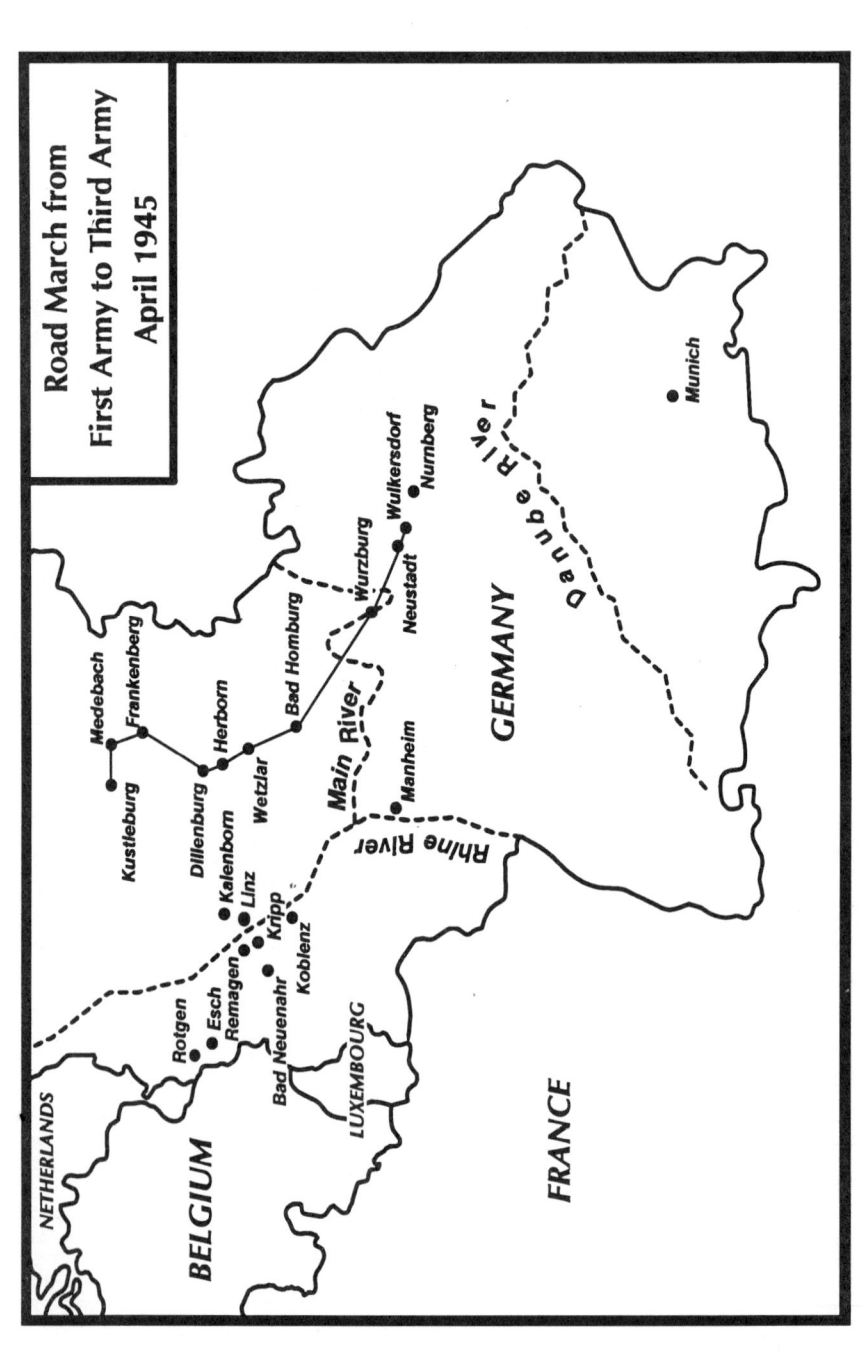

led it to a bivouac area near Wulkersdorf. Prior to midnight the heavy equipment convoy moved in, completing the battalion move. It was now prepared for work in the Third United States Army area of operations. By 2200 hours that evening, the unit had been reassigned to its old standby, the 1111th Engineer Combat Group (ECG), commanded still by Colonel Anderson.

— Assault Crossing of the Danube River at Ingolstadt —

On April 19, the battle for Nuremberg ended when the 3d Division penetrated its walls and entered the heart of the city. The city collapsed on April 20, Hitler's birthday, as did the right wing of the German First Army. A gap opened between the German First and Seventh Armies, and the United States Third Army began its drive to the southeast through this opening. With III Corps freshly assigned, Third Army was ready to exploit the gap in an assault which actually began on April 19.[4]

On April 21 the battalion went into close combat support of the 86th, or Blackhawk, Infantry Division. Their shoulder patch was a spread eagle configuration of a black hawk. The battalion's first work included the removal of enemy roadblocks to allow for two-way traffic, the posting of directional signs on the main supply routes, removing destroyed tanks and vehicles that obstructed traffic, sweeping the roads and shoulders out to twenty feet for mines, widening bridges, and filling craters.

Five days later, Fraser ordered Company A to build a class 40 treadway bridge across the Danube River in Ingolstadt. At that point the Danube River flows from west to east and is approximately 324 feet wide. That portion of Ingolstadt located on the north side of the river was the original townsite dating back to medieval times. Most of a high rock wall encircling the town was still in place. Intelligence reports stated that 300 German Schutzstaffel (SS) Troopers were in buildings on the south side of the river, ready to defend against any crossing at that location.[5]

Everyone knew that the war would end in a matter of days, but nobody knew just when. No commander of troops wanted to take an action that would get anyone killed if there was any honorable way to get around it. This applied to all commanders from First Lieutenant Floyd Wright of Company A, 51st ECB, to Major General Harris M. Melasky, commander of the 86th Infantry Division. Attempts to balance this rationale with a strong desire to end the war as soon as possible caused king-sized headaches for all commanders.

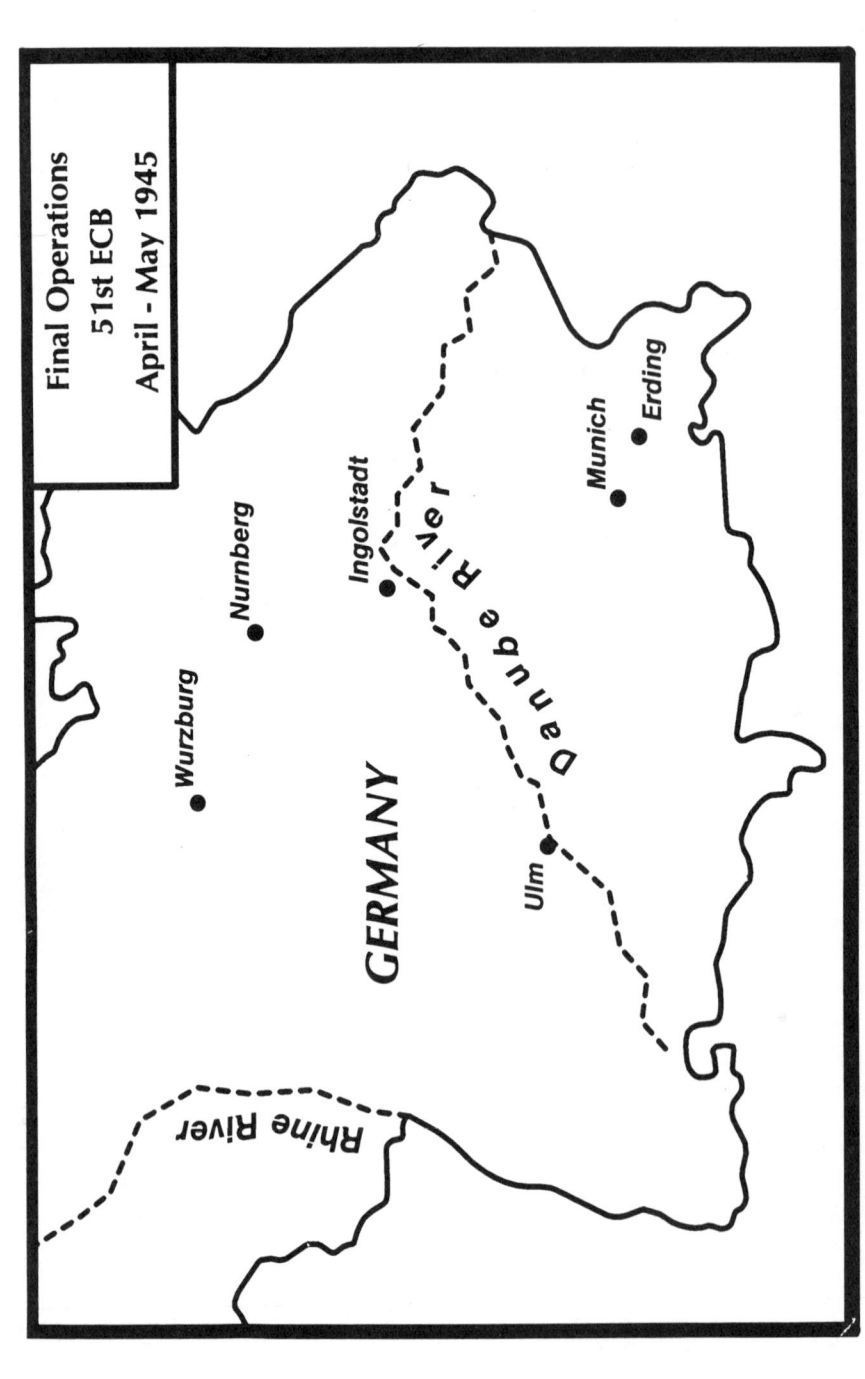

On receiving Fraser's orders, Wright suggested that Company B or C be brought up, because Company A had been the forward company and completed the last two or three missions assigned to the battalion. But that would take too long. General Melasky had told Fraser that one of his regiments had taken Ingolstadt and controlled everything on the near bank (north side) of the Danube. Late in the afternoon of April 26, Fraser and Wright went to Ingolstadt to find a suitable site for the bridge. Fraser led with his jeep and Wright followed in his.

After passing through the rock wall around the city, and going half the distance between the wall and the river, both jeeps came under a hail of rifle and machine gun fire from the buildings on each side of the street. The colonel's driver turned into the first alley he saw, with Wright's jeep close behind. In the relative safety of the alley, a very brief conversation was held which went something like this: "What the hell is going on? We are supposed to have an infantry regiment in this town. Let's get the hell out of here!" By taking the alleys and back streets, the two jeeps got out of town with no injuries to the occupants. Later it was learned that the American regiment was in town, but had occupied the basements of the buildings. The Germans still occupied and controlled everything above ground within Ingolstadt.

The next stop was General Melasky's headquarters. Fraser told him of the situation, advising that the inflated pneumatic floats and other bridge equipment would be destroyed by small arms fire if moved into town under the present situation. That would mean that the bridge could not be built, and the 51st would take numerous casualties trying.

Melasky either did not believe Fraser or did not want to hear what he was being told. He reached for the field phone on his desk and started cranking the handle. As he did so, he stated that he would inform the III Corps commanding general that he had an Engineer battalion commander down here who did not want to carry out his instructions. At this point, Fraser reached over and removed the phone from the hands of the general and informed him, "We'll build your bridge sir!" On this happy note, the two Engineers departed for Company A's CP.

In the Company A command post, Wright sat on a box smoking one cigarette after another while Fraser paced back and forth. They discussed the mission and considered alternate means for bridging the river. After several minutes of this, Colonel Fraser said in effect, "Damn, Floyd, give me a cigarette." At this point Wright learned that Scrappy had decided several weeks before to quit smoking.

Gradually a plan unfolded. During the remaining daylight hours, Company A inflated the pneumatic floats supplied by the 998th Engineer

THE 51ST AGAIN!

Treadway Bridge Company, commanded by Captain G. E. Hancock, near the company command post. The men loaded two floats on each bridge truck. Although they were a large target, they would greatly speed up construction once the Engineers were on the river bank. Their use would also reduce the amount of heavy equipment required, cutting the noise at the crossing site. Noise reduction was essential because the Germans also controlled the south side of the river.

About 2300 hours that night, Company A and the 998th Treadway Bridge Company made a motor march to the edge of town. Here the 1st Platoon, became an advance guard on foot to clear any Germans that might still be in the buildings on either side of the street leading to the crossing site. Fraser and Wright positioned themselves as the point in front of the advance guard, one on each side of the road. The 2d Platoon rode shotgun on the bridge trucks. The 3d Platoon remained motorized and followed the bridge trucks as a rear guard.

The night was still dark when the column reached the bank of the river. Fraser went one way, Wright another, to find a crossing site. Wright was walking on the muddy bank as quietly as he could when someone tapped him on the shoulder from behind and said in a low, but reassuring voice, "I think you can get started now." This scared the daylights out of Wright. He turned around and in spite of the darkness recognized Colonel Anderson, Commanding Officer, 1111th ECG. With the group commander and the battalion commander at the bridge site every soldier knew that somehow everything was going to be OK, even though the Germans still controlled the far bank. The commander's presence at the site of an operation is one of the fibers that holds a unit together and keeps it on track, even when its basic instincts tell it to run like hell. That fiber also converts a good outfit into an outstanding outfit such as the 51st ECB. Scrappy Fraser was always at the scene of the action, continually moving among the troops and gently slapping them on the rump, at the same time encouraging them with the same words: "Hurry up, hurry up, hurry up." For the men in Company A he was known as "Hurry-up Harvey," but never in his presence.

Wright deployed one platoon on the bank of the river with .30 and .50-caliber machine guns. They were to place as much fire as they could on the German-occupied barracks and buildings on the far shore. Melasky had furnished the battalion an M-8 armored vehicle with a .50-caliber machine gun and a 37-mm. gun, and this was used to good advantage. The orders were not to fire first. The plan called for doing as much as could be done under cover of darkness, and still have the bridge ready when the 86th needed it.

Many aspects of that bridge project were extremely unusual. In the first place, the enemy controlled the far shore. There, the treadway bridge had to be built out into the river from the near shore by successive sections, using bridle lines, both upstream and downstream, anchored on the near shore. A section of bridge was placed in the water, then pushed out to make room for another section. This was repeated until the first section of the bridge reached the far bank.

Moreover, there were no power boats to push sections into place. The 998th Treadway Bridge Company's boats had been swamped in the Rhine River crossing, and each section had to be pulled into place by hand with ropes. With the bridge extended some 300 or more feet into a river into a current of 7 miles per hour, pulling sections into place by hand was difficult. To encourage the men of Company A to move a little faster, Colonel Fraser stationed himself on the lead section of the bridge, and remained there until the bridge was completed.

At the break of day, the lead section of the bridge was about 40 feet from the far bank. German rifles and machine guns opened up from the barracks about 200 feet from the edge of the river. The defensive platoon, now reinforced with two squads from the 86th's 311th ECB immediately laid down a heavy volume of fire. That greatly reduced the fire from the barracks and permitted the bridge building to continue. The M-8 with its 37-mm. gun was instrumental in silencing fire from the round building. As Technician Fifth Class John P. (Kelly) Watson recalled, the M-8 fired its first shot shortly after Fraser broke the silence and yelled back from the lead ponton, "to give them everything we've got if the burp gun fires again."

About that time, at a distance of about 1,000 feet upstream, assault boats loaded with infantrymen headed for the far bank. The first thoughts of the men of Company A was, "Damn! This action should have occurred before the bridge was started." Their second thought was that somebody must have reasoned that the bridge, sticking out in the river like a dagger with its point only a few feet from the far shore, would receive all the attention and fire from the Germans in the barracks. Their third thought was that they were happy as hell to see the infantry moving over.

In any event, the assault boats reached the far shore without receiving a single shot. Because they were made of plywood, a couple of bullet holes in the side could easily sink any of the boats. As the infantrymen debarked and climbed the ten-foot bank of the river, they formed a skirmish line to advance on the barracks. As the action developed, they received small arms fire from the barracks and began to drop. Those

SECURITY PLATOON FIRING ON THE FAR SHORE. INGOLSTADT, GERMANY. APRIL 1945.
From the collection of Al Bolha

WHEN THE LEAD FLOAT TOUCHED THE FAR SHORE, AMBULANCES WERE BACKED ACROSS TO EVACUATE THE WOUNDED. 51ST ECB. INGOLSTADT, GERMANY. APRIL 1945.
From the collection of Al Bolha

GERMAN POWS MOVING TO THE NEAR SHORE OF THE BRIDGE AT INGOLSTADT, GERMANY. APRIL 1945.

From the collection of Al Bolha

CROSSING THE DANUBE WITH DRY FEET, COURTESY OF COMPANY A, 51ST AGAIN. INGOLSTADT, GERMANY. APRIL 1945.

From the collection of Al Bolha

who were able rolled themselves like logs to the bank of the river, and then down the slope toward the water, taking advantage of the only cover available. Those unable to roll were dragged to cover near the water's edge by the medics. As if controlled by some magnetic force, these men managed to move toward the treadway bridge. By that time, the leading section of the bridge had reached the far shore.

Once the lead section of the bridge touched the far shore, normal operations were suspended. Ambulances backed across the bridge to pick up the wounded men and get them to an aid station as quickly as possible. When the evacuation was completed, the bridge was secured. Steel treadways were then placed between the last floating section and the bearing plates. Finally, bridle lines were moved to the far shore, to be anchored on the bank both upstream and downstream, to hold the bridge in place. The bridge was finished about 0800 hours on April 27.

Corporal Lenart A. Fahlander and Private Reno V. Pisano, along with some other men, handled the bridle lines attached to the lead section of the bridge. Pisano was the first man to reach the far shore as he waded through knee deep water to haul the bridle lines up the steep bank to anchor the bridge. At this time, with the Blackhawk infantrymen hugging the ground about 500 feet from the enemy barracks, 400 German soldiers came out of the barracks with white flags and surrendered to Company A. They were immediately moved across the bridge.

While that was going on, Private Pisano walked behind a building and discovered about 35 Germans coming toward him in a column of twos. The man in front had both of his hands over his head with a white handkerchief in one of them. He was followed by two officers. Although Pisano did not have his rifle, the group surrendered to him. Pisano led them to another group of prisoners who were waiting to cross the bridge. Among the prisoners were many older men and teenagers. At that point Pisano realized "that the war was essentially over."

The prisoners crossed even before friendly forces secured the far shore. The Engineers were quick to relieve the Germans of their Luger pistols, bottles of schnapps, cognac, and other goodies. The infantrymen of the 86th began yelling unprintable words at the engineers to the effect that, "Hey! Those are our prisoners, not yours."

After the prisoners had crossed to the American side, the 86th began moving across the bridge in force. With all of that activity, a mudhole began to develop close to the approaches to the bridge. The company put 20 to 30 prisoners to work placing rubble from a nearby rock wall in the holes so that division traffic could continue across the bridge. All elements of the division crossed the Danube and continued their drive to the south. Miraculously, Company A had no casualties during the construction of the bridge.

On to the Isar Canal

On the same day that the 51st finished the bridge over the Danube, Company B assumed responsibility for maintaining roads from Ellingen to Eichstatt. That duty included maintaining a Bailey bridge and filling in a bomb crater. Company C moved to Ingolstadt and began maintaining roads from there to Eichstatt. Signs were posted for Route "A" from Eichstatt to Ingolstadt by H&S Company, and the battalion set up headquarters in Gaimersheim, Germany.

The next day all three line companies were busy maintaining roads, and removing obstacles from the roadway. During April 29 and 30, the battalion worked on opening a section of the Autobahn from Frankfurt to Munich. The efforts of Company A on this task consisted of filling in two craters, installing a culvert, and constructing a 70-foot, double-single, class 40 Bailey bridge. Company B repaired one bridge and constructed a timber-trestle bent to reinforce another bridge. Both of these were on the Autobahn. Company C maintained and guarded a Bailey bridge on April 29 and a treadway bridge on April 30. It also cleared debris from ditches and filled craters.

During the month of April the battalion turned in large amounts of German and Allied guns and ammunition, clothing, and other salvageable material to salvage dumps. For example, it salvaged over 1,100 jerry cans.[6]

The battalion continued in direct support of the 86th during the first four days of May, but it was obvious that the war was winding down. It maintained the divisional MSR, and removed German roadblocks and destroyed vehicles from the roadway to permit two-way traffic. Enemy ammunition left alongside roads was removed and destroyed.

At 1730 hours on May 1, Company A began its longest and last portable fixed bridge of the war. That was a 130-foot double-double, class 40 Bailey bridge across the Isar Canal at Neider Ding, Germany, about 25 miles northeast of Munich. Before dark set in, a German fighter plane flew over the bridge site at an altitude of about 100 feet but did not fire. At its low altitude the plane was overhead and out of sight before anyone on the ground could open fire. The pilot may have been trying to get the occupants to where they could surrender to the Americans and not to the Russians.

SIDE VIEW OF 120 FEET OF CLASS 40, DOUBLE-DOUBLE, BAILEY BRIDGE ACROSS ISAR CANAL AT BERGLERN, GERMANY. CONSTRUCTED BY COMPANY B.
Courtesy of National Archives

APPROACH VIEW OF CLASS 40, DOUBLE-DOUBLE, BAILEY BRIDGE CONSTRUCTED BY COMPANY A, ACROSS THE ISAR CANAL AT NEIDER DING, GERMANY.
Courtesy of National Archives

During construction of the bridge, a heavy snowfall and an exceptionally dark night slowed down the work. Shortly after the launching nose touched the rocking rollers on the far abutment, a soldier fell from the nose to the ground below. Fortunately he landed on a pile of sand, formerly the core of the stone arch bridge before it was destroyed. The soldier, somewhat shaken, was sent to the rear for a checkup by Doc Maxson.

When all of the bridge trucks were unloaded and an inventory completed, four end-posts were discovered missing. These were required to complete the bridge on the near abutment. A truck was sent to obtain the end-posts from the nearest Engineer depot. At this stage of the war, all depots were many miles to the rear. These four small pieces of bridge material delayed the completion of the project about three hours. The bridge opened for traffic at 0530 hours on May 2.

On the same day Company B started a 120-foot double-double Bailey bridge across the Isar near Berglern, Germany. Construction started at 2030 hours and was completed the next morning at 0830 hours. This bridge relieved traffic congestion on the Erding to Freising road.

From May 5 until the end of the war on May 8, the battalion maintained the III Corps MSR, guarded the Bailey bridges constructed by Companies A and B and a treadway bridge at Freising. To help control the traffic, weight classification signs were posted on all bridges and culverts within the battalion area of responsibility.

An unfortunate accident occurred on May 7. Staff Sergeant Alex George, a platoon sergeant in Company B, was killed, and Technician 5th Grade William Schenker was injured when a premature blast occurred during the destruction of unserviceable explosives.

When the war ended, some members of the "51st Again" celebrated by trying to consume any and all alcoholic beverages that could be confiscated, bought, borrowed or bartered for, within the immediate area. Others turned to God. Then came the sobering thought for each individual—What next?

CHAPTER X

POSTWAR OCCUPATION

The day for which all Allied Forces in Europe had been waiting arrived on May 8, 1945. General Eisenhower issued an Order for the Day declaring that "Full victory in Europe has been attained." He added: "Even before the final week of the conflict, you had put five million of the enemy out of the war."[1]

VE Day Reactions

The Victory in Europe (VE) Day reaction of the officers and enlisted men of the battalion was complex. Captain Preston Hodges went to church to say thanks for the victory and pray for the men who had died. Nevertheless, he wanted to finish the business in the Pacific, in the hope that there would be no more wars once this one was finished. Staff Sergeant Fred Beckler, a platoon sergeant in Company C, agreed. "There was no celebration," he wrote his sister, on hearing that the war in Europe was over. "Our minds were too much on what Truman was going to do about Japan." Hodges also saw a letdown from the everyday intensity of the Engineer job in combat to the bewildering slow pace of a normal, daily activity.[2]

Private First Class Larry Senger, a water supply specialist in the S-4 section, H&S Company, was at a 51st ECB water point in the vicinity of Augsburg, Germany on VE Day. Nearby were located a German prison camp, and an Air Force prison hospital. He went to the hospital and spent some time with the prisoners. He sampled the stew prepared by the nuns at the hospital and found it was fairly good. Dressed in striped clothing, a few hungry captives from the nearby concentration camp at Dachau approached him. He offered them some bread and spam, which they ate like it was steak.[3]

But some celebrating did go on. Hodges had saved several barrels of choice brandy for the occasion. On VE Day he delivered one to each platoon in his company; one to each of the other companies in the battalion; one to the 1111th Engineer Combat Group (ECG); and one to the battalion. He kept one for himself. The latter came in handy a short time later when he had to be hospitalized and was able to share some with his doctor.[4]

As corps troops, the engineers often felt that they stayed with the fighting after the divisions were sent back for rest. But there were two occasions that Lieutenant Milgram remembered wherein the engineers tasted the fruits—and drinks—of victory.

The first was in the city of Rheims where the 51st was among the first to enter after the tanks. Milgram still remembers the gifts of flowers, the wine, and the tearfully happy faces of the people lining the streets, hanging out of the windows, or running out among the jeeps and trucks to hand the men their treasured bottles of champagne. He also remembers the hilarity of the people along the curb as he, riding in a jeep and having popped a cork of some champagne, tried to drink from the bottle and almost strangled on the bubbly.

The 51st was early to enter Bastogne the first time through. There again the men were greeted most warmly by the people of the town. It was a sunny day and warm. Everyone seemed to be out on the streets, smiling and trying to talk with the engineers. Happiness was in the air. Again they were given bottles of wine, but Milgram remembers best the taste and wonderful look of those lovely open-faced apple and peach cakes that had obviously just been baked in honor of the liberators. They were so especially Belgian.

Not all occasions were so happy. Company C had been pulled back to the Marche area after its stand and relief by the 505th Parachute Infantry at Trois Ponts. There they remained for some days as the westernmost portion of the Bulge was still in active combat. As the 2d Armored Division began the mopping up at Celles, a general retreat of the German forces took place. Some days later, having been alerted by members of their unit, several men from the 51st visited the town of Bande, not far from Marche. There Milgram and others heard of the recent massacre of townspeople, and the destruction in the town wrought by the retreating Germans.

Engineer trucks can and do carry lots of unofficial items like blankets, pillows, useful clothing and items of comfort. The engineers delivered everything they had in their trucks to those poor people, who had so little, and had been through so much. In return they were toasted afterward by the grateful mayor and townspeople with a delicious apricot liqueur of local origin.

In the early part of 1945 the 51st was near the Moosberg prisoner of war compound just after it was liberated by the tanks of Third Army. The freed American prisoners of war came through the engineer's positions. The men of the 51st were filled with pity for them. Every one of them was skinny and pasty looking. All were hungry. Many had lost their teeth. They called our ordinary white bread "cake." The prisoners were passed back to the rear echelons for care, but the engineers gave food to many, and all of their private hoards of chocolate, cigarettes, any goodies, were dug out of barracks bags and footlockers for these bedraggled wretches before they left. The engineers wrote letters to their families. Many, who had been fliers, had been confined since 1942. These prisoners had been some of the best, strongest, and healthiest young American men before their capture and imprisonment.[5]

The end of the war in Europe did not mean complete relaxation for the officers and enlisted men of the battalion. Company A, located in Marzling, continued maintaining roads. Company B, in Erding, maintained and guarded Bailey bridges. One platoon of Company C remained guarding the command post of the 1111th ECG. At that time Company C's command post was located in Breitasch, and the 51st ECB and H&S Company command posts were located in Kirchasch.

On May 11 the entire battalion moved to new locations. The battalion headquarters and H&S Company moved to Biebelried, Company A to Theilheim, and Companies B and C to Westheim. The battalion was relieved of the guarding and maintenance of bridges so it could prepare for the move. All vehicles were thoroughly checked for the 187-mile road march. Once the move was completed, the men turned to routine maintenance of equipment, and organized athletics.

On May 12, Colonel Fraser called the battalion together to address them as a group for the first time. Fraser recalled and paid tribute to

POSTWAR OCCUPATION

those men who gave their lives in the war. Marche, Hotton, Trois Ponts, and Ciney, were only a few of the places he mentioned that would be recalled by the men of the battalion in the days to come. The list of numbers he called off sounded like a quarterback calling signals—82d, 75th, 9th, 84th, 86th, 87th—but in reality it was just a list of divisions the 51st had supported in the Allied drive across Europe.[6]

Fraser reminisced about his first three days in the battalion when he visited the sawmills and pubs. Then the bottom fell out when the Germans attacked in the Ardennes and the 51st had not sawed lumber since. He also noted that the battalion took VE Day in stride.

> As to what will happen to the 51st, I do not know, Colonel Anderson assured me he doesn't know, that the Corps commander doesn't know, that he doubted whether General Patton knew, but he hoped that maybe General Eisenhower knew what in the hell will happen to the 51st.[7]

With the war over, it was time for formal inspections of both individual and organizational equipment. Fraser inspected the companies the week of May 14. His first inspections in December 1944 had revealed many shortcomings. Now all companies passed.

Fraser left his mark in other ways. When he arrived in the 51st he had wanted to establish a unique identity. Most engineer outfits put signs on their bridges which said "Built by the 88th Engr Bn." Fraser hit on the idea of a sign which said, "51st Again," a reference to the many bridges built by the 51st Engineer Combat Battalion across Belgium and Germany.

It was plain that the name stuck. Soon after the war ended the battalion had an opportunity to send some people to the Riviera on Rest and Recuperation (R&R). Fraser took one group by truck from Wurzburg to Luxembourg City where there was a special train for the troops to go south. There were probably 300 to 400 officers and enlisted men waiting there while someone called the roll of units, such as 84th Field Artillery, 97th Signal Battalion, and so forth. When he called "51st Engineer Combat Battalion" the whole place exploded simultaneously with "51st Again." Obviously Fraser's strategy had worked. People from all over the First and Third United States Armies had seen and experienced the work of the 51st Engineer Combat Battalion.

When the war ended in Europe, the 51st was anticipating a combat crossing of the Inn River with Third Army. With the war over the battalion turned from combat operations to repair of damage, first in Wurzburg, then in Nurenburg.

On May 17, when the 51st moved to Wurzburg as part of the army of occupation, Colonel Fraser was made area engineer for the area. Wurz-

LTC HARVEY R. FRASER, COMMANDING OFFICER, 51ST ENGINEER COMBAT BATTALION, ADDRESSING BATTALION AFTER VE DAY, MAY 12, 1945.
Courtesy of National Archives

SGT MAJ CHARLES W. BEST AT THE END OF THE WAR.
From the collection of Charles W. Best

POSTWAR OCCUPATION

burg is a large city on the Mainz River and a busy transportation and rail center. River barge traffic was important in the German economy. The Allies had hit the city with a devastating fire bombing late in the war, and it was said that not a single roof remained unburned in the city. In addition, there was significant regular bomb damage to bridges and municipal buildings in the area. The area engineer had orders to revive the civilian economy. A Theater Order prohibited dealing with former Nazi personnel, but General Patton was not overly concerned about who the troops dealt with as long as they got the job done. Of course, when asked, no German admitted to being a Nazi. Fraser knew that the Nazis held significant positions in the German economic machine and that he had to deal with them to get the job done. Interestingly, General Patton was relieved of command of Third Army a few months later, largely because he permitted coordination with Nazis in the rebuilding of Germany.[8]

The Wurzburg city water and sewer systems were out of service, the Mainz River was blocked by numerous highway and railroad bridges that had been dropped in the stream by German demolitions, and barge traffic was at a standstill. The highways were not only bomb damaged, but were full of pot holes due to poor maintenance by the Nazis in the latter days of the war. Getting people to repair the economy was only half the problem. The construction supply system was not only depleted, but the whole system was broken down. The battalion supply officer and the intelligence section scoured the area for building supplies. One company was assigned to open the river to barge traffic and the repair of the hospital for use by American forces, one company the city sanitation systems and city roads, and a third company the rural road system. Highway responsibilities included operating rock quarries and asphalt plants, and replacing temporary bridges with more permanent structures.

Progress was seriously hampered by the demobilization system which returned personnel to the United States after the war. Higher headquarters often replaced experienced engineer commissioned and non-commissioned officers with infantry and artillery officers and non-commissioned officers.

Fraser established and maintained good rapport with the civilian and government construction personnel, as well as with the area highway personnel, and the systems gradually returned to somewhat normal operations. The sanitation system limped along after a couple of weeks, and even the city swimming pool was back in operation by early July. By the middle of July the battalion moved to the Nurenburg area for similar construction duties.

THE 51ST AGAIN!

The Army soon established a point system to determine eligibility for departure to the States and separation from the service. The system gave 1 point for every month in the Army, 1 for every month overseas, 5 for each decoration or campaign, and 12 for each child up to a limit of 3 children. The criterion for discharge on May 20, 1945 was 85 points. Because of the diligent work of the battalion personnel section and company commanders, all enlisted men who met the standard were on their way to the States the next day.

Through *Stars and Stripes* the men learned that most of the combat troops scheduled to go from Europe to the Pacific would be redeployed through the United States. Most of the supply forces, however, would be redeployed "directly from this theatre." The routing of 4,000,000 American soldiers and vast stores of equipment seemed to be a greater problem than the War Department faced in getting them to Europe. The military necessities involved in beating Japan threatened to hold in Europe many soldiers who would otherwise have been eligible for discharges. Under the new priority system, transportation to the States was available to the sick and wounded first, next to the liberated prisoners of war, then to units bound for the Pacific, and last to those awaiting discharge. In order to build installations rapidly, construction and aviation engineers would be the first to go to the Pacific.

Machinery had been set in motion to classify all units into one of four classes. Class one units were to remain in Europe on occupational and service duties. Class two units were to be redeployed to active theaters, either directly from Europe, or indirectly through the United States. Class three units were to be broken up into categories one or two. Class four units were to be returned to the United States for inactivation.

Units with the least number of men over the critical score of 85 fell into the class two category. Units with the greatest number of men over the critical score became class four. Individuals whose scores did not approximate the average score of their outfit would be transferred. In other words, a man with a low score would be transferred to a new unit, either class one or two, while those with high scores went to a class four category unit.

Although some or all of the point system information had come or would soon arrive through official Army channels, it did not always get to every man in the unit. But *The Stars and Stripes* was distributed throughout the battalion on the basis of one copy per ten men, so everyone learned about the point system. Morale was high because every soldier had a good idea where he stood as far as rotation was concerned.

Because the battle for Germany was broken into three separate campaigns, the point system for rotation and discharge was soon modified.

The change added ten points to nearly all the men in the battalion. Colonel Anderson and Lieutenant Colonel Fraser kept morale high when they both declared that no officer in the group would be declared essential if he had the points for rotation to the United States.

On June 21, *The Stars and Stripes* listed the officer's critical score for rotation as 85 points. This meant that any officer with less than 85 points would more than likely return to the States with the 51st.

During this period of concern about going home three former sergeants of H&S Company returned to pay a visit to the battalion but this time as second lieutenants. The three lieutenants fresh from the Infantry Officer Candidate School (OCS) and sporting shiny gold bars were Matthew Carlisle, George Turner, and Arnold Parker.

Occupation Duties

During June, the 51st and its companies remained in their areas, a welcome relief from the frequent moves of the past six months. The major task of the battalion continued to be repair and maintenance of all roads within the Army road net. The roads were in poor condition and it was necessary to resurface entire sections. The battalion sent out search teams for German equipment and materials to do the work, and they discovered seven road rollers, thirteen tar pots, and two ¾-yard cement mixers.

The secondary task of the battalion, the operation of sawmills, was a throwback to the autumn of 1944. Company A began work on the sawmills on June 2. They were manned by the civilian owners under the supervision of Company A. German prisoners were used daily in transporting the finished lumber to an engineer supply dump in Zell. Company C began operating the dump at Zell on June 6 before starting its own sawmill operations on the 11th.

Company B continued its work on the repair of the German hospital in Wurzburg using both prisoners of war and displaced persons. They finished on June 12. On that day the battalion was relieved from III Corps and assigned to XII Corps.

On June 18, the battalion turned to clearing a channel of the Main River for barge traffic in the battalion area after a reconnaissance of the area showed 26 bridges obstructing the channel. Company B supervised the operation of civilian dredges and cranes removing debris from the channel with civilian labor. Two days later the company began construction of a railroad bridge at Kitzingen.

PUTTING THEIR LIVES BACK TOGETHER. ASCHAFFENBERG, GERMANY. SEPTEMBER 7, 1945.
From the collection of Al Bolha

FEEDING HUNGRY CHILDREN. MICHELOU, GERMANY, AFTER THE WAR.
From the collection of Al Bolha

LEAVING GERMANY. CPL ALBERT BOLHA AND SGT HAINES. SEPTEMBER 13, 1945. "THE 300TH AT LAST" REFERS TO AN INCIDENT AT ROCHEFORT IN WHICH ELEMENTS OF THE 300TH RELIEVED PART OF THE 51ST AGAIN.

From the collection of Floyd D. Wright

THE 51ST ECB'S LAST PARADE. CAMP PATRICK HENRY, VIRGINIA. OCTOBER 27, 1945.

From the collection of Al Bolha

THE 51ST AGAIN!

That same day the 51st became a "Category IV" unit, one that was to return to the United States for inactivation. The new designation required changes in personnel and represented the preliminary steps in the readjustment program.

Through June, the battalion continued road maintenance, sawmill operations, operating the engineer supply dump, and clearing the Main River barge channel. It also received new assignments, expanding its involvement in reconstructing Germany. Company B started repair of the Custom House in Wurzburg, and Company C began operating cold mix units and a crusher and screening plant at a rock quarry. H&S Company took on the operation of a carbon dioxide plant in Kitzingen.

By July major USO shows were coming to the battalion area. They included the Jack Benny Show featuring Larry Adler, Ingrid Bergman and Martha Tilton. When Ingrid Bergman came to Wurzburg, the 51st built a stage in the city square for the show.

On July 3 morale of the officers and men of the battalion hit a high note when it was learned that Army policy would be to keep all men with 70 points or more in the unit as long as possible. About two-thirds of the battalion had between 70 and 85 points, so would be staying together.

Twelve officers with over 85 points to their credit, left on July 7, the first officers of the 51st to return home. Leaving the battalion to take command of the 299th ECB was the highly esteemed battalion commander Lieutenant Colonel Harvey R. Fraser. Having assumed command of the battalion a mere two days before the start of the German Ardennes Offensive that brought the war into the unit's front yard, he soon showed all that he was an outstanding leader of men with superior tactical capabilities. Fraser, having served almost the entire war overseas, both in the Pacific and European Theaters, had more points than anyone in the battalion, but was not considered eligible for rotation because of his Regular Army status.

The change in officers continued for the next two months. On July 8, Major Wyman P. Boynton arrived from the 145th ECB to take command of the battalion. On July 9, First Sergeant Samuel Hall, H&S Company, left for another engineer battalion in Germany. Four officers from the battalion left on July 28 by air for the States, including Captain Preston Hodges.

On July 17 the battalion was relieved of all assigned duties by the 336th ECB, and the next day moved to Lichtenfels, where it moved into two school buildings in an undamaged town. The men enjoyed the thermal bath house equipped with Turkish baths. Company A moved to

Michelau and Company B to Mistelbach. Not to be outdone in living standards, Captain Sam Scheuber, Company C, had his unit located in what appeared to be a castle in Seehof. Huge oil paintings covered every wall. Even some of the ceilings had ornate paintings. There was elaborate brass work in nearly every room, and formal chandeliers throughout the building. Some of the walls were papered with hand painted silk. The owner, a baron, still lived there, trying to protect his property.

The battalion was assigned to the 1123d ECG and immediately assumed responsibility of the area under the control of the 283d ECB and one half the area of the 145th ECB. In addition to road maintenance and the operation of 32 sawmills, the battalion repaired 3 autobahn bridges, constructed a small arms range, and operated a corps map depot in Bamberg. It also ran prefabrication plants, paper factories, coal mines, metal works, tar factories, and a nail factory. Over 450 POWs and 400 civilians supplemented the understrength 51st.

On July 31 word spread that XV Corps was planning to deactivate the 51st in the European Theater of Operations following the disposition of all personnel and property. The tentative date for this final action was not yet known. As a result, more officers continued to leave. Sam Scheuber was reassigned for duty in Japan. He was to fill a field grade position as an experienced petroleum engineer. Twelve days later, Floyd Wright left. Most of the old-timers in the 51st ECB were gone by that time. By the end of July there were 20 officers, 3 warrant officers, and 411 enlisted men in the battalion.

During August, the battalion continued its maintenance and repair of roads, while at the same time operating 32 sawmills, and 16 industries. It constructed a landing strip in Bamburg and repaired a building for the Quartermaster. At the same time the S-2 continued its efforts to find work for the battalion. He reconnoitered a machine factory, a lime factory, the existing river gauges on the Main River, a Feldspar plant, and the entire area for electrical industries.

The Road Home

By the end of August, the battalion had begun its long preparation for movement home. Captain Coats, the senior of the 11 remaining officers, assumed command on August 22. Two days later the 51st was relieved of all work assignments by the 145th ECB and ordered to turn in all engineer equipment to Engineer Dump, E-55, located in Michelau, Germany. The entire battalion moved into one building in Michelau, and on August 27, the unit received verbal instructions that instead of deactivation, it would return to the United States with a readiness date of September 11, and an availability date of September 21. The 51st was to be brought up to authorized strength plus 10 percent prior to shipment. Fillers began arriving in about two days. By the end of the month battalion strength almost doubled from 10 officers, 3 warrant officers, and 133 enlisted men, to 11 officers, 3 warrant officers, and 253 enlisted men.

On September 2, Major Arthur Baiden, Jr., arrived from the 178th ECB, and assumed command from Captain Coats. During the first few days of the month personnel continued streaming in from various units throughout a wide area. By September 10, the battalion strength was 25 officers, 6 warrant officers, and 671 enlisted men. It became extremely difficult to cope with the personnel and records problems because most of the old key people had left. The battalion now consisted almost entirely of new men. That resulted in an almost entirely new unit being organized with the consequent necessity of having to prepare it for overseas movement to the States.

Lieutenant Colonel John W. Cofer arrived from the 1106th ECG on September 4 and assumed command from Major Baiden. After working feverishly on the personnel and supply records in compliance with European Theatre of Operations-Preparation for Overseas Movement-Redeployment, SOP 61, the 51st Engineer Combat Battalion was ready to leave. It left Aschaffenberg at 0500 hours on September 12 and arrived at Camp Philadelphia in the Assembly Area Command at Mourmelon, France, at 1330 hours the next day. Company A had left by train on September 11 and joined the battalion there. The recomputation of scores based on new SOPs complicated the personnel procedure. However, by working nights, the personnel section completed separation center rosters, and embarkation rosters in sufficient time to rest a few days before the battalion departure on September 24 for the Calas Staging Area near Marseilles, France, in the Delta Base Section.

The 51st arrived there about 1630 hours on September 26 and immediately began re-processing in accordance with the new lower critical score for discharge. All roster stencils had to be recut because of the switch from reception stations to separation centers. In addition, officers and warrant officers who had indicated their desire to remain in the service and enlisted men who had applied for civilian positions in the ETO required further reprocessing.

Finally, on October 13, the personnel turnover stabilized so that the battalion staff could complete preparations for return to the States. The battalion boarded the SS *Eufala Victory* at Marseilles, France, at

POSTWAR OCCUPATION

1500 hours, October 16, and sailed the next morning. The voyage home was different than the voyage over to North Africa. The food aboard ship was reasonably good. Everyone ate at tables and was served by waiters.

The ship had a daily newspaper entitled *You Follow Log*, which printed world and stateside news, including professional football scores. The paper also listed the movies shown on board ship. Listed in the October 22 edition were Van Johnson in "Three Men in White" at number 3 hatch, and William Bendix in "Taxi Mister" at number 4 hatch. The paper also published the progress of the ship for the previous 24 hours. For example, the same issue reported: distance, 415 miles, speed, 17.129 knots, and miles to go, 1,921. Unlike the first voyage, there were no lookouts or navy personnel manning 37-mm. guns and .50-caliber machine guns.

The 51st arrived at Hampton Roads on October 27, debarked at 1030 hours, and moved by motor convoy to Camp Patrick Henry, Virginia. The process of deactivation began immediately. At midnight, after slightly over two years and seven months of existence, with two years less eighteen days overseas, the 51st Engineer Combat Battalion was inactivated under the provisions of General Orders Number 84, Army Service Forces, Headquarters, Camp Patrick Henry, Virginia, dated October 27, 1945. Final morning reports were submitted, property records cleared, funds turned in, and records boxed and listed for permanent file. The administrative procedure for the inactivation of units at Camp Patrick Henry was by far the smoothest, most efficient and well-planned administrative and supply procedure encountered by the 51st anywhere in the United States or overseas.

Only four of the original officers remained in the unit. They were Captains John Poronsky, the battalion dental officer, and Maurice E. Coats, the battalion S-4, and Lieutenants William R. Mueller, the battalion S-1, and David Henry, the battalion Motor Officer. These officers were with the 51st throughout its existence. They continued on together to Camp Atterbury, Indiana where they were separated and left for home.

Some of the men who had served their career overseas with the 51st ECB and returned with it to Camp Patrick Henry, Virginia, included Technical Sergeant Paul E. Thomas, Staff Sergeant James W. Baker, Corporal Frank Lee, Private First Class Lawrence Senger, Technician Fifth Grade Wilson Roberts, Master Sergeant Kenneth Kelly, and Technicians Fourth Grade Frank Iczkowski, Eldridge Walker, and Harry Wdzcieczny (Weber), H&S Company; Staff Sergeants Herbert L. Kelly and Leonard Weil, Sergeant William T. Saunders, Corporal Albert Bolha, Technicians

THE 51ST AGAIN!

Fifth Grade Harold D. Dudley, Eugene Fox, Raymond Mitchell, and William E. Robinson, and Privates First Class Felix B. Gay, Gordon G. Morgan, Ernest F. Minyard, Elfido Vigil, and Ervin W. Anderson, Company A; Floyd W. Catherman, Company B; and Corporals Howard B. Beam, and George W. Fincher, Private First Class Lloyd Randolph, and Staff Sergeant Frederick C. Beckler, Company C.

The 51st Engineer Combat Battalion, though gone, would not be soon forgotten.

Epilogue
THE FIRST REUNION

Over 40 years ago, the 51st Engineer Combat Battalion was inactivated on its return from Europe on October 27, 1945. Just 16 months before, it had landed at Normandy and fought and built its way across France, Belgium, and Germany. Now, on April 18-20, 1986, the battalion held its first reunion. Men from all over the country, accompanied by wives and friends, made their way to the Remada Renaissance in Washington, D.C. to reminisce about a period of their lives that few could have forgotten, and to meet old friends they had not seen for 40 years.

Brigadier General Harvey R. Fraser, Retired, Commanding Officer, 51st Engineer Combat Battalion, from December 14, 1944 to June 1945, welcomed the assembled.

> There is a unique and lasting camaraderie generated when men put their lives on line with each other day after day. This camaraderie is not eroded with the passage of time but is in fact cultivated and seasoned. Such camaraderie was generated during all of World War II by the 51st Engineer Combat Battalion, but especially during the Battle of the Bulge, and the combat crossings of the Roer, Rhine, and Danube Rivers.
>
> This weekend we are gathered to renew and nurture that camaraderie, and to expose our spouses to the '51st Again' spirit of the battalion. It was my privilege to command this battalion during its acute operations in Europe. I am proud to be a part of this group which has engrained its enviable record across the history books of World War II.
>
> We were fortunate to minimize our casualties during our operations, but it does not mean we have forgotten those who have paid the ultimate price on the field of battle. We remember and salute them, and also those who have passed to their reward since the war.
>
> I welcome all my comrades and their spouses to this reunion, and I hope you will enjoy the program as we spin the tales and enhance our camaraderie.

THE 51ST AGAIN!

Colonel Charles Attardo, Retired, brought the veterans together for their first reunion. Harold Puntch, Company B, spoke on reunion fever, then Colonel Floyd Wright, Retired, described the "Most Memorable Moments with the 51st ECB and the Battalion's Lineage and Honors." He said:

> Now for a few closing comments about the Lineage and Honors of the 51st. You have noticed that all the honors for the unit, up to this day, were earned by you people out there, and all the other men who were with us during WW II. Each one of you has accomplished something that very few people are able to do during the time that God has allotted to them here on earth. During this time, most people bear children who will keep their memory alive for a few generations, if they are lucky, but all members of the 51st have earned honors for themselves and their unit that will never be forgotten. Two thousand years or more from now, if our great nation of liberty and freedom needs the 51st Engineers, it will be called to active duty. Brave young men will once again stand proudly at attention, wearing the same distinctive unit insignia that you are wearing today, with the distinctive blue ribbon over their right breast pocket. They will stand before the same unit flag, with its battle honors, in front of them, and their shoulders will be thrown back as the adjutant reads the lineage and honors of the 51st that I have read to you today. You have set the standard of courage and honor that they will be asked to achieve, and hopefully, to exceed. Now I think that is something to be mighty proud of. I salute you.

On Saturday, Major General John Barnes, Retired, presented "Historical Highlights" of the battalion up to the Battle of the Bulge, and Dr. Barry W. Fowle, a Corps of Engineers historian, covered the battalion in the Battle of the Bulge, the Rhine River crossing, and the Danube crossing. Major General William A. Carter, Retired, First U.S. Army Engineer, followed with "A Look from the Top," then Frank Lee, Headquarters & Service Company, Carlton Moore, Company A, Lezar Caldwell, Company B, and Ralph K. Middleton, Company C, presented their "A Look from Below."

The participants toured Washington in the afternoon and in the evening attended the banquet where Lieutenant General Elvin R. Heiberg III, Chief of Engineers, made the main speech. The ceremony began with the pledge of allegiance after which Preston C. Hodges asked a representative from each company to light a candle in memory of those who had passed on.

The reunion wrap-up came the next morning when, under the heading of "Confessions and Comments by Senior NCOs," Charles Best, Donald Bonifay, George M. Verrall, and Raymond Millard spoke. General Fraser ended the reunion with a few remarks. The members of the 51st decided to meet again in Nashville, Tennessee in two years.

EPILOGUE

In his talk on Saturday evening, General Heiberg discussed the Corps of Engineers in today's Army, pointing out all of the functions engineers now perform. Noting the 51st's Croix de Guerre and Presidential Unit Citation, General Heiberg said engineers knew the 51st's achievements and were proud of everyone associated with the unit. He concluded that their examples set a high standard for today's engineers to emulate.

Appendix A

AWARDS

LEGION OF MERIT

FRASER, LTC Harvey R.   Hqrs

SILVER STAR

CONNELLY, T/5 Oliver M.	Co A	SCHEUBER, CPT Sam C.	Co C
HODGES, CPT Preston C.	Co B	YATES, MAJ Robert B	Hqrs
MILGRAM, 1LT JOSEPH E. JR	Co C		

BRONZE STAR MEDAL W/OAK LEAF CLUSTER

FRASER, LTC Harvey R.   Hqrs

BRONZE STAR MEDAL

BONIFAY, S/SGT Donald	Co A	MACK, PFC Jessie R.	Co C
CHASTAIN, PFC Winford C.	Med Det	MARQUEZ, PFC Jose E.	Co C
CLARK, SGT Fayne B.	Co C	MORIN, CWO Wilfred G.	H&S
COATS, CPT Maurice E.	Hqrs	MUELLER, 1LT William R.	Hqrs
CUNDIFF, SGT William S.	Co C	NABORS, 1LT Fred L.	Co C
GOLDSMITH, SGT Elvin	Co C	PEDERSEN, CPT Karl G.	Co A
GOSSARD, SGT Evers	Co C	REYNOLDS, SGT Payton E.	Co A
GREEN, 1LT Richard I.	Hqrs	STIFTINGER, SGT John J.	Co A
HODGES, CPT Preston C.	Co B	WALKER, PVT Morris S.	Co C
HORECKA, WOJG JULIUS J.	H&S	WRIGHT, 1LT Floyd D.	Co A
ISHMAEL, PVT Lee J.	H&S	WRIGHT, PFC Philip F.	Med
JAMISON, 1LT Bruce W.	Co B	YATES, MAJ Robert B.	Hqrs
KECK, T/5 Paul H.	Co C		

SOLDIERS MEDAL

BANKS, T/5 Thomas G.	H/S	MURPHY, 2LT J. A.	Co B
BARNES, CPT J. W.	Hqrs	RAPER, M/SGT M. L.	H&S
CASH, PFC G. M.	H/S	YATES, MAJ ROBERT B.	Hqrs
HENRY, 1LT D. H.	Hqrs		

PURPLE HEART

ABBOTT, William H.	Co A	JOYNER, Marvin C.	Co B
BAILEY, THEODORE O.	Co C	KENNEDY, Earlie	Co A
BANKS, Thomas G.	H&S	LIVERMORE, Thomas W.	Co B
BARCO, Colon A.	Co C	MCFARLAND, Dewey A.	Co B
BLACKBURN, Cecil C.	Co C	MCFARLING, Thadius J.	Co B
BOOTH, Larry C.	Co B	MCBEE, Earl C.	Co B
BROWN, Clyde R.	Co A	MALCOLM, Barnett R.	Co C
BROWN, Gerald C.	Co C	MAPLES, Lehn	Co C
CAPPS, Glenn L.	Co B	MARQUEZ, Jose E.	Co C
CARLISLE, Matthew R.	H&S	MATHIS, Edgar L.	Co B
CARNEY, Warren K.	Co B	MIDDLETON, Hervie L.	Co B
CARROLL, Nelson	Co A	MIMS, David C.	Co B
CARRUTH, John N.	Co B	MONTGOMERY, Edgar F.	Co C
CASADOS, Casimiro	Co A	MORGAN, Gordon G.	Co A
CONLEY, L. D.	Co B	NABORS, Fred A.	Co C
CONNELLY, Oliver M.	Co A	NELSON, Charles	Co A
CONNER, Grover C.	Co C	OCHSON, Joseph H.	Co A
COWEN, Thearndeen	Co A	PALMER, Anthony J.	Co A
CREWS, Charley E.	Co C	PEALE, John B.	Co A
CURTIS, Paul W.	Co A	PEDERSEN, Karl G.	Co A
CUTBERTH, Russell R.	Co C	PHILLIPS, Charles	Co A
DIEFFENBACH, Patrick A.	Co C	PICKARD, Ossie L.	Co C
DONATO, Andrew A.	Co C	PRATT, Clifton M.	Co A
DOUCET, Emile J.	Co A	PRESTON, Bennett	Co C
DUNLAP, John G.	Co A	RANKIN, William W.	Co C
ELLIOTT, Frank J.	Co A	ROBERTS, Wilson	H&S
EVANS, William D.	Co B	ROMANO, Frank B.	Co C
FAIRCHILD, Houston M.	Co A	ROSE, Winston W.	Co C
FERNANDES, Emiliano	Co A	SALAZAR, Andres G.	Co C
FORMBY, Doyle M.	Co C	SCENNA, Frank	Co A
GEORGE, Alex	Co B	SHERWOOD, George	Co A
GOSSARD, Evers	Co C	SMITH, Coy D.	Co A
GREEN, Richard I.	Co C	SMITH, Harold B.	Co A
GREENWOOD, Leo O.	Co C	SMITH, Philip G.	Co B
GROCE, William M.	Co B	SNOW, James M.	Co C
GURNSEY, Edward B.	Co C	SPIVY, Radford	Co C
GYURE, Joseph	Co C	STEPHENS, Jerry R.	Co A
HARMON, Bill	Co B	STRAWSER, Carl	Co C
HAYWOOD, Ray	Co A	TILLMAN, Raligh	Co B
HERRIN, Mimz C.	Co C	TRAFFORD, Raymond A.	Co A
HIGHFIELD, James E.	Co A	TRITT, William D.	Co C
HINDMAN, Charlie S.	Co C	WARZECHOWSKI, Stanley	Co B
HODGES, Preston C.	Co B	WHEATLEY, James T. Jr	H&S
HOUDLETTE, Clarence E.	Co C	WILLIAMS, Arthur F.	Co C
HOWRY, Lamont	Co B	WININGER, Marion M.	Co C
HUEHN, Carl L.	Co A	WOTTON, David L.	Co C
ISHMAEL, Lee J.	Co B	WRIGHT, FLoyd D.	Co A
JENKINS, Edgar L.	Co B	YEATES, Buster	Co B

The names listed are those found in the records of the 51st ECB. There may have been men wounded who received the Purple Heart after transferring out of the unit, but there are no records to indicate who they might be.

Appendix B

DEPARTMENT OF THE ARMY
Lineage and Honors
51st Engineer Battalion

Parent unit constituted 5 May 1942 in the Army of the United States as 51st Engineers (Combat)

Activated 13 June 1942 at Camp Bowie, Texas

Reorganized and redesignated 1 August 1942 as 51st Engineer Combat Regiment

Regiment broken up 1 April 1943, and elements reorganized and redesignated as follows:

1st Battalion as 51st Engineer Combat Battalion

(Headquarters and Headquarters and Service Company as Headquarters and Headquarters Company, 1111th Engineer Combat Group; 2d Battalion as 238th Engineer Combat Battalion; separate lineages)

51st Engineer Combat Battalion inactivated 27 October 1945 at Camp Patrick Henry, Virginia

Redesignated 8 November 1951 as 51st Armored Engineer Battalion and allotted to the Regular Army

Activated 27 November 1951 at Fort Leonard Wood, Missouri

Inactivated 16 March 1956 at Fort Leonard Wood, Missouri

Redesignated 10 May 1967 as 51st Engineer Battalion

Activated 1 October 1967 at Fort Campbell, Kentucky

Inactivated 31 August 1971 at Fort Campbell, Kentucky

APPENDIX B

CAMPAIGN PARTICIPATION CREDIT

<u>World War II</u>
Normandy
Northern France
Rhineland
Ardennes-Alsace
Central Europe

DECORATIONS

Presidential Unit Citation (Army), Streamer embroidered ARDENNES

French Croix de Guerre with Silver Star, World War II, Streamer embroidered ARDENNES

By Order of the Secretary of the Army:

/s/Kenneth G. Wickham
/t/KENNETH G. WICKHAM
Major General, USA
The Adjutant General

Appendix C

The Engineer Officer Candidate Course
The Engineer School
April 4, 1942 to June 24, 1942

Subject	Hours
Close Order & Extended Order Drill	21
Ceremonies and Inspection	11
Physical Training	16
Defense against Chemicals	6
Military Discipline and Courtesy	8
Current Military Operations	12
Sanitation and First Aid	8
Military Organization	13
Map and Aerial Photo Reading	31
Military Sketching	17
Training Management	7
Administration	28
Interior Guard	2
Mess Management	3
Law	11
Command & Leadership	6
Engineer Reconnaissance	5
Infantry Weapons	49
Musketry	10
Defense against Aircraft	5
Combat Principles	26
Marches and Camps	21
Scouting and Patrolling	8
Field Fortifications	11
Demolitions	20
Camouflage	10
Defense against Mechanized Attack	10

APPENDIX C

Organization of Ground	18
Assault Tactics	6
Obstacles	12
Fixed Bridges	30
Floating Bridges	37
Roads	11
Motors and Heavy Equipment	17
Water Supply	9
Engineer Tools and Rigging	13
Traffic Control	14
Signal Communication	6

Appendix D

Panel Bridge, Bailey Type, M2

The Bailey bridge provided a rapid means of bridging streams and ravines for all military loads. It could be assembled in different ways for various spans and classes.*

The bridge (fig. 1) is a through-truss bridge supported by two main trusses formed from 10-foot steel truss sections called panels. A roadway of wood chess (flooring) laid on steel stringers is supported by transoms (transverse members) laid between the two main trusses. Steel ribands (curbs) hold down the chess; steel ramps support the flooring at the ends of the bridge. Footwalks can be added outside the trusses on each side. Each 10-foot section of bridge is called a bay. Each bridge set includes 126 panels, 56 transoms, 96 stringers, 48 ramps, 48 ribands, chess, end posts, bracing, accessories, and erection equipment. One set provides a 130-foot double-double bridge or two 80-foot double-single bridges.

Major items of equipment are described below:

1. Panels are truss sections about 10 feet long and 5 feet 1 inch high. They weigh 577 pounds. They are connected end-to-end by panel pins to form a truss. Trusses are placed side by side and also one above the other to form bridges of greater capacity.

2. Transoms are the principal transverse members of the bridge. They are clamped across the bottom panel chords and they support the stringers and flooring. Each transom is made from a 10-inch I-beam reinforced with 5/16 inch cover plates. A transom is 19 feet 11 inches long and weighs 618 pounds.

3. Stringers are placed on transoms to carry flooring. There are two types: plain stringers weighing 260 pounds and button stringers weighing 267 pounds. They are identical except that the latter has 12 buttons which serve to space the chess. Each is 10 feet long and is made from three 4-inch I-beams separated by stiffeners. Four plain stringers are used under the center of the roadway of each bay and one button stringer is used on each side.

4. Ramps are similar to stringers. However, they are made from 5-inch I-beams and the lower flange is tapered slightly at each end. They support the portion of the flooring leading from ground level to the bridge.

APPENDIX D

5. Ribands are steel curbs which are placed over the ends of chess and bolted to button stringers. Each is 13 feet 10 inches long and weighs 215 pounds.

6. Chess are 8¾ by 2 inch timbers. Each is 13 feet 10 inches long and weighs 65 pounds.

7. End posts are built-up steel columns which are pinned to the end panels of trusses to take the shear at the end of the bridge. There are male posts weighing 121 pounds and female end posts weighing 130 pounds. A bearing block at the bottom of each post fits over a steel bearing which is supported by timber cribbing.

Trusses may be one, two, or three panels wide and up to three panels high. Standard types of assembly include: single truss, single story (SS); double truss, single story (DS); triple truss, single story (TS); double truss, double story (DD); triple truss, double story (TD); double truss, triple story (DT); and triple truss, triple story (TT). Overhead bracing must be used for triple-story bridges with all three stories above the floor system.

For detailed assembly of the bay of a double-double bridge, see (Fig. 2).

One bridge set can be transported on forty-one 2½-ton dump trucks and twelve 2½-ton pole-type trailers. There are 1 spares load, 2 grillage loads, 8 ramp loads, 6 launching nose loads, 2 footwalk loads, 24 bay loads, 8 supplementary panel loads, and 2 supplementary transom loads.

The bridge is assembled on rollers on the near bank. When launched by the normal cantilever method, a skeleton length of the bridge is assembled on the forward end for a launching nose. Launching links are placed in the bottom chords of the launching nose trusses to overcome sag or to reach a high bank. The bridge is then cantilevered across the gap until it touches the rollers on the far (shore fig. 3). After the bridge is pushed into position, the launching nose is removed, the bridge is jacked down on bearing plates, and ramps are added.

Bailey bridge parts can be formed to make panel crib piers (see fig. 4), two-lane bridges (see fig. 5), or a floating bridge (see fig. 6).

*All narrative and figures in this appendix are from Department of Army Technical Manual TM 5-260, *Principles of Bridging*, U.S. Government Printing Office, 1955, pp. 97-104.

FIGURE 1. DOUBLE-DOUBLE BAILEY BRIDGE.

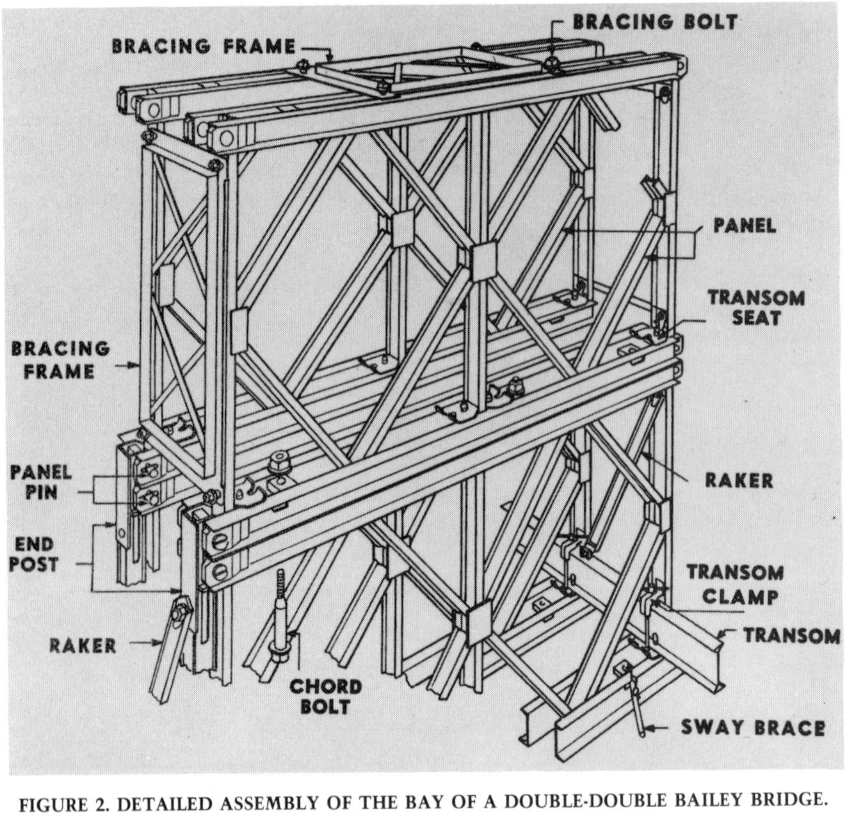

FIGURE 2. DETAILED ASSEMBLY OF THE BAY OF A DOUBLE-DOUBLE BAILEY BRIDGE.

FIGURE 3. BRIDGE BEING CANTILEVERED ACROSS A GAP.

FIGURE 4. PANEL CRIB PIER.

FIGURE 5. TWO LANE BAILEY BRIDGE.

FIGURE 6. FLOATING BAILEY BRIDGE.

Appendix E

Letter of Appreciation

From: Colonel Louis P. Leone
       Commanding Officer
       Field Force Replacement Depot #4

Thru: Channels

To: Commanding Officer
       51st Engineer Combat Battalion
       First United States Army

1. Company "B" of the 51st Engineer Combat Battalion, 1st U.S. Army, has been attached to this command as a training organization for the training of replacement soldiers during the period of 21 February 1944 to date (2 Apr 44). The mission assigned the company was the organizing of training teams to instruct and train replacements, both soldiers and officers, of the several branches of the service represented here.

2. This company has fulfilled its responsibilities here and has accomplished its assigned mission in a superior manner while operating under difficult field conditions and lacking many training aids and facilities.

3. The pride of the individual soldier and officer in the unit's appearance, discipline and conduct is outstanding. The individual and collective enthusiasm of these soldiers integrated in the unit's discharge of its duties, together with their untiring effort and application of initiative and ingenuity in the improvisation of training aids, and the construction of field training facilities reflects the highest credit upon the company. There is no doubt this unit has obtained in its training a superior degree of technical and tactical proficiency and preparedness.

THE 51ST AGAIN!

4. It is desired to commend each officer and enlisted man in the unit not only for their individual and collective soldierly accomplishments, but for the unit's high contribution to the training of replacement officers and soldiers. It is also desired to especially mention and commend the commanding officer of this company, Captain Preston C. Hodges, 0110139. Without doubt the unit's high standards have been reached through Captain Hodges' untiring efforts and his outstanding and exemplary leadership.

/s/ Louis P. Leone
/t/ LOUIS P. LEONE
    Colonel,   Inf
    Commanding

Appendix F

Memorandum Commemorating Activation Day
Saturday, 18 March 1944

    To each and every member of this command I extend my heartiest congratulations on the excellent work you have performed during the year. You have made this battalion the best battalion in the Army. I am proud indeed to have been selected to command this organization. In the future I shall depend on the unquestionable loyalty you have shown to me in the past, and we shall by team effort work together in doing our part to bring this War to a successful conclusion.

    For each and everyone of you I ask God's blessing in the task which lies ahead of us. May He see fit to give us all the courage to give our lives willingly if necessary in our struggle to maintain the freedom to which our Country has been dedicated. May He help us all in winning the War quickly that we may return home safely and speedily to the loved ones we have left behind.

                                               /s/ VICTOR J. REAFSNYDER
                                                  Major, C.E.
                                                  Commanding

Appendix G

Courses of Instruction and Instructors for Two-Week Specialist School

CLASS	INSTRUCTOR	ASS'T INSTRUCTOR(S)	NUMBER OF STUDENTS
1st Sergeant	CWO Morin	1st Sgt Milgram 1st Sgt Abbott	7
Co Motor Sgt	1LT Henry	S/Sgt Williamson S/Sgt Rankin S/Sgt Hall	4
Supply Sgt	CPT Coats	T/Sgt Pugh S/Sgt Strauss S/Sgt May	4
Company Clerk	T/Sgt Best	Cpl Beam Cpl Foreman	7
Platoon Sgt	1LT Wright	S/Sgt Sherwood	17
Chemical Sgt	Sgt Bargar		2
Classification Sgt	T/4 Wheeler		3
Air Compressor Operator	M/Sgt Raper	T/5 Helton	9
Squad Leader	1LT Green		54
Auto Mechanic	1LT Henry	T/4 Bell T/4 Carmichael T/4 Harrison	12
Electrician	1st Sgt Bothra	T/4 Madison	6
Clerk General	T/4 Jones		9
Radio Repairman	CPT Carver	Sgt Newcomer	7

Appendix H

Officer and First Sergeant assignments, 51st ECB, on Departure from England

Headquarters
LTC V. J. Reafsnyder, Commanding
Major R. B. Yates, Executive Officer
1LT W. R. Mueller, S-1
CWO Morin, Personnel Officer
CPT A. H. Carver, S-2
CPT Huxman, S-3
CPT J. W. Barnes, ADE
1LT C. J. Attardo, Asst S-3
CPT M. E. Coats, S-4
CWO P. H. Pugh, Asst S-4
1LT D. Henry, Motor Officer
CWO J. J. Horecka, Asst Motor Officer
CPT S. Weinstein, Surgeon
CPT J. A. Poronsky, Dental Officer

H&S Company
CPT A. E. Radford, Commanding
First Sgt S. Hall

Company B
CPT P. C. Hodges, Commanding
First Sgt H. L. Middleton
1LT B. W. Jamison
1LT V. J. Harwood
1LT L. Nolan
2LT L. Senger

Company A
CPT K. G. Pedersen, Commanding
First Sgt W. H. Abbott
1LT F. D. Wright
1LT H. L. O'Neil
1LT R. C. Trafford
2LT J. H. Kelley

Company C
1LT S. Scheuber, Commanding
First Sgt R. Millard
1LT R. I. Green
1LT F. L. Nabors
2LT J. B. Milgram, Jr.
2LT J. Norton

When the 51st Engineer Combat Battalion left England it had 29 officers, 3 warrant officers, and 622 enlisted men.

Appendix I

HEADQUARTERS
505th PARACHUTE INFANTRY
APO 469   U.S. ARMY

24 December 1944

SUBJECT: Commendation
TO   :   Commanding Officer, 51st Engineer Combat Battalion.
             (Thru: Commanding General, 82nd Airborne Division).

    1.   On 19 December 1944, when this unit advanced to seize critical terrain at TROIS PONTS, BELGIUM, the Regimental Commander found your unit in complete command of the town and bridge across the SALM RIVER at that point, thereby greatly assisting this unit in the accomplishing of its mission. Although they had been completely isolated for four days and nights, they continued to assist in maintaining control of the situation for another forty-eight hours.

    2.   Although isolated, your unit was staying in position and repelling attacks by the Germans, including armor. The spirit and courage displayed by your men and officers in this engagement of your small arms against armor was worthy of the highest tradition of the service.

    3.   Please convey to the officers and men of your unit the thanks of the officers and men of this regiment for their cooperation and support.

                                                 /s/ William E. Ekman
                                                 /t/ WILLIAM E. EKMAN
                                                       Colonel, Infantry
                                                        Commanding

TRUE COPY
/s/ Karl G. Pedersen
/t/ KARL G. PEDERSEN
Capt.   CE
    ADJUTANT

Appendix J

PRESIDENTIAL UNIT CITATION

Unit citation awarded to battalion per Sec I, GO #29, Hq., First U.S. Army, 17 February 1945

The 51st Engineer Combat Battalion, United States Army, is cited for outstanding performance of duty in action against the enemy from 17 to 22 December 1944, in Belgium. When German forces had penetrated deep into friendly lines on 17 December 1944, and were rolling westward rapidly, the 51st Engineer Combat Battalion was ordered into strongpoint defensive positions in the vicinity of Trois Ponts, Hotton and Marche, Belgium with the mission of impeding and containing the enemy advance at strategic points. Faced by numerically superior forces in armor, firepower and manpower, the battalion quickly constructed and stubbornly defended roadblocks, prepared vital bridges for demolition and served as infantrymen. By their determination and devotion to duty, regardless of the odds, the battalion denied the enemy important avenues of advance, thus permitting strong friendly forces to move into counterattack positions. By skillful use of the weapons at hand, excellent terrain appreciation and the use of ingenious ruses, the enemy was led to believe that strong formations confronted them and that they were being rapidly reinforced. When German tanks attacked repeatedly, fierce fire from rocket launchers destroyed them; infantry attacks, supported by intense artillery barrages, were met by a hail of small arms fire with heavy losses on enemy ranks; when bridges could no longer be held, they were demolished at the last possible moment, denying their use to the hostile advancing forces. Throughout the five-day period, the enemy was never able to penetrate the defenses manned by the officers and men of the 51st Engineer Combat Battalion. Their courageous actions and fortitude contributed materially to the ultimate defeat of German offensive plans in this area and are worthy of high praise.

Appendix K

RÉPUBLIQUE FRANÇAISE

Guerre 1939-1945

CITATION

EXTRAIT DE LA DECISION N° 246

SUR la proposition du Ministre de la DEFENSE NATIONALE
LE PRESIDENT DU GOUVERNEMENT PROVISOIRE DE LA REPUBLIQUE

CITE A L'ORDRE DE LA DIVISION

51st Engineer Combat Battalion

"Unité d'élite qui s'est particulièrement fait remarquer au cours de l'offensive allemande des ARDENNES. Lancée dans la brèche avec mission de contenir l'avance ennemie dans l'Axe LIGNEUVILLE-STAVELOT TROIS PONTS a, pendant la période du 17 au 22 décembre 1944, malgré le manque d'armes lourdes et bien qu'attaquée par un adversaire très supérieur en nombre, gardé les positions qui lui avaient été assignées, faisant ainsi preuve des plus belles qualités de courage et de discipline militaire".

Ces citations comportent l'attribution de la Croix de Guerre avec Etoile d'Argent

PARIS, le 15 juillet 1946

P.O. Le Général d'Armée JUIN
Chef d'Etat-Major Général
de la Défense Nationale

Signé : A. JUIN

EXTRAIT CERTIFIEE CONFORME
Paris, le **06 SEP. 1988**
Pour le Ministre et par autorisation
Le Chef du Bureau des Décorations

D. CADILHAC.

TRANSLATION OF APPENDIX K

Extract of Decision No 246

Upon the proposal of the Minister for National Defense The President of the Provisional Government of the Republic

Cites

The 51st Combat Engineer Battalion

An Elite unit which particularly distinguished itself during the German offensive in the Ardennes. Thrown into the breach with the mission of containing the enemy advance on the LIGNEUVILLE-STAVELOT-TROIS PONTS axis, it, during the period from 17 to 22 December 1944, despite the lack of heavy weapons and although attacked by an adversary very superior in number, held the positions which had been assigned to it, demonstrating proof of admirable qualities of courage and military discipline.

These citations carry the award of the Croix de Guerre with Silver Star.

Appendix L

THE 51ST PROVERB

(To all the 51st Wives)

Verily I say unto you, bewarest an Army Engineer, for the Army Engineer is a strange being possessed by anything moving; yea, he speaketh in parables which he calleth regulations, and he wieldeth a big stick which he calleth a shovel. He hath but one Bible—a training manual.

He talketh often of a man called Bailey, whom thou knowest not. He showeth both smile and deep thought, until one knoweth not his inner workings; he speaketh in his sleep of strange objects called treadways, half-tracks, jeeps, dozers and tanks. Often he speaketh in strange tongues which soundeth like "Je vous aime beaucoup." Thou inquireth not, and accepteth his ramblings in good faith, for thou knowest not their meaning.

He refereth often to "the old Man," which thou interpreteth as sacrilegious reference to a supreme being. Yet thou forgiveth his trespasses, as thou expecteth him to forgiveth thy own.

In his gaze, he carrieth a faraway look as he rambleth on of places beyond the sea which thou knowest not. He speaketh of Bowie, Plattsburgh, and Casablanca; HST Andes, which he describeth as with a slippery cafeteria; Utah Beach and Marche; Trois Ponts, Rochefort and Champlon Crossroads. And always he speaketh the number "51." Verily, thou asketh of him, "What meaneth this '51'?" He respondeth with some strange explanation of men whom he calleth "Engineers." Thou knowest better than to further displayeth thy ignorance; and inquireth not when he speaketh further of the "Battle of the Bulge," for thou darest not mention the matter of his spare tire, where once grewest a fertile plain.

Tho' he groweth gray and sparse on top, he forgeteth not his youth nor his buddies, and he speaketh with much enthusiasm of DC and Nashville, and of something he calleth a "reunion." Thou detecteth a glowing light in his eyes when he so speaketh, and thou determineth to shareth in his glory, for thou lovest him with all thy heart.

He is thy special "51st Engineer."

Edna M. Wright
(Mrs. Floyd D. Wright)

Appendix M

SALUTE TO THE ENGINEERS

Now it's all very fair to fly through the air
Or to humor a heavy gun,
Or to ride in tanks through the ranks
Of the crushed and battered Huns,
And it's nice to think when the U-boats sink
Of the glory that outlives years,
But whoever heard one vaunting word
For the MUDDY OLD ENGINEERS?

Now you mustn't feel when you read this spiel
That the engineer is a jealous knave,
That he joined the ranks for a vote of thanks
In search of a hero's grave.
No, your mechanized cavalry's quite all right
And your Doughboy has few peers,
But where in hell would the lot of them be
If it weren't for the Engineers?

Oh, they look like tramps, but they build your camps,
And they sometimes lead the advance,
And they sweat red blood to bridge the flood
To give you a fighting chance.
Who stays behind when it gets too hot
To blow up the roads in your rear?
Just tell your wife that you owe your life
To some MUDDY OLD ENGINEERS.

*Why "Heni soit qui mal y pense" is a
   gruesome sort of phrase,
But their modest claim to immortal fame
Has probably reached your ears.
The first to arrive and last to leave
Are the MUDDY OLD ENGINEERS.

-Johnnie-

(Reprinted from "Army Poets" column in *Stars and Stripes* — 1944 or 45)

*"Evil to him who thinks evil."
 (Motto of the Order of the Garter)

Appendix N

ACRONYMS, ABBREVIATIONS, AND INITIALS

AD	Armored Division
ADE	Assistant Division Engineer
ASP	Ammunition Supply Point
AT	Anti-tank
BN	Battalion
CG	Commanding General
Co	Company
CO	Commanding Officer
COE	Chief of Engineers
CP	Command Post
CPX	Command Post Exercise
DP	Displaced Person
ETO	European Theater of Operations
FM	Field Manual
FO	Forward Observer
FUSA	First United States Army
H&S	Headquarters and Service
ID	Infantry Division
IP	Initial Point
LCVP	Landing Craft, Vehicle and Personnel
MLR	Main Line of Resistance
MSR	Main Supply Route
NCO	Noncommissioned Officer
PI	Parachute Infantry
POE	Port of Embarkation
POL	Petroleum, Oil, and Lubricants
POW	Prisoner of War
REGT	Regiment
R&R	Rest & Recuperation
S-1	Special Staff, Personnel
S-2	Special Staff, Intelligence
S-3	Special Staff, Operations
S-4	Special Staff, Supply
SOP	Standard Operating Procedures

APPENDIX N

TOE	Table of Organization & Equipment
TM	Technical Manual
T/3	Technician Third Grade
T/4	Technician Fourth Grade
T/5	Technician Fifth Grade
TI&E	Troop Information and Education
VE Day	Victory in Europe Day

Endnotes

Chapter One

1. Information about the 51st is from the Official Records, 51st Engineer Combat Battalion, Modern Military Records Branch, National Archives, Suitland, Maryland. Department of the Army, Lineage and Honors of the 51st Engineer Combat Battalion is at Appendix B.

2. Unit History, 1111th Engineer Combat Group (formerly 51st Engineer Combat Regiment), Modern Military Records Branch, National Archives, Suitland, Maryland.

3. Subjects and hours of the Sixth Engineer Officer Candidate Course, The Engineer School, April 4, 1942 to June 24, 1942, is at Appendix C.

4. Related by Preston Hodges at the first reunion of the 51st in Washington, D.C. in April 1986.

5. Department of the Army, ROTC Manual No. 145-20, *American Military History 1607-1953* (U.S. Government Printing Office, Washington, D.C. July 1956), pp. 30, 368-371.

6. A technician rating was for enlisted men doing specialized work. Technicians could have been of the third, fourth, or fifth grade. A technician third grade had a rank equivalent to that of a staff sergeant with equal pay and privileges. However, a technician third grade was outranked by a staff sergeant regardless of length of service. A technician fourth grade was equivalent to a sergeant in the same way, and a technician fifth grade to a corporal.

Chapter Two

1. Information about the 51st is from the Official Records, 51st Engineer Combat Battalion, Modern Military Records Branch, National Archives, Suitland, Maryland.

2. Unit History, 1111th Engineer Combat Group (old designation, 51st Engineer Combat Regiment), Modern Records Branch, National Archives, Suitland, Maryland. By authority of Unnumbered Circular, War Department, Subject: "Redesignation and Reorganization of Engineer Combat Regiments," file: AG320.2 (3-2-43) OB-I-GNGCT-M, 5 March 1943, and letter, Hqs, XIII Corps, same subject, 17 March 1943.

3. Organizational Diary, 51st Engineer Combat Battalion, Modern Records Branch, National Archives.

4. Ibid, p. 3. Scores for H&S Company not given.

5. Unit History, 1111th Engineer Combat Group.

6. Department of the Army Technical Manual TM 5-260, Principles of Bridging, U.S. Government Printing Office, 1955, pp. 97-8. All technical data on the Bailey bridge is from this manual.

7. Memoirs of Colonel Charles J. Attardo, AUS, Retired, former Assistant S-3, 51st Engineer Combat Battalion.

8. Ibid.

9. Letter Thomas A. Banks to LTC Maurice E. Coats, AUS, Retired, dtd. 31 January 1989.

Chapter Three

1. Information about the 51st is from the Official Records, 51st Engineer Combat Battalion, Modern Military Records branch, National Archives, Suitland, Maryland.

2. Department of the Army, ROTC Manual No. 145-20, *American Military History 1607-1954* (U.S. Government Printing Office, Washington, D.C., July, 1956), p. 99.

3. Memoirs of Colonel Charles J. Attardo, AUS, Retired, a member of the 51st ECB from 1943 to 1945.

4. Letter, dated 1988, Thomas G. Banks to Lieutenant Colonel Maurice E. Coats, AUS, Retired.

5. Stewart Richardson, *The Secret History of World War II* (New York: Richardson & Steirman, Inc., 1986), p. 145.

6. Memoirs of Colonel Charles J. Attardo.

7. Ibid; letter, Banks to Coats.

8. Letter, dated March 23, 1989, Lieutenant Colonel Maurice E. Coats, AUS, Retired, to Barry W. Fowle.

9. See Appendix E for a copy of Colonel Leone's letter.

10. See Appendix F for Major Reafsnyder's memorandum.

11. See Appendix G for instructors and courses of instruction.

12. Omar N. Bradley, *A Soldier's Story* (New York: Rand McNally & Company, 1951), p. 267.

13. See Appendix H for a list of officer and first sergeant assignments as the 51st ECB prepared to leave England.

ENDNOTES — PAGES 46 TO 68

Chapter Four

1. Information about the 51st Engineer Combat Battalion is from the Official Records, 51st Engineer Combat Battalion, Modern Military Records Branch, National Archives, Suitland, Maryland.

2. Omar N. Bradley, *A Soldier's Story* (New York: Rand McNally Company, 1951), p. 302.

3. Organizational Diary, 51st Engineer Combat Battalion (ECB).

4. Memoirs of Colonel Charles J. Attardo, AUS., in possession of the authors.

5. Organizational Diary, 51st ECB; Gordon A. Harrison, *Cross Channel Attack* (Washington, D.C.: Government Printing Office, 1951), Map XXV.

6. Memoirs, Attardo.

7. Ibid.

8. Ibid.

9. Ibid.

10. The following personnel received the Soldier's Medal for their efforts in putting out the ammunition dump fire: Major Robert B. Yates, Captain John W. Barnes, 1/Lt D.H. Henry, 2/Lt J.A. Murphy, M/Sgt Lee N. Raper, and Pfc G.M. Cash.

11. Memoir, Attardo.

12. Organizational Diary, 51st ECB.

13. Martin Blumenson, *Break-out and Pursuit* (Washington, D.C.: Government Printing Office, 1951), pp. 229, 234-236.

14. Ibid. p. 234.

15. Organizational Diary, 51st ECB.

16. Sergeants Leonard Weil, Harry E. (Cotton) Wimberly, and Corporal Ossie L. Pickard, rejoined the battalion after being hospitalized in England.

17. Blumenson, p. 690.

18. Information and bridge drawings for this period of time in France and Belgium were contributed by Major General John W. Barnes, USA, Retired, former S-3, 51st Engineer Combat Battalion.

19. Bradley, pp. 444-5.

20. War Correspondent Report, Ivan H. (Cy) Peterman, *Philadelphia Inquirer*, dated February 7, (Delayed) 1945. Unit Diary, 51st ECB.

21. Oral History Interview, Brigadier General Harvey R. Fraser, USA, Retired, July, 1987, by Barry W. Fowle.

22. Dwight D. Eisenhower, *Crusade in Europe* (New York: Permabooks, 1952), pp. 377-8.

Chapter Five

1. Except where noted, material in this chapter is taken from Ken Hechler, *Holding the Line*, Studies in Military Engineering Number 4, Washington, D.C.; Battalion History, 51st Engineer Combat Battalion (ECB), Modern Military Records Branch, National Archives, Suitland, Maryland.

2. Ibid. An excerpt from a speech prepared by Doctor T. Reed Maxson, for presentation at the 2d Reunion, 51st Engineer Combat Battalion, Nashville, Tennessee, April 1988, but not delivered.

3. Ibid.

4. Battalion History, 51st ECB.

5. Hugh M. Cole, *The Ardennes: Battle of the Bulge*, United States Army in World War II (Washington, 1965), pp. 51-56.

6. Ibid., pp. 69-70; 264-5.

7. Ibid., pp. 264-7.

8. The 51st ECB was under the control of the Commanding Officer, 158th Engineer Combat Battalion, the Area Defense Commander, Area 2. S-2 & S-3 Log, 51st ECB, until 1930 hours December 19.

9. Phone call between Floyd D. Wright and John T. Oliver, July 1, 1989.

10. Letter, Joseph B. Milgram, Jr. to Barry W. Fowle, dated May 12, 1988.

11. Ibid.

12. Ibid.

13. Ibid.

14. The Official Military Record. See also Janice Holt Giles, *The Damned Engineers*, Reprint, 1985.

ENDNOTES — PAGES 77 TO 86

15. Letter, Milgram, dated May 12, 1988. Milgram is not sure if the vehicle was an open top self propelled gun or a tank destroyer.

16. Ibid.

17. S-2 & S-3 Log, 51st ECB.

18. Ibid.

19. Ibid.

20. Letter, Milgram, dated May 12, 1988.

21. Article by Joseph B. Milgram, dated July 26, 1949.

22. Letter, Milgram, dated May 12, 1988. Milgram later learned it was the 30th Infantry Division Artillery firing on Company C in Trois Ponts.

23. Letter, Milgram, dated May 12, 1988.

24. Ibid.

25. Ibid.

26. Ibid. General Eisenhower placed Field Marshal Sir Bernard L. Montgomery in command of all Allied forces on the north flank of the bulge.

27. Colonel William E. Ekman, Commanding officer, 505th Parachute Infantry, sent a letter of Commendation to the 51st ECB for the cooperation and support received from Company C. The letter is at Appendix I.

28. Article, Milgram, dated July 26, 1949.

29. Ibid.

30. Ibid.

31. Ibid.

32. Ibid.

33. Cole, *The Ardennes*, pp. 267, 670-1.

34. Cole, *The Ardennes*, pp. 268, 670-1. Cole, in a footnote on the 51st Engineer Combat Battalion, said, "The ubiquitous 51st Engineer Combat Battalion will crop up at many points in this narrative. The battalion was awarded a Presidential Citation." In this and the next chapter it can be seen that the 51st became involved in much of the action in this area of Belgium during the Battle of the Bulge.

ENDNOTES — PAGES 87 TO 96

Chapter Six

1. S-2 & S-3 Log, 51st Engineer Combat Battalion, Modern Military Branch, National Archives, Suitland, Maryland. Except where otherwise noted, the information in this chapter is from the S-2 & S-3 Log, and the Battalion History, 51st ECB, National Archives, and from Ken Hechler's *Holding the Line*, Studies in Military Engineering Number 4, (Washington, D.C.: Government Printing Office, 1988).

2. The Area Defense Commander of Area 2 was the CO, 158th ECB. When the 158th ECB left the area for the Bastogne area, Lieutenant Colonel Fraser took charge of Area 2 at 1930 hours, December 19.

3. Letter from Brigadier General Harvey R. Fraser, USA, Retired, to Barry W. Fowle dated May 4, 1988.

4. Excerpt from a speech prepared by Doctor T. Reed Maxson for presentation at the second reunion of the 51st Engineer Combat Battalion at Nashville, Tennessee, in April 1988, but not given.

5. Ibid.

6. Letter, Fraser to Fowle, dated October 23, 1988.

7. Hugh M. Cole, *The Ardennes: Battle of the Bulge* (Washington, D.C.: Government Printing Office, 1965), p. 429.

8. Information for the Battle of Hotton has been taken from Ken Hechler's *Holding the Line*.

9. Letter from Colonel Floyd D. Wright, USA, Retired, to Barry W. Fowle, dated September 9, 1988. Wright's letter was based on his interviews with Bill Saunders, Harry Wimberly, Leonard Weil, Floyd Johnson, Lee Ishmael, and others at the second reunion of the 51st ECB, during April 1988.

10. Ibid.

11. Ibid.

12. Ibid; Letter from Floyd Johnston to Colonel Floyd D. Wright dated January 31, 1988.

13. Cole, pp. 381-2.

14. Cole, pp. 430-1.

15. Letter, Wright to Fowle, dated September 9, 1988. With Curtis were Squad Sergeants Joseph H. Ochson, William T. Saunders, and Harry S. Wimberly; Corporal Ado Severi; and PFCs Herbert L. Kelly and Edward W. Borowski. In the half-track from company headquarters with Staff Sergeant Leonard Weil were

ENDNOTES — PAGES 96 TO 107

Pfc Felix H. Gay on the .50-caliber machine gun and Technician Fifth John Hendrix driving. In June 1945, Lieutenant Curtis's mother responded to a letter from the commander, Company A, concerning the death of her son. She challenged all the young men who came back from the war to work unceasingly for a peaceful world.

16. Cole, pp. 429-31. This account of Captain Alfred E. Radford's experience with delaying action on N4 is taken from a letter written to his wife on December 29, 1944 and sent to BG Harvey R. Fraser for inclusion in the unit history.

17. This account of Wright's 1st Platoon at Jamelle was supplied by letter, Wright to Fowle, dated March 13, 1989.

18. Cole, pp. 435-6.

19. Cole, pp. 431-2.

20. The battalion history for December 23, 1944 describes the vehicle striking the mine and Trafford and Fairchild as being evacuated to the hospital. The rest of the information on the incident is based on a letter from Trafford to Wright dated April 30, 1989 and a follow-up phone call on May 15, 1989.

21. Material on the Battle of Rochefort was supplied by Wright from his personal experience using the unit records to "jog" his memory. Cole, pp. 432-3.

22. Cole, pp. 433-4.

23. At the first reunion of the 51st Engineer (C) Battalion in April 1986, a banner was proudly displayed by the men of Company A. The banner was made by the late Corporal Albert Bolha of the 1st Platoon. On one half of a canvas pup tent he had painted, among other things, "The 51st Again" across the top, and "The 300th At Last" on the bottom. This referred to the lieutenant from the 300th ECB who came to Rochefort to relieve the 1st Platoon of Company A.

24. Letter, Charles G. Kroen to Floyd D. Wright, dated August 2, 1988.

25. Cole, pp. 436-8.

26. Charles B. MacDonald, *A Time for Trumpets*, (William Morrow and Company: New York, 1985), p. 568-9.

27. Cole, pp. 438-9.

28. Letter, Donald A. Bonifay to Floyd D. Wright, dated February 13, 1988.

29. Ibid.

30. Ibid.

31. Cole, pp. 439-440.

32. Information concerning Major Yates' capture and subsequent escape and return to the 51st ECB is contained in a letter from Fraser to Fowle dated July 2, 1991.

33. Varrall is unsure as to who the man was that jumped into the slit-trench, either Jim Gregory or Jack M. Childress. A "Most Memorable Moment" sent in by George Verrall, Company B, for the first reunion of the 51st ECB, April 1986, Washington, DC.

34. Letter, Fraser to Fowle dated May 4, 1988.

35. Ibid.

36. A copy of the citation is at Appendix J. This is the highest honor that any unit can be given for heroic achievement. The Distinguished Unit Citation is awarded to units of the Armed Forces of the United States and cobelligerent nations for extraordinary heroism in action against the armed enemy occurring on or after December 7, 1941. The unit must display such gallantry, determination, and esprit de corps in accomplishing its mission under extremely difficult and hazardous conditions as to set it apart and above other units participating in the same campaign. The degree of heroism required is the same as that which would warrant award of a Distinguished Service Cross (DSC) to an individual. The DSC for an individual is second only to the highest award for an individual, the Congressional Medal of Honor. The French Croix de Guerre is the highest honor that the French government gives to a unit. A copy of this citation is at Appendix K as is a translation from French to English.

37. Letter, Fraser to Fowle, dated May 4, 1988.

Chapter Seven

1. Charles B. MacDonald, *The Last Offensive*, (Washington, D.C.: Government Printing Office, 1973), pp. 25-27.

2. Ibid. pp. 28-29.

3. After Action Report, 51st Engineer Combat Battalion, January 1945. Unless otherwise stated, material concerning the 51st Engineer Combat Battalion is from the Official History, 51st ECB, Modern Military Branch, National Archives.

4. Letter, Colonel Floyd D. Wright, USA, Retired to Barry W. Fowle, dated September 25, 1988. The story concerning bridge support comes from this letter.

5. Unit History, 1111th Engineer Combat Group, January 1945.

6. Ibid.

ENDNOTES — PAGES 120 TO 141

7. Ibid.

8. Letter, Wright to Fowle, dated September 25, 1988. The complete story of the 1st Platoon at Grand Halleux is from this letter.

9. Unit History, 1111th Engineer Combat Group.

10. Letter, BG Harvey R. Fraser, USA, Retired, to Barry W. Fowle dated September 16, 1988.

11. Letter, Wright to Fowle, dated September 25, 1988. The complete story of 1st Platoon's support of the 32d Cavalry Squadron comes from this letter.

12. Unit History, 1111th ECG.

13. MacDonald, *The Last Offensive*, pp. 73-83.

14. Excerpt from a speech prepared by Doctor T. Reed Maxson for presentation at the 2d Reunion, 51st ECB, Nashville, Tennessee, April 1988, but not given due to illness.

15. Ibid.

16. Letter, Joseph B. Milgram, Jr. to Barry W. Fowle, dated October 1989. The story of "Whatever Happened to the Town of Schmidt" is told by Milgram in his own words.

17. Letter, Fraser to Fowle, dated November 6, 1988.

18. Letter, Fraser to Fowle, dated May 4, 1988. Lieutenant Colonel Edwin A. Bedell was the Commanding Officer, 307th Engineer Combat Battalion, 82d Airborne Division.

19. Letter, Sam Scheuber to Barry W. Fowle, dated December 14, 1988.

20. Letter, Fraser to Fowle, dated July 2, 1991.

21. Letter, Wright to Fowle, dated July 9, 1991.

Chapter Eight

1. Oral history interview with General William M. Hoge, Colonel George Robertson, 1977. Unless otherwise indicated, all material used in this chapter comes from the official records of the 51st Engineer Combat Battalion.

2. Oral history interview with Lieutenant Colonel Harvey R. Fraser, Commanding Officer, 51st Engineer Combat Battalion, and Major Robert Yates, Executive Officer, 51st Engineer Combat Battalion, by Captain Ken W. Hechler and Lieutenant Robert E. Maxwell, 2d Information & History Service; and from a talk by BG Harvey R. Fraser, "The Bridges at Remagen," to an Engineer Officer Advance Class, Fort Belvoir, Virginia, May 5, 1987.

3. Ibid.

4. Ibid.

5. Ibid.

6. Ibid.

7. Ibid.

8. "Action taken by First Army Just prior to and During Seizure of Remagen Bridgehead," Colonel Russell F. Akins, Assistant G-3, First United States Army.

9. After Action Report, Rhine River Crossings, III Corps.

10. Ibid.

11. Ibid.

12. Ibid.

13. For the uninitiated, a Class VI ration is the monthly alcoholic beverage allotment.

14. "Pill Peddler's Palaver," by Doctor T. Reed Maxson.

15. Ibid.

16. Ibid.

Chapter Nine

1. Charles B. MacDonald, *The Last Offensive*, (Washington, D.C.: Government Printing Office, 1973), p. 425. Except where otherwise noted, information is from the Official History, 51st Engineer Combat Battalion, and Floyd D. Wright's "Assault Crossing of the Danube River."

2. After Action Report, April 1-30, 1945, 51st Engineer Combat Battalion. Carleton (Carl) E. Moore's presentation, first reunion, 51st ECB, Washington, D.C., April 1945.

3. Ibid.

4. MacDonald, p. 425.

5. Schutzstaffel Troopers (SS) were classified as elite guard forces.

6. After Action Report, 51st ECB, April 1-30, 1945. A jerry can is a flat-sided, narrow can with about a five-gallon capacity. It is easily stacked and transportable and can be adapted by special openings for discharging fuel.

ENDNOTES — PAGES 172 TO 177

Chapter Ten

1. Except where noted, this chapter is based on the experiences of Lieutenant Colonel Maurice E. Coats, AUS, Retired, and the Official Records, 51st Engineer Combat Battalion, Modern Records Branch, Suitland, Maryland.

2. Letter, Captain Preston C. Hodges to his father, W. D. Hodges. Letter from Fred Beckler to Maurice E. Coats, February 9, 1988.

3. Letter, Larry Senger to Maurice E. Coats, February 9, 1988.

4. Letter, Preston C. Hodges to Maurice E. Coats, February 9, 1988.

5. Letter, Joseph B. Milgram, Jr. to Barry W. Fowle describing some of the happy and some not so happy times during the war for the civilian population and POWs, October 29, 1989.

6. The battalion newspaper, *Poop and Patter*, dated May 13, 1945.

7. Ibid.

8. Information concerning occupation duties is contained in a letter from Fraser to Fowle dated July 2, 1991, and from the Official Records.

Index

Aachen, Germany, 127
Aberdeen Proving Grounds, Maryland, 24, 25
Ahr River, 139, 144
Ambleve River, 73, 77-79, 82, 84, 113, 117
Anderson, PFC Ervin H., 124 (picture), 186
Anderson, Col. H. Wallis, vi, 4, 7-8, 15-16, 27, 40, 42 (picture), 77-79, 81, 97, 137, 150 (picture), 161, 164, 175, 179
Ardennes area, 68-69, 72-73, 76, 110
Ardennes campaign (see also Battle of the Bulge), 17, 71-72, 127, 182

Bad Neuenhauer, Germany, 153
Bahe, Maj. Gordon A., 103-106
Baiden, Maj. Arthur Jr., 184
Bailey, 2d Lt. Raymond L., 8
Baird, 2d Lt. Earle D., 7
Baker, S/Sgt. James W., 185
Baldwin, 2d Lt. (later 1st Lt.) Elmer G., 8, 26
Barco, Pvt. Colon A., 51
Barnes, 2d Lt. (later Maj. Gen.) John W., xi, 4, 13, 32, 36-37, 43, 52, 58-59, 64 (picture), 94-95, 157, 188
Bastogne, Belgium, vi, 59, 92, 97, 100, 113, 173
Battle of the Bulge (see also Ardennes Campaign), v, x, 17, 73, 102, 106, 111, 112, 187-188
Baugh, 2d Lt. Lyle C., 21
Beam, Cpl. Howard B., 186
Beckler, S/Sgt. Frederick C., 172, 186
Bedell, Lt. Col. Edwin A., 134
Berger, Chaplain Harold E., 149 (picture)
Best, Sgt. Major Charles W., 176 (picture), 188
Blackburn, PFC Cecil C., 153
Blankenship, Pvt. Ernest V., 60
Boies, Lt. Jack E., 36, 58
Bolha, Cpl. Albert, 181 (picture), 185
Bolling, Maj. Gen. Alexander R., 94-95, 101, 103

Bonifay, S/Sgt. Donald A., 93, 98, 102-103, 104, 107, 121, 188
Boynton, Maj. Wyman P., 182
Bradford, PFC Gordon L., 123 (picture)
Bradley, Lt. Gen. Omar N., 38, 47, 68-69, 141
Bridges
    Bailey bridge, 20 (picture), 21-22, 25, 28 (picture), 39, 41, 56, 58-59, 102-103, 114, 116, 118 (picture), 120, 124, 135-137, 148 (picture), 155-157, 169, 170 (pictures), 171, 174, 196-197 (description), 198-200 (pictures)
    floating bridge, 11, 15, 40, 133, 135
    H-10 steel bridge, 12, 25
    pneumatic floating bridge, 11, 41, 144, 163
    ponton bridge, 11, 20 (picture), 25, 29, 142, 144, 145 (pictures), 146 (picture), 151 (sketch), 152-154
    tactical (fixed) bridge, 11, 41, 154, 169
    timber trestle bridge, 11, 20 (picture), 25, 41, 59-62, 63 (pictures), 67, 76, 84, 148 (picture), 156
    treadway bridge, 15, 59, 109, 119, 133-135, 142, 144, 155-156, 161, 165, 168-169, 171
Brilon, Germany, 156
Brown, Pvt. Gerald C., 133
Brucker, 2d Lt. Frederic L., 21
Bruck-Hetzingen, Germany, 135-136

Caldwell, S/Sgt. Leazar M., 188
Camp Bowie, Texas, 1, 5, 7, 27
Camp Don B. Passage, Algeria, 37
Camp Patrick Henry, Virginia, 32, 181 (picture), 185
Camp Philadelphia, France, 184
Canada
    9th Forestry Company, 90-91, 97
Cannon, PFC Elder D., 146 (picture)
Carlisle, T/Sgt. (later 2d Lt.) Matthew R., 81, 179

- 225 -

Carter, Col. (later Maj. Gen.) William A. Jr., vi, 153, 188
Carver, 2d Lt. (later 1st Lt.) Arnold H., 3, 15
Carville, Lt. Richard A., 7
Casablanca, Morocco, 37, 47
Cash, Pvt. G. M., 52
Catherman, PFC Floyd W., 186
Champlon Crossroads, Belgium, viii, 91, 97, 99-100, 112
Ciergnon, Belgium, 107
Ciney, Belgium, 175
Clavan, Sgt. Bernard P., 58
Coats, 2d Lt. (later Capt.) Maurice E., xi, 26, 38-39, 41 (picture), 49, 144, 149 (picture), 183-185
COBRA operation, 53
Cofer, Lt. Col. John W., 184
Collins, Maj. Gen. J. Lawton, 101, 103
Conklin, 2d Lt. Robert S., 21
Conley, Sgt. L. D., 153
Connelly, T/5 Oliver M., 111
Craighill, Lt. Col. Edley, 39
Crandall, Lt. Col. Riel S., 119
Curtis, 1st Lt. Paul W. Jr., 59, 93, 96

Danube River, v, 161, 163, 166, 167 (pictures), 168-169, 181, 188
Dattenberg, Germany, 142-144
Davis, West Virginia, 28
Dawley, Lt. Col. Jay P., 119
Dietrich, Gen. Josef, 73
Doucet, PFC Emile K., 121, 124
Driggs, Pvt. Stanley A., 93
Dudley, T/5 Harold D., 186

Eisenhower, Gen. Dwight D., 69, 73, 113, 172
Ekman, Col. William E., 82, 206
Elkins, West Virginia, 27-28, 32
Engeman, Lt. Col. Leonard E., 139, 141

Fahlander, Cpl. Lenart A., 168
Faust, Cpl. Odis C., 84
Fent, PFC Roy G., 123 (picture)
Fields, Col. Kenneth E., 137, 142, 144
Fincher, Cpl. George W., 186
Finn, Pvt. Henry A., 98
Fleurus, Algeria, 36
Fort Belvoir, Virginia, v, 3-4, 8, 13, 17, 24, 29-30
Fort Dix, New Jersey, 30-32
Fossett, 2d Lt. Harry W., 21
Fowle, Dr. Barry W., xii, 188
Fox, T/5 Eugene, 186
Frankenhouser, PFC Ray, 123 (picture)
Fraser, Lt. Col. (later Brig. Gen.) Harvey R., v, vi, ix, x, xi, 68, 71-72, 87, 90-91, 93-94, 96-97, 108-111, 114-116, 119, 121-122, 134, 136-137, 142-144, 149 (picture), 150 (picture), 152, 154, 156-157, 159, 161, 163-165, 174-175, 176 (picture), 177, 179, 182, 187

Gaimersheim, Germany, 169
Garrity, 2d Lt. William F., 21
Gavin, Maj. Gen. James M., 114, 133-134
Gay, PFC Felix B., 186
George, S/Sgt. Alex, 171
German Army units
    5th Armored Panzer Army, vii, viii, 85-86, 96
    6th SS Panzer Army, viii, 73, 85
    LVIII Panzer Corps, viii, 96
    1st SS Panzer Division, vii, 73, 85
    2d Panzer Division, 92, 99, 103, 106
    9th SS Panzer Division (Panzer Lehr), 104, 106, 108
    116th Panzer Division, 92, 96
    1st Panzer Regiment, vii
    304th Panzer Grenadier Regiment, 100
Germenter, Germany, 130-131 (pictures), 134
Givet, Belgium, 105-107
Gloucester, England, 38-39, 43-44
Goldsmith, Sgt. Elvin, 84
Gossard, Sgt. Evers, 80
Grand Halleux, Belgium, 120-121, 124
Green, 2d Lt. (later 1st Lt.) Richard I., 8, 17, 19 (picture), 43, 74, 78-81, 136, 149 (picture)
Gullesheim, Germany, 155
Gurnsey, PFC Edward, 74
Gyure, Sgt. Joseph, 83

Haines, Sgt., 181 (picture)
Hall, 1st Sgt. Samuel, 182
Ham, Sgt. Benjamin C., 60, 90, 121, 124 (picture)
Hampteau, Belgium, 91-93
Hampton Roads, Virginia, 33, 185
Hancock, Capt. G. E., 164
Hardcastle, S/Sgt. Robert L., 121
Hardin, Brig. Gen. John, v
Harwood, Lt. Vincent J., 43
Haywood, Pvt. Ray, 137
Hebert, Normandy, France, 48
Heiberg, Lt. Gen. Elvin R., 111, 186, 189
Henry, 2d Lt. (later 1st Lt.) David H., 3, 15, 52, 109, 159, 185
Highnam Court, England, 38-39, 44-45
HMS *Andes*, 37-38
Hodges, 2d Lt. (later Capt.) Preston C., xi, 2 (picture), 3-4, 13, 15, 19 (picture), 28 (picture), 39, 47, 93-96, 110, 143, 149 (picture), 172-173, 182, 188, 202
Hoge, Brig. Gen. (later Gen.) William M., 68, 139, 141
Homme, L' River, 103-104, 106

INDEX

Horecka, WOJG Julius J., 32, 55, 150 (picture)
Hotton, Belgium, vii, viii, 89, 91, 93-96, 98, 108, 111-112, 114, 175, 207
Huertgen Forest, Germany, 129
Hulce, 2d Lt. Durwood C., 21
Huxman, Capt. Richard F., 26, 35, 58

Iczkowski, T/4 Frank, 185
Ingolstadt, Germany, 161, 163, 166-167 (pictures), 169
Isar Canal, 169, 170 (picture)
Ishmael, Pvt. Lee J., 94, 96

Jamison, 2d Lt. Bruce W., 24, 93-95
Jewett, Capt. Robert N., 77-79
Johnson, 2d Lt. Elmo F., 21
Johnston, T/5 Floyd, 94-95, 98, 103-104, 115-116
Jordan, PFC Clinton L., 98, 103-104

Kalenborn, Germany, 155
Kall River, 129, 133
Keck, T/5 Paul H., 84-85
Keesing, CWO Walter J., 31
Kelly, S/Sgt. Herbert L., 96, 98, 185
Kelly, Lt. Jay H., 110
Kelly, M/Sgt. Kenneth, 185
Kelso, 2d Lt. Richard W., 21
Kennedy, PFC Earlie, 137
Ketchum, Col. Edwin P., 2
Kirkland, Maj. (later Lt. Col.) James H., 7, 15, 77, 81
Kitzingen, Germany, 179, 182
Koblenz, Germany, 141
Kripp, Germany, 142-144, 151
Kroen, Sgt. Charles G., 104, 107, 121
Krueger, Gen. Walter, viii, 96

Lake Champlain, New York, 5, 7, 11
Lape, Cpl. Claude N., 59
La Roche, Belgium, 100-101
Lauchert, Col. Meinrad von, 99
Lee, Cpl. Frank, 185, 188
Leonard, Maj. Gen. John, 141
Leone, Col. Louis P., 39, 201-202
Levitus, 2d Lt. George I., 21
Lichtenfels, Germany, 182
Lienne River, 117, 119
Linz, Germany, 143
Liverpool, England, 37-38
Llanelly, Wales, 38
Ludendorff Bridge (see also Remagen), 139, 141-144
Lungberg, Capt. A. P., 86
Lyons, Capt. F. Russell, 141, 144, 150 (picture), 154

McCollam, Capt. (later Maj.) Albert E., 4, 7, 13, 15, 27
Macomb Reservation, New York, 7-8, 13, 15-18, 19-20 (pictures), 21, 26
Maffe, Belgium, 109-110
Main River, 177, 179, 182-183
Malmedy, Belgium, 67, 74
Manteuffel, Gen. Hasso-Eckard von, viii
Marburg, Germany, 155
Marche, Belgium, viii, 67, 71-72, 85, 90, 92, 94-109, 111, 114, 173-175, 207
Marquez, Pvt. Jose E., 84
Marseilles, France, 184
Massoglia, 1st Lt. (later Capt.) Martin F., 2-4, 7, 15
Mathis, Pvt. Edgar L., 153
Maxson, Dr. (also Capt.) T. Reed, xi, 60, 72, 90, 11, 128, 129, 149 (picture), 154, 157, 171
Melasky, Maj. Gen. Harris M., 161, 163-164
Melraux, Belgium, 91
Meuse River, vi, vii, ix, 73, 87, 96, 99, 104, 106-107, 111
Michelau, Germany, 183
Middleton, Sgt. (later 2d Lt.) Hervie L., 24, 143
Middleton, Ralph K., 188
Milgram, Lt. Joseph E. Jr., xi, 76, 81, 83-85, 133, 173-174
Millard, Sgt. Raymond, 188
Miller, Sgt. Jean D., 82
Milliken, Maj. Gen. John, 153
Milne, Lt., 42 (picture)
mines—clearance and removal, 117, 119, 124-126, 133, 137, 156
Minyard, PFC Ernest F., 120, 186
Mitchell, T/5 Raymond, 124 (picture), 186
Mock, Pvt. Jessie R., 84
Modave, Belgium, 79
Moore, PFC Carlton E., 56, 159, 188
Moosberg, Germany, 174
Morgan, PFC Gordon G., 137, 186
Morin, WOJG (later CWO) Wilfred G., 30, 32, 149 (picture)
Mueller, 2d Lt. (later 1st Lt.) William R., 26, 37, 149 (picture), 185
Munich, Germany, 169
Murphy, Lt. James H. Jr., 52
Mussomeli, Capt. Marino, 60, 149 (picture), 157
Myer, PFC Robert, 52

Nabors, 2d Lt. Fred L., 8, 42 (picture), 79, 81
Namur, Belgium, 90
Neustadt, Germany, 155, 159
Neider Ding, Germany, 169, 170 (picture)
Noiseux, Belgium, 114, 119
Nolan, 2d Lt. Leo, 24, 33

THE 51ST AGAIN!

Norton, 1st Lt. John J., 42 (picture), 84
Nuremberg, Germany, 159, 161, 175, 177

Oberdorf, 2d Lt., 4-5
Ochson, Sgt. Joseph H., 96
Oliver, Sgt. John T., 74, 76
OMAHA Beach, 47
O'Neill, 2d Lt. (later 1st Lt.) Harold L., 26
Oran, Algeria, 35-37, 47
Ortheuville, Belgium, viii, 59, 92, 96-97, 99
Ourthe River, vi, vii, 59, 89, 90-92, 94, 96, 111, 114

Paris, France, v, 57
Parker, 2d Lt. Arnold, 179
Patton, Lt. Gen. George S., 113, 125, 157-158, 177
Pedersen, 2d Lt. (later Capt.) Karl G., 3-5, 7, 12-13, 30, 33, 52, 99-100, 107-108, 149 (picture), 156, 206
Peiper, Lt. Col. Joachim, vii, 73, 80, 85
Pendergrass, Sgt. James A., 60
Pergrin, Lt. Col. David E., 74
Perles, France, 58
Petrini, 2d Lt. Nevio (Pete), 5, 21
Pisano, Pvt. Reno V., 168
Plattsburg, New York, 5, 8, 16, 18 (pictures), 23, 25, 27, 31, 117
Plattsburg Barracks, New York, 5, 6 (pictures), 8, 15-16, 19 (picture), 26-27
Poronsky, Dr. (also 1st Lt., later Capt.), John G., 3, 185
Pratt, T/5 Clifton M., 93
Pugh, S/Sgt. Paris, 38
Pulawski, 2d Lt. Richard, 24
Puntch, Harold, 187

Radford, 2d Lt. (later Capt.) Albert E., 3, 15, 32, 96, 97, 98, 128, 129, 149 (picture), 159
Randolph, PFC Lloyd, 186
Rankin, S/Sgt. William, 83
Raper, M/Sgt. Lee N., 51
Rawlins, Capt. Alfred H., 21, 24
Reafsnyder, Maj. (later Lt. Col.) Victor J., 24, 33, 39, 40, 43, 52, 203
Red Ball Express, 57-58
Remagen, Germany (see also Ludendorff Bridge), v, 139, 141-142, 144, 154
Rheims, France, 173
Rhine River, v, vi, 137, 139, 141-142, 144, 154, 156, 187-188
Ridgeway, Maj. Gen. (later Gen.) Matthew B., 101, 113
Roberts, T/5 Wilson, 97, 185
Robinson, T/5 William E., 123 (picture), 186
Rochefort, Belgium, 92, 99, 101-106, 108, 112
Roer River, v, 127-128, 132 (picture), 133-135, 187

Ross, 2d Lt. James A. Jr., 3, 25, 127
Rotgen, Germany, 128-129, 137
Rozich, PFC George A., 153
Ruhr Pocket, 156, 158-159

St. Vith, Belgium, 113, 126-127
Ste. Mere-Eglise, France, 48-49
Salazar, PFC Andrew, 78
Salm River, 73, 77-79, 82-84, 120, 206
Salmon Lake, 16
Saunders, Sgt. William T., 96, 185
Scheuber, Capt. Sam C., vi, vii, xi, 42 (picture), 77, 84-86, 135-136, 149 (picture), 157, 183
Schmidt, Germany, 133-135
Schonberg, Belgium, 127
Schroff, 2d Lt. (later Capt.) Clifford P., 3-5, 13, 25-26, 35-36
Self, T/5 Harold, 97
Senger, PFC Lawrence, 173, 185
Shanes, PFC James M., 53
Sheletsky, PFC John F., 123 (picture)
Sherwood, S/Sgt. George M., 99
Simoni, T/5 Frank, 74, 76
Snow, PFC James W. Jr., 80
Solis, Sgt. Maj. Gilberto G., 15
Southhampton, England, 45-46
Spa, Belgium, vi
Spearmin, 2d Lt., 91
Spurrier, 2d Lt. James D., 4
Stann, Lt. Col. Eugene J., 141-142
Stavelot, Belgium, 77-79, 81, 113, 208-209
Stearns, Capt., 48
Stephens, T/5 Elmer C., 60
Stevens, Cpl. Jerry, 93
Stiftinger, Sgt. John J., 104, 121-122
Strawser, Pvt. Carl, 83
Sweatt, Cpl. Loyd E., 2, 107

Thomas, T/Sgt. Paul E., 185
Tillman, PFC Raligh, 153
TNT—*use in demolition*, 11, 22-23, 84, 97-99, 101, 157
Tompkins, Maj. William F., 153
Trafford, 2d Lt. (later 1st Lt.) Raymond A., 32, 43, 99-100, 102
Trois Ponts, Belgium, vi, vii, viii, 67, 73-74, 76-77, 79-80, 82-83, 85, 87, 89, 108, 112-113, 119-120, 173, 175, 206-209
Turner, Sgt. (later 2d Lt.) George, 59, 179

United States Army
Army
    1st United States Army, v, ix, 39-40, 44, 48, 55, 58, 69, 80, 90, 113, 127, 134, 139, 141, 153, 156-159, 175, 188, 204, 207
    3d United States Army, 69, 113, 125, 141, 157-159, 161, 174, 175, 177

INDEX

Corps
  III Corps, 134-135, 143-144, 153-159, 161, 163, 179
  V Corps, 58-59
  VI Corps, 5, 10
  VII Corps, 58, 100-102, 111, 113-114
  VIII Corps, 158
  XII Corps, 179
  XIII Corps, 10, 17, 27-28
  XVIII Airborne Corps, 101, 113, 127
Division
  82d Airborne Division, vii, viii, 51, 82-83, 112, 114, 119, 125-129, 133, 134
  101st Airborne Division, 51
  2d Armored Division, viii, ix, 55, 100, 102, 104, 109, 112, 114, 116
  3d Armored Division, viii, 55, 93-94, 96, 101-102, 112, 114
  7th Armored Division, 61, 77, 97
  9th Armored Division, 139, 141, 143
  22d Armored Division, 32
  1st Infantry Division, 134-135
  4th Infantry Division, 55
  9th Infantry Division, v, 55, 131, 133-135, 137, 141, 154, 156-157, 175
  30th Infantry Division, 53, 55
  75th Infantry Division, 102, 113-114, 120, 122, 175
  78th Infantry Division, 141, 143
  83d Infantry Division, 114
  84th Infantry Division, viii, 94-97, 100-103, 107, 109-110, 112-113, 175
  86th Infantry Division, 161, 164-165, 168-169, 175
  87th Infantry Division, 125-126, 175
  106th Infantry Division, 74, 90
Regiment
  37th Engineer Combat Regiment, 2-3
  39th Engineer Combat Regiment, 2
  51st Engineer Combat Regiment, 1, 3-5, 7, 10, 13-15, 117
  335th Infantry Regiment, 103-104, 107
  504th Parachute Infantry Regiment, 125
  505th Parachute Infantry Regiment, 82-85, 173
  508th Parachute Infantry Regiment, 125
Group
  1106th Engineer Combat Group, 184
  1110th Engineer Combat Group, 110
  1111th Engineer Combat Group, vi, ix, 15, 17, 22, 27, 39-40, 44, 49, 71, 74, 77, 80, 89, 114, 117, 125, 128-129, 137, 154-158, 161, 164, 173
  1123d Engineer Combat Group, 183
  1128th Engineer Combat Group, 38-39
  1159th Engineer Combat Group, 137, 142, 144, 154, 156
Battalion
  440th Antiaircraft Artillery Battalion, 91-92, 108
  526th Armored Infantry Battalion, 77-79
  23d Armored Engineer Combat Battalion, 93
  49th Engineer Combat Battalion, 33
  51st Engineer Combat Battalion, v-xi, 15, 17, 22, 25-32, 35-40, 43-44, 47-49, 51, 53, 55, 57-68, 61, 67-68, 71, 73-74, 77-78, 82-83, 85-86, 89-91, 93-95, 97, 100-101, 103-105, 107-109, 111-112, 114, 117, 119-120, 125, 127-129, 130 (picture), 133-135, 142-143, 145 (picture), 148-150 (pictures), 152-157, 159, 161, 163, 166-167 (pictures), 171, 173-175, 179, 181 (picture), 182-184, 187-189, 192, 193 (lineage and honors), 201, 203, 206-210
  61st Engineer Combat Battalion, 110
  145th Engineer Combat Battalion, 182-183
  158th Engineer Combat Battalion, vii, 74, 91-92, 99
  163d Engineer Combat Battalion, 17, 21
  178th Engineer Combat Battalion, 184
  237th Engineer Combat Battalion, 33
  238th Engineer Combat Battalion, 15, 17, 117, 119
  275th Engineer Combat Battalion, 110, 114, 120
  291st Engineer Combat Battalion, 44, 73-74, 77, 82, 110, 142, 144, 152-153
  296th Engineer Combat Battalion, 44
  299th Engineer Combat Battalion, 182
  300th Engineer Combat Battalion, 103-104, 119
  307th Engineer Combat Battalion, 82, 114, 120, 125, 133
  309th Engineer Combat Battalion, 104, 109
  311th Engineer Combat Battalion, 165
  1262d Engineer Combat Battalion, 156
  181st Engineer Heavy Ponton Bridge Battalion, 142, 153
  552d Engineer Heavy Ponton Bridge Battalion, 142, 153
  638th Tank Destroyer Battalion, 104
Squadron
  32d Cavalry Reconnaissance Squadron, 125-126
  85th Reconnaissance Squadron, 82

THE 51ST AGAIN!

Trains
    3d Armored Division Trains, vii, 94-95
    7th Armored Division Trains, viii, 100
Company
    51st ECR Company A, 2, 4, 7, 9, 12
    51st ECR Company B, 2, 4, 9, 13
    51st ECR Company C, 2, 4, 9
    51st ECR Company D, 2
    51st ECR Company E, 2, 3
    51st ECR Company F, 2, 3
    51st ECR H&S Company, 1, 3, 4, 9
    51st ECB Company A, viii, xi, 15, 17, 19 (picture), 23-25, 28-30, 32-33, 36, 38, 46, 48, 52-53, 56, 60-61, 67, 87, 89, 91-93, 96-101, 107, 109-112, 114, 118-120, 123-124 (pictures), 125-126, 129, 133-134, 136-137, 142, 146 (picture), 148 (pictures), 154, 156-157, 159, 161-165, 167 (picture), 168-169, 171, 174, 179, 182, 184, 186, 188
    51st ECB Company B, vii, xi, 15, 17, 24, 26, 28-29, 33, 38-40, 43, 46, 56, 59-61, 87, 89, 91-94, 96, 101, 108-110, 112, 119, 124, 127, 129, 131, 132 (pictures), 134-135, 142-144, 153, 155-156, 159, 161, 163, 169, 171, 174, 179, 182-183, 186, 188, 201
    51st ECB Company C, vi, xi, 15, 17, 24, 26, 28-29, 33, 36, 38, 40, 46, 48, 51-53, 56, 59-61, 67, 73-74, 76-87, 108-110, 112, 118 (picture), 119, 123 (picture), 124, 128-129, 133-134, 136, 142, 153, 155-157, 159, 161, 163, 169, 172-174, 179, 182-183, 186, 188
    51st ECB Headquarters and Service Company, 15, 24, 29, 33, 37-38, 44, 46, 51-52, 56, 60, 95-97, 112, 128, 149 (picture), 156, 159, 161, 169, 173-174, 185, 188
    501st Engineer Light Ponton Company, 117, 129
    629th Engineer Light Equipment Company, 117
    988th Engineer Treadway Bridge Company, 142
    994th Engineer Treadway Bridge Company, 117
    998th Engineer Treadway Bridge Company, 142, 155-156, 163-165
USS *Abiel Foster*, 46, 48
USS *Calvin Coolidge*, 33
USS *Charles D. Poston*, 46
USS *Eufala Victory*, 184-185
USS *Joseph H. Johnson*, 46
USS *Richard Rush*, 33
Unkel, Germany, 144
UTAH Beach, 47, 49, 50 (picture)

Verrall, T/4 George M., 110, 188
Vielsalm, Belgium, 120, 124
Vigil, PFC Elfido, 186

Walker, T/4 Eldridge, 185
Walker, Pvt. Maurice S., 84
Walters, Lt. Albert J., 77, 82
Watson, T/5 John P. (Kelly), 165
Watson, S/Sgt. Russell E., 43, 143
Wdzcieczny (Weber), T/4 Harry, 185
Weil, Sgt. Leonard, 107, 185
Weinstein, Capt. Seymour, 53
Westmoreland, Col. (later Gen.) William C., 133
Wied River, 156
Wimberly, Sgt. Harry S., 96
Winchester, Virginia, 29
Wittwer, 2d Lt. Glade S., 4, 7
Wood, PFC Sidney L., 124 (picture)
Wooten, PFC David L., 153
Wright, Edna M. (Ed), xi, 210
Wright, 2d Lt. (later Col.) Floyd B., xi, 3, 4, 15, 18 (picture), 23-24, 29, 92-95, 98-99, 101-108, 115-117, 149 (picture), 157-158, 161, 163-164, 183, 188
Wurzburg, Germany, 159, 161, 175, 177, 179, 182

Xhoris, Belgium, 119

Yates, Capt. (later Maj.) Robert B., vi, vii, 7, 10, 13, 15, 17, 19 (picture), 23-24, 27, 33, 38-39, 52, 56-57, 68, 71, 79-85, 108-109, 136, 144-145, 152, 154, 156-157

Zerkall, Germany, 132 (picture), 135